AQUINAS AND THE METAPHYSICS

OF CREATION

AQUINAS AND
THE METAPHYSICS
OF CREATION

GAVEN KERR

OXFORD
UNIVERSITY PRESS

Oxford University Press is a department of the University of Oxford. It furthers the University's objective of excellence in research, scholarship, and education by publishing worldwide. Oxford is a registered trade mark of Oxford University Press in the UK and certain other countries.

Published in the United States of America by Oxford University Press
198 Madison Avenue, New York, NY 10016, United States of America.

© Oxford University Press 2019

Library of Congress Cataloging-in-Publication Data
Names: Kerr, Gaven, author.
Title: Aquinas and the metaphysics of creation / Gaven Kerr.
Description: New York : Oxford University Press, 2019. |
Includes bibliographical references and index.
Identifiers: LCCN 2019009761 (print) | LCCN 2019015412 (ebook) |
ISBN 9780190941314 (updf) | ISBN 9780190941321 (epub) |
ISBN 9780190941307 (hardcover) | ISBN 9780190941338 (online content)
Subjects: LCSH: Thomas, Aquinas, Saint, 1225–1274. | Creation.
Classification: LCC B765.T54 (ebook) | LCC B765.T54 K474 2019 (print) |
DDC 110.92—dc23
LC record available at https://lccn.loc.gov/2019009761

9 8 7 6 5 4 3 2

Printed by Sheridan Books, Inc., United States of America

CONTENTS

ACKNOWLEDGEMENTS

It is a privilege to acknowledge publicly a number of people and groups of people who have aided in the completion of this work.

I would like to thank Cynthia Read and the team at Oxford University Press for once again working with me to produce this work. I cannot thank them enough for their professionalism and support.

In an age of social media I have been able to benefit from the advice and expertise of a number of individuals whom I have not personally met. There are so many individuals to thank in this respect that, if I may be permitted, I would like to thank all at once the contributors to the Facebook Thomism Discussion Group. This group and its members are an invaluable resource to the Thomist for chasing up references, airing views and interpretations, and even engaging with dissenting voices. I thank all the members for their continual advice and engagement on all Thomist-related matters.

A substantial portion of this book was completed while I was working for one year at Maynooth University Ireland. My colleagues there provided me with an atmosphere in which research could flourish and my work was supported. I wish to thank in this regard

Mette Lebech, Cyril McDonnell, Amos Edelheit, Susan Gottloeber, Simon Nolan, William Desmond, and Hadyn Gurmin for providing such a collegial atmosphere in which to work.

Moving from the professional to the personal, I wish to thank my families. The first family I want to thank are my Dominican brethren of the Irish province. By their love and support they continually remind me that it is not enough to love God with all my mind, but that I must love Him also with all my heart. Many of those Dominicans portray in their lives the truth of that reality about which I often think and write. In particular I would like to thank Eamonn and Leah Gaines, Christina Martin, Michael O'Toole, Kirsten Peterson, Fr John Walsh, and Fr Conor McDonough.

Turning then to my other family, I wish to thank my wife, Collette, and my children, Evelyn, Dominic, and Joseph. They often have to deal with a husband and father distracted and drowning in the depths of Thomist philosophy: with all my heart—thank you.

Finally, there is nothing that I have and nothing that I can do if not for God, the cause of my being. It is only right then, in a book devoted to considering Him as our first beginning and final end, that I acknowledge God for His goodness to me in all things. Meagre and imperfect as they are, I dedicate these thoughts to Him.

The material in Chapter 7 on per se series and final causality originally appeared in 'Essentially Ordered Series Reconsidered Once Again', *American Catholic Philosophical Quarterly,* 91:2 (2017), 155–174. I thank the *ACPQ* for permission to use that material here.

INTRODUCTION

ST THOMAS AQUINAS IS A thinker whose considerable intellectual energies were devoted to an understanding and articulation
of the nature of God and the relation of creatures to Him. Casual
readers will be aware that he is famous for his demonstrations for
God's existence; the more specialized reader will lament that this is
all the casual reader is aware of concerning the thought of Aquinas.

St Thomas is rightly famous for his demonstrations of God's
existence; I am certainly of the opinion that we should read and
ponder his thought in this regard for the perennial insight that
the very existence of things is what is at stake in the question of
God's existence. Behind considerations of change, causality, possibility and necessity, etc., there is the insight that existing things
may as well not exist; it is not in their natures to be. Hence, essence
and existence are distinct therein, so that unless there is something
that is pure existence itself on which all depend for their existence,
there would be nothing.[1] This is what God's primacy consists in,
not being first in some linear chain, but that on which all depend
for their existence, He Himself depending on nothing.[2]

---

1. Aquinas's argument for God from the *De Ente et Essentia*, Cap. 4, is developed along
   these lines, and I defend it in *Aquinas's Way to God: The Proof in* De Ente et Essentia
   (New York: Oxford University Press, 2015).
2. Edward Feser, *Five Proofs of the Existence of God* (San Francisco: Ignatius Press,
   2017), p. 64: 'what is meant by a "first" cause . . . is not merely "the cause that comes
   before the second, third, fourth, and so on", or "the one which happens to be at
   the head of the queue". Rather, a "first cause" is one having *un*derived or "primary"
   causal power, in contrast to those which have their causal power in only a derivative
   or "secondary" way.'

The latter in turn has implications for how we think about God as creator, since He is so not in terms of being there before the beginning of all things (for instance, prior to the big bang) and giving the first push into existence, or something like that; rather God is creator because of the complete dependency of all things on Him for their existence. It was this key insight into the nature of God as creator which permitted Thomas to affirm the possibility, though not the actuality, of a beginningless created universe, since such a universe would not exist in itself and so would still require a cause of existence.

My previous book, *Aquinas's Way to God: The Proof in* De Ente et Essentia, focussed on a demonstration of God's existence the central argumentative strategy of which was to show that the very existence of things calls for a source of existence without which nothing would be. Such argumentation led me naturally to conclude with a brief account of what a Thomistic metaphysics of creation would look like. In that final chapter I was able to offer nothing more than a brief overview. This work substantially enlarges on that overview and comes as the natural completion of the demonstration of God's existence in the *De Ente et Essentia*.

It should be noted however that whereas the proof of God in the *De Ente et Essentia* appears in a single paragraph of a single chapter of a small treatise devoted to metaphysics, Aquinas's metaphysics of creation is spread throughout his works. To be sure there are magisterial treatments of the issue in his *Sentences* commentary (Lib. II, dist. 1, qu. 1), his disputed questions (*Quaestiones Disputatae De Potentia Dei*, qu. 3), and his two *Summae* (*Summa Contra Gentiles*, Lib. II, Cap. 6–38; *Summa Theologiae*, Ia, qq. 44–49); and it is to be noted that each of these treatments is remarkably similar in the issues with which it deals and the philosophical principles on which it depends. Nevertheless, there is no single treatment of the issue of creation as there is of the proof of God based on essence and existence that we find in *De Ente et Essentia*, Cap. 4. Yet Aquinas's metaphysics of creation wherein God is conceived as the absolute source of all that exists is the backbone of his philosophical theology. Throughout his writings, there is ever present the framework of the absolute dependence of creatures on God and the independence of God as pure existence itself. Indeed, one who has not understood this aspect of Aquinas's philosophical thought cannot hope to understand his philosophy of God. Given the importance of this outlook in Aquinas's thinking and its omnipresence in his system, I have endeavoured in this work to tease out key aspects of the metaphysics of creation and to present them as signifying Aquinas's synthetic view on the matter.

One might immediately raise a procedural issue at this point to the effect that outlining the metaphysics of creation as I propose to do in this book cannot be done unless the very fact of creation, i.e. the absolute dependence of all things on God, is itself taken for granted beforehand. But we cannot demonstrate the absolute dependence of all things on God unless we outline the metaphysics of creation. Hence, we have a circle.[3]

I think the way out of this is to focus clearly on which metaphysical issues are necessary to demonstrate God's existence and the dependence of all things on Him as their cause. So if we can demonstrate God as the cause of all things *without* presupposing the fact of creation we are free to go forward in outlining the metaphysics of creation. Now as I argued in my previous book, we can demonstrate God's existence on the basis of the distinction of essence and *esse* and a denial of an infinite regress of causes in a per se ordered series. Neither of these metaphysical teachings presuppose creation in their premises; rather they go to establish that there is a being on which all things depend for their existence, i.e. God. Having established that God exists as the source of all things

---

3. Focusing on the articles on creation in the *Summa Theologiae*, Ia, qu. 44, Rudi te Velde highlights this circularity in *Aquinas on God: The 'Divine Science' of the 'Summa Theologiae'* (Aldershot: Ashgate, 2006), p. 129; note in particular what he says on p. 129: 'The argument for creation appears to be a circular argument. Proving that all things are caused by God, and proving that God exists as the first cause of all things, are two sides of the same circular argument, since God is known from creatures as their cause.'

and this without presupposing creation as a premise, we are then free to articulate the metaphysical thought explaining the absolute dependency of things on God, i.e. the metaphysics of creation. And this is what I did in a summary fashion at the end of my 2015 book after God's existence had already been demonstrated, and which I now enlarge on in this book.

So now we are at a point where we can presuppose the existence of God as established in the *De Ente et Essentia* and defended in *Aquinas's Way to God*, and I thus proceed to outline the metaphysics of creation. Thus far nothing controversial has been presupposed which is not buttressed by argumentation taken from natural reasoning.[4]

Following on from this I would like to reiterate something I have said elsewhere about Aquinas's mode of procedure in metaphysics.[5] When it comes to metaphysics, Thomas is committed to thinking through the issues involved therein on the basis of natural reason. What this entails is that if we arrive at an affirmation of the existence of God, or in this case come to conclusions about what it is for God to be creator and for creatures to have a relation to Him, we must do so on the basis of a wider metaphysical view as to

4. Te Velde adopts a similar resolution to the circularity problem by focusing on the fact that the cause of all things, i.e. God, can be known by means of His effects, i.e. creatures or essence/*esse* composites, and as so known He can be known as the ground of the being of all things. With this in mind, we can conceive of essence/*esse* composites as participating in the causal activity of God for their being. We are thus led not into a vicious circle but a speculative circle whereby we can see how creatures are related to God, their creator, by participation; see *Aquinas on God*, pp. 132–142. My only problem with te Velde's approach is that he grants that there is a circularity to Aquinas's reasoning. I don't think there is such circularity; rather Thomas simply moves from a consideration of effects, known to be so because of the composition of essence and *esse*, to their cause, which is pure *esse* itself. Moving from effects to cause in such a manner thus brings us to a level whereby we can say that all things are dependent on this cause, which cause is thereby the ground of being of all things, i.e. a creator. This seems to me to be straightforward causal reasoning with nothing circular about it.

5. See *Aquinas's Way to God*, pp. xiii–xvii; 'Thomist *Esse* and Analytical Philosophy', *International Philosophical Quarterly*, 55:1 (2015), 28–31.

the constitution of reality, a view that does not presuppose divine truths but can indeed establish them.[6]

With that in mind then metaphysics is an investigation of the being that is proportionate to our natural reason, what Thomas labels *ens commune*.[7] Whilst all sciences are concerned with investigating being in some way, they are distinguished by their formal objects.[8] Sciences take such diverse formal objects precisely because of the distinct focus that the investigator in that domain has with regard to being. And in metaphysics, the formal object of study is the being that is common to all beings, such that the focus is not narrowed to some individual being or domain of beings.

Accordingly, whilst all scientists are engaged with being, some are concerned with being as subject to matter and motion both for its being and for its being understood, and such a focus pertains to natural science. Others are concerned with being as subject to matter and motion for its being but not for its being understood, and such a focus pertains to mathematics. Finally, some are concerned with being as subject to matter and motion neither for its being nor for its being understood, i.e. with what is immaterial. The latter investigation subdivides into a consideration of what is in itself essentially immaterial such that it could never be found to be in material things, e.g. God and Angels; and what is immaterial

---

6. Aquinas's somewhat magisterial teaching of the issue of the divisions and methods of the sciences is to be found in *Super Boethium De Trinitate* (Rome: Commissio Leonina, and Paris: Les Éditions du Cerf, 1992), qq. 5–6; this section of the commentary has been translated by Armand Maurer as *Thomas Aquinas: The Divisions and Methods of the Sciences* (Toronto: Pontifical Institute of Medieval Studies, 1986). For metaphysics in particular as a science that considers being in itself and does not presuppose the existence of divine being, see qu. 5, art. 4.

7. For a treatment of Aquinas's thinking on *ens commune*, see my article 'The Meaning of *Ens Commune* in the Thought of Thomas Aquinas', *Yearbook of the Irish Philosophical Society* (2008), 32–60. For a more general discussion of the subject matter of metaphysics, see John Wippel, *The Metaphysical Thought of Thomas Aquinas: From Finite Being to Uncreated Being* (Washington, DC: Catholic University of America Press, 2000), Chapter 1.

8. *Super Boethium De Trinitate*, qu. 5, art. 1.

yet can be found to pertain to material things, e.g. being, potency, form, act, etc. The latter categories are applicable both to material and immaterial substances, and so pertain to being in general. It is the task of the metaphysician to consider the latter since these can be investigated without appeal to revelation, whereas the theologian proper considers the former and requires the aid of revelation.[9]

My point here is not to go over Aquinas's hierarchy of the sciences but to make clear that when we are considering the metaphysics of creation, we are not turning our intellects to some isolated domain of reality to which only metaphysicians have privileged access. Rather we are looking at the world around us and thinking about it in terms of its being. Nevertheless, thinking of beings in terms of their being is a way of thinking distinct from that employed in natural science and mathematics. Aquinas maintains that the latter two sciences are committed to thinking about real things by means of a certain kind of intellectual operation distinct from that employed by the metaphysician; the former he calls 'abstraction' whereas the latter he calls 'separation'.[10]

The natural scientist and mathematician make use of a kind of thinking that focuses on the essence of a thing, but overlooks its very existing, what Aquinas frequently calls its *esse*. On the other hand, there is a kind of thinking about things which does not overlook the actual existing of things, but which focuses on the *esse* of things. Now insofar as the thinking characteristic of the natural scientist and mathematician pertains only to the essences of things, one can conceptually differentiate intelligible components of essences so considered without those components themselves being separate in reality. For instance, the natural scientist can distinguish between the universal nature that pertains to several instances of it without that nature itself being separable from those instances, and the mathematician can distinguish between

---

9. Ibid., aa. 1 & 4.
10. Ibid., art. 3.

accidental features such as quantity and figure without those features being separable from the things thereby considered.

The metaphysician on the other hand, insofar as he is concerned with the actual existence of things, cannot abstract from the actual constitution of the thing's existence, but must consider the thing in terms of its existing. This then restricts the metaphysician to considering those aspects of things that are constitutive of them in their very being such as their matter and form, essence and *esse*. Once we are at a level of thinking of things in terms of their actual existence and not passing over that in favour of conceptual abstractions pertaining to features of their essences, we have entered upon a metaphysical consideration of things. And as it is focussed on the very existence of things, Aquinas's metaphysics can be described as an existentialist metaphysics.

This characterization of Thomist metaphysics as existentialist is useful insofar as it distinguishes it from the dominant approaches to metaphysics found in the analytical philosophical tradition whilst at the same time recapturing something of the metaphysical awareness of the reality, the sheer thereness, of things that is lost in the Sartrean philosophical project.

To begin with analytical approaches. The two central ways of doing metaphysics that became dominant in the latter half of twentieth-century analytic philosophy focussed on either (i) what there is, or (ii) how it is that what there is is actual as opposed to merely possible. The first approach was that of Quine, who saw the project of metaphysics as one of ontology whereby the philosopher need only regiment our best science by means of a suitably constructed mathematical logic and thence determine what that science commits us to through an interrogation of the existentially quantified propositions in the logical regimentation of science.[11]

On the other hand, developments in quantified modal logic and the use of possible worlds to ascertain the truth conditions

11. See Quine's presentation of this project in 'On What There Is', in *From a Logical Point of View* (New York: Harper and Row, 1964), 1–20.

of modal statements led thinkers such as Saul Kripke and Alvin Plantinga to some interesting conclusions about the nature of what actually exists. In particular these thinkers argued that we can arrive at some kind of essentialism through a consideration of the properties that a thing has in all possible worlds in which it exists. Not only that, they held that there is something about this actual world that distinguishes it from the various possible worlds, something that is philosophically interesting of which we need to take account. Such reasoning paved the way for a focus on the actuality of actual things, as opposed to their mere possibility, which arguably returned philosophy to a focus on the reality of the real.[12]

Elsewhere I have argued in greater depth against these approaches to metaphysics from a Thomistic perspective.[13] What I wish to say here is that neither approach focuses the philosopher on the very existence of things. The Quinean approach of deciphering what we are ontologically committed to focuses on what exists, but it does not consider that the very existence of what exists could be philosophically illuminating. Indeed, the interpretation of existence in terms of quantification cannot recognize the Thomistic view that there is a metaphysical principle of things constituting them as existing, in which case Thomist *esse* is not akin to the denial of the number zero, a predicate of predicates etc., but it is that whereby there is anything at all. On the other hand, it is arguable that the turn to actualism in modal metaphysics ushered in by Kripke and Plantinga takes us closer to a view where the actual existence of things is seen to be something of philosophical interest. But when we explore actualism, we see that the existence of things is not thought through on the basis of an advertence to some metaphysical principle like *esse* constitutive of the things that exist;

---

12. See Saul Kripke, *Naming and Necessity* (Oxford: Blackwell, 1981); Alvin Plantinga, *The Nature of Necessity* (Oxford: Clarendon Press, 1974); Robert Adams, 'Theories of Actuality', *Noûs*, 8:3 (1974), 211–231.

13. See *Aquinas's Way to God*, Chapters 2–3, and 'Thomist *Esse* and Analytical Philosophy'.

rather, the actuality of things is accounted for on the basis of what distinguishes the actual world from all other possible worlds, such as its obtaining or being true. This makes possibility explanatorily more basic than actuality, so that the latter must be explicated on the basis of the former; and that is alien to a Thomistic approach to metaphysics, which seeks to account for things in terms of their very existence, which is itself what is most basic and most fundamental, for without it there would be nothing.

Turning then to the existentialism of Sartre, his project is not so much a metaphysics but a philosophy of life, such that one exists but one is not an existing essence. Hence one's existence is not limited to a particular essence; one must make a choice, a fundamental project, to determine one's existence accordingly.[14] If we can wrestle anything of a metaphysics from this view, it is such that existence is real or present as undifferentiated prior to one's free choices to determine it on the basis of one's project. Hence existence is somewhat unlimited unless funnelled and moulded by one's choices. But as an entryway into evaluation we may ask: what is it that exists so as to make free choices? It has to have some features characteristic of its essence, otherwise it couldn't even make such choices. And it is precisely in figuring out these features, such as intelligence and freedom, that we are permitted to speak of a thing that exists, an existing essence. On the basis of the latter then, we can inquire into the very being of the thing that exists, and think it through in terms of the metaphysical principles that Aquinas outlines.

The existentialist metaphysics of Aquinas has the benefit of distancing us from these projects, since we are not taking an inventory of what there is, nor are we turning to a privileged realm of possible worlds by means of which we can get a handle on the reality of things, nor indeed are we envisioning a philosophy of life by means of which our existence is determined by our choices.

---

14. For a summary outline of this view see Jean-Paul Sartre, *Existentialism Is a Humanism* (York, England: Methuen, 2007).

Rather, what we are doing is focussing on reality in a very particular way and considering it in terms of what it is for things to be
rather than not to be. The metaphysics that thus ensues is illuminative of that reality, just as natural science and mathematics are.
Yet precisely because metaphysics considers things in their very
being, without which such things would not be, it is a more fundamental science than natural science and mathematics, because it
investigates and considers what the other sciences merely presuppose. Not only that, insofar as metaphysics seeks to offer an explanatory account of the being of things, it is illuminative for the other
sciences. This is not to say that the metaphysician can enter natural
science or mathematics and proceed to draw conclusions proper
to those sciences. Rather it is to say that insofar as these sciences
presuppose the being of things, and thus the intelligibility of such
being, they intrinsically depend on the work of the metaphysician
in making such being intelligible, feeding off that presupposed intelligibility as it were.

Furthermore, insofar as metaphysics considers the very being
of things and does not limit itself in such a consideration, metaphysics is first philosophy; for only after the being of things has
been considered can we consider how such being is known (epistemology) and how we ought to act in relation to being (moral
philosophy). Hence, in what follows, I will frequently speak of
Aquinas's philosophy of creation and his metaphysics of creation.
I mean the same by both. Technically speaking we are dealing with
the metaphysics of creation, since we are constraining ourselves
to a consideration of the very being of things and how that is dependent on God. Whilst metaphysics is first philosophy, philosophy has a wider signification than metaphysics, involving also
epistemology, ethics, etc. My use of 'philosophy of creation' as a
stand-in for 'metaphysics of creation' is merely stylistic and should
not be taken as signifying a move into a domain of consideration
outside metaphysics (though of course considerations of the metaphysics of creation will impact relevant considerations in other
branches of philosophy—such is the nature of first philosophy).

Now insofar as metaphysics is a fundamental science which illuminates the very being of things and which the other sciences implicitly presuppose, it cannot be inconsistent with other sciences, since they depend on it for their intelligibility. Hence, if our metaphysics of creation does end up affirming something that is inconsistent with a well-established fact in some other science, we have a problem.

The significance of Aquinas's metaphysics, especially his metaphysics of creation, in regard to this problem is that it is not concentrated on a domain of reality on which some science other than metaphysics is also focussed. Rather, all sciences are concentrated on being, but they have a certain focus that distinguishes their formal objects. It follows then that insofar as the conclusions of the various sciences must be consistent with each other, their explanations of reality are not in competition with one another; and their conclusions must be devised with this in mind. So a genuine metaphysics, and hence a genuine metaphysics of creation, cannot in itself be inconsistent with natural science. And this is something that I will show with Aquinas's metaphysics of creation, especially when it comes to issues pertaining to the beginning of creation and the origin and development of living things. Hence, developments in the other sciences are never threatening to a Thomistic metaphysics of creation, because it has arrived at a set of truths about things that the other sciences presuppose but do not establish (and truths that they certainly cannot dispute unless a transition is made to a metaphysical mode of thinking).

My presentation of Aquinas's metaphysics of creation will proceed with all this in mind. I will be considering the very being of things, and in particular what it is about things that makes them to be as opposed to not to be. Automatically this project takes us deep into the heart of Thomistic metaphysics, yet I am not here concerned with explicating Thomistic metaphysics pure and simple; rather I am interested in how Aquinas interprets creation with his metaphysics already established. That metaphysics is the metaphysics of *esse,* which Aquinas articulates as early as the *De Ente et*

Essentia and which remains with him throughout his career. I shall delve into some of the details of this in Chapter 2 but not in any significant depth. It is presupposed here that the reader will already have some familiarity with Aquinas's metaphysical thought, especially since this work follows upon the successful demonstration of God's existence as presented in *De Ente et Essentia*, Cap. 4; nevertheless explanatory footnotes and guides to further reading will be offered throughout. With all that in mind, the layout will be as follows.

Chapter 1 presents something of a prolegomenon that considers the philosophical heritage on which Aquinas builds his metaphysics of creation. This is no mere exercise in the history of philosophy. As I will show, Aquinas reads the history of philosophy in this regard as being on a certain trajectory, moving from a particular and insufficient consideration of being to a universal consideration wherein one can arrive at the affirmation of a cause of the very being of things and hence at a creator. Thus, Thomas's consideration of the history of the philosophy of creation will tell us exactly in what an appropriate metaphysics of creation must consist.

Chapter 2 explores Aquinas's thinking on the agent of creation. This will involve a consideration of God as intelligent, volitional, and powerful—all key divine attributes that Aquinas maintains any creator must possess. This chapter will not establish the existence of God, since this whole book is concerned with what creation is like, given that God exists and causes all things to be. Hence I take as given the successful demonstration of God's existence (something that I take Aquinas to have established in *De Ente et Essentia*, Cap. 4) and proceed from there to consider creation.

Having considered the history of the philosophy of creation and the nature of the agent of creation, I move on in Chapter 3 to consider the nature of creation itself. This chapter offers a definition of creation and teases out of that what it is to be created *ex nihilo*. Furthermore, I will explore Aquinas's notion of creation as an asymmetrical dependence relation of creatures on God, thereby permitting an interpretation of creation in causal terms.

Chapter 4 makes a start in considering the causality of creation. This chapter focuses on God as the originating source of the existence of things, in which case it will consider Him somewhat as the primary efficient cause of all. It is pointed out in this chapter that God's being the primary cause does not consist in His being first in a linear causal chain but in His being the primary source of the actuality, the *esse*, that all creatures have.

God having been considered as originating cause in Chapter 4, the next two chapters consider aspects of what has been originated. Chapter 5 considers the object of creation, i.e. what exactly is originated by God in the act of creation, and how all of the diverse metaphysical components of a creature can simultaneously depend on God for their being. Chapter 6 considers the history of creation, and it focuses on two issues: (i) the beginning (or otherwise) of creation and its standing in relation to God, and (ii) the development of created things over time, particularly with regard to the scriptural interpretation of such development.

Finally, in Chapter 7 I consider the end of creation, and in this chapter I return to a consideration of causality. Whereas Chapter 4 focussed on God as the originating source of all things, Chapter 7 considers God as the final end of such things, humanity in particular. In this chapter I integrate the causal framework of Chapter 4, within which God is the originating primary cause, with a causal framework wherein God is seen to be the absolute final cause. In doing so I show how it is possible to conceive of God as both primary cause and ultimate end. Thus not only do creatures come from God, but they also strive to return to Him. I end this final chapter with a discussion of humanity's return to God and how Aquinas believes that can be achieved.

Beyond the fine details of such metaphysical reasoning about God and creation, Aquinas's thinking in this regard is ordered to give one an intellectual grasp of how God is the source and summit of the being of all creatures. As I will show, nothing would be if not for Him, and all things are radically incomplete, humans in particular, unless they return to Him. Whilst Aquinas's metaphysics does not presuppose any spirituality and is capable of being affirmed on the basis of natural reason, it can indeed function in the context of a spiritual life, and in Aquinas's case, the life of a saint. Being an expert metaphysician will not make one a saint; but sometimes endeavouring to become a saint will entail that one excels in metaphysics. As I said at the beginning, Aquinas's intellectual energies were devoted to an understanding and articulation of the nature of God and the relation of creatures to Him. The urge that pushed him deeper into metaphysics was the urge to love God, which love drew from St Thomas the desire to come to know Him Whom he loved. An understanding and mastery of the Thomistic metaphysics of creation will not entail that one loves God as Thomas did, but it will bring to the fore the realization that through no motivation other than the sheer ecstatic love He has for Himself, God brings into existence things other than Himself that they may share in that love. This may motivate us to seek to know God and in turn to love Him; it may not. For Aquinas at least, his metaphysics is an instance of his striving to come to know God, and the metaphysics of creation offers us a taste of that knowledge.

1

PHILOSOPHIES OF CREATION

THE CENTRAL INSIGHT OF AQUINAS'S philosophy of God is that He is the unique subsisting source of being from which all existing things come. So much is clear from Aquinas's demonstrations of God, especially that of the *De Ente et Essentia*, Cap. 4, wherein Thomas establishes that whereas all other things are composites of essence and *esse*, God is pure *esse* itself on which all essence/*esse* composites depend. All creatures then exist precisely because they depend on God for their existence. This is a position that Aquinas sees as having been slowly arrived at in the history of philosophical reflection on the notion of creation. Indeed, he reads the history of philosophy in this respect as incrementally progressing towards that which scripture simply reveals and what the greatest philosophers only grasped with difficulty. In two particular texts Aquinas outlines the direction of philosophical speculation on these matters.

In the *Quaestiones Disputatae De Potentia Dei* he writes:

[i] It should be said that the ancients proceeded according to the order of human cognition in the consideration of the nature of things. So insofar as human cognition begins with sense and proceeds to understanding, the earlier [priores] philosophers were occupied with sensible things and gradually moved from there to the consideration of intelligible things. And insofar as accidental forms are in themselves sensible, not substantial, the earlier philosophers held that all forms are accidents and that the only substance is material substance; and insofar as substance is such

that it is the cause of accidents, which are caused from the principles of substance, the earlier philosophers postulated no other cause beyond matter; rather out of that they held that all that is seen to come forth in sensible things is caused. Hence, they did not think to posit any cause of matter, and they completely neglected the efficient cause. [ii] Later [posteriores] philosophers began to consider certain substantial forms to a certain degree. They did not however arrive at the consideration of universals, but their whole focus was concerned with particular forms [formas speciales]. Consequently, they posited certain agent causes, not as universally conferring being [esse] on things, but as changing matter to this or that form, such as intellect, love, and hate, whose action they took to divide and unite. Hence, not even these philosophers held that all beings proceed from the efficient cause, but that matter is presupposed for the action of the agent cause. [iii] Later philosophers, such as Plato, Aristotle, and their followers came upon the consideration of universal being [esse] itself, and therefore they alone held that there is some universal cause of things from which all things come forth into being [esse], as is clear from Augustine [De Civitate Dei, Lib. 8, Cap. 4]. And in this their thought is in agreement with the Catholic faith.[1]

---

1. Aquinas, *De Potentia Dei* (Turin: Marietti, 1927), qu. 3, art. 5: 'Dicendum, quod secundum ordinem cognitionis humanae processerunt antiqui in consideratione naturae rerum. Unde cum cognitio humana a sensu incipiens in intellectum perveniat priores philosophi circa sensibilia fuerunt occupati, et ex his paulatim in intelligibilia pervenerunt. Et quia accidentales formae sunt secundum se sensibiles, non autem substantiales, ideo primi philosophi omnes formas accidentia esse dixerunt, et solam materiam esse substantiam. Et quia substantia sufficit ad hoc quod sit accidentium causa, quae ex principiis substantiae causantur, inde est quod primi philosophi, praeter materiam, nullam aliam causam posuerunt; sed ex ea causari dicebant omnia quae in rebus sensibilibus provenire videntur; unde ponere cogebantur materiae causam non esse, et negare totaliter causam efficientem. Posteriores vero philosophi, substantiales formas aliquatenus considerare coeperunt; non tamen pervenerunt ad cognitionem universalium, sed tota eorum intentio circa formas speciales versabatur: et ideo posuerunt quidam aliquas causas agentes, non tamen quae universaliter rebus esse conferrent, sed quae ad hanc vel ad illam formam, materiam permutarent; sicut intellectum et amicitiam et litem,

And again in the *Summa Theologiae* he writes:

[i] The ancient philosophers gradually and step by step entered into the understanding [cognitionem] of truth. Being of cruder mind in the beginning, they did not think that there were any beings other than sensible bodies. Those among them who held that there is motion in sensible bodies did not consider it except as pertaining to certain accidents, for example through rarefaction and condensation, uniting and dividing. And supposing the very substance of bodies to be uncreated, they assigned certain causes for the change of accidents, for example, love, hate, intellect, and such like. [ii] Later thinkers understood the distinction between substantial form and matter, which matter they held to be uncreated; and they perceived the change that occurred in corporeal things to be according to essential forms. They posited certain universal causes for such changes, such as the oblique circle, according to Aristotle, or the ideas, according to Plato. But it should be considered that through form matter is contracted to a determinate species, just as the substance of a certain species is contracted by accidents coming to it and thereby determining its mode of being, as a man is contracted by whiteness. Each of these positions considered being in a particular way, as it is this or that being, and thus they assigned particular agent causes for things. [iii] Finally others rose to the consideration of being as being, and they considered the cause of things, not simply insofar as they are this or that, but insofar as they are beings. What is the cause of

---

quorum actionem ponebant in segregando et congregando; et ideo etiam secundum ipsos non omnia entia a causa efficiente procedebant, sed materia actioni causae agentis praesupponebatur. Posteriores vero philosophi, ut Plato, Aristoteles et eorum sequaces, pervenerunt ad considerationem ipsius esse universalis; et ideo ipsi soli posuerunt aliquam universalem causam rerum, a qua omnia alia in esse prodirent, ut patet per Augustinum. Cui quidem sententiae etiam Catholica fides consentit.' I will discuss the historical veracity of Aquinas's treatment of his predecessors below, but for a brief evaluation of the historicity of this passage, see Fernand Van Steenberghen, *Le problème de l'existence de Dieu dans les Écrits de s. Thomas d'Aquin* (Louvain: Éditions de l'institut supérieur de philosophie, 1980), p. 138.

things insofar as they are beings is a cause of things not simply as they are such through accidental forms, or according as they are these [kinds of things] through substantial forms, but is a cause of things with respect to all that pertains to their being [esse] in whatever mode.[2]

Both texts clearly maintain that historically speaking there has been an upward ascent in the consideration of things, from thinking of them as material and subject to certain accidental forms and rising to a consideration of things in terms of their being, which consideration brings about an awareness of the cause of such being. It is the final stage wherein things are considered in terms of their very being at which the notion of creation is reached in a philosophical sense in accord with Catholicism. So clearly then Aquinas sees the philosophical tradition as playing a decisive

2. Aquinas, *Summa Theologiae* (Turin: Marietti, 1926), Ia, qu. 44, art. 2: 'Antiqui philosophi paulatim, et quasi pedetentim, intraverunt in cognitionem veritatis. A principio enim, quasi grossiores existentes, non existimabant esse entia nisi corpora sensibilia. Quorum qui ponebant in eis motum, non considerabant motum nisi secundum aliqua accidentia, ut puta secundum raritatem et densitatem, congregationem et segregationem. Et supponentes ipsam substantiam corporum increatam, assignabant aliquas causas huiusmodi accidentalium transmutationum, ut puta amicitiam, litem, intellectum, aut aliquid huiusmodi. Ulterius vero procedentes, distinxerunt per intellectum inter formam substantialem et materiam, quam ponebant increatam; et perceperunt transmutationem fieri in corporibus secundum formas essentiales. Quarum transmutationum quasdam causas universaliores ponebant, ut obliquum circulum, secundum Aristotelem, vel ideas, secundum Platonem. Sed considerandum est quod materia per formam contrahitur ad determinatam speciem; sicut substantia alicuius speciei per accidens ei adveniens contrahitur ad determinatum modum essendi, ut homo contrahitur per album. Utrique igitur consideraverunt ens particulari quadam consideratione, vel inquantum est hoc ens, vel inquantum est tale ens. Et sic rebus causas agentes particulares assignaverunt. Et ulterius aliqui erexerunt se ad considerandum ens inquantum est ens, et consideraverunt causam rerum, non solum secundum quod sunt haec vel talia, sed secundum quod sunt entia. Hoc igitur quod est causa rerum inquantum sunt entia, oportet esse causam rerum, non solum secundum quod sunt talia per formas accidentales, nec secundum quod sunt haec per formas substantiales, sed etiam secundum omne illud quod pertinet ad esse illorum quocumque modo.' Unless otherwise stated, all translations are my own.

role in forming a philosophy of creation that he takes to be true and in accord with the Catholic faith.[3]

These two texts illustrate Thomas's reading of the trajectory of the history of philosophy with respect to the philosophical treatment of creation; so they provide us with an invaluable insight into those philosophical traditions with which he dialogued in working out his own doctrine of creation. It is clear from both texts that for Thomas creation can only be arrived at once we consider the very being of things, i.e. once we come to a consideration of what it is for a thing to be and not restrict ourselves to considering the accidental or essential features of things. Only when we have arrived at a consideration of the being that all things possess and account for that in terms of a primary cause without which nothing would be, only then have we arrived at a satisfactory doctrine of creation.

Both texts clearly locate the beginnings of philosophical reflection on creation in the Presocratic philosophers with their stress, in Thomas's eyes, on the primacy of matter. Now, in the *De Potentia Dei*, Aquinas places in the second category certain Presocratics who came to an understanding of a cause of motion somewhat independent of matter, such as love/hate/intellect. (As will be seen, this is a reference to Empedocles and Anaxagoras.) Moving on, in the same text, Aquinas places Plato and Aristotle in

---

3. As an aside, this would entail that Gilson's notion of a Christian philosophy, being a philosophy done in the context of questions and issues made pressing by Christian revelation, is problematic at least in regard to the notion of creation; for whilst Aquinas undoubtedly maintained that the creation of things in time was a matter of revelation, we see him in these texts maintaining that a philosophical reflection on the nature of things can give us a notion of creation in accord with the Catholic faith, in which case we have a philosophy (a metaphysics to be exact) worked out independently of revelation but which agrees with revelation. However, as will be seen, the Gilsonian reading of these texts, especially with regard to the depths into which the unaided reason of Plato and Aristotle penetrated the notion of creation, does not lend itself to the straightforward reading I (and others) have given it here. For some details on Gilson's notion of Christian philosophy see John Wippel, 'Thomas Aquinas and the Problem of Christian Philosophy', in *Metaphysical Themes in Thomas Aquinas* (Washington, DC: Catholic University of America Press, 1984), Chapter 1.

the third, the most profound, group of philosophers who arrived at a consideration of the being that all things possess. Philosophers of this category managed to understand the nature of creation and God as creator insofar they rose up to a consideration of that being without which nothing would be and the cause on which all things depend.

Nevertheless, when we turn to the *Summa Theologiae* text, on one reading (favoured by Gilson), Aquinas seems to say that Plato and Aristotle did not arrive at an account of creation but stopped short of the consideration of the being of things. He appears to say in this text that they remained only with a particular consideration of things, investigating them in terms of their essences but not their being. Hence, on this reading Aquinas relegates Plato and Aristotle to the second category representing a definite advance over the first but not yet having arrived at the profundity of the *aliqui* of the third category. The latter according to Thomas managed to arrive at a consideration of the being of things, and thence to a notion of creation. Consequently, on this reading, as profound as Plato and Aristotle's development over the Presocratics was, it was not profound enough to arrive at an account of creation proper.[4]

These two texts set the stage for Aquinas's philosophy of creation. So in the remainder of this chapter I will consider the stages of philosophical reflection which in Thomas's mind eventually culminated in a genuine appreciation of the doctrine of creation. Doing so will help to convey the philosophical problematic in which Aquinas locates his thought on creation.

4. Commenting on the *Summa* text Gilson writes in *The Christian Philosophy of St Thomas Aquinas* (Notre Dame, IN: University of Notre Dame Press, 1956), p. 131: 'To explain the existence of a being is to explain the existence of the whole being. Now the pre-Socratics had, indeed, justified the existence of individuals as such. Plato and Aristotle had justified the existence of substances as such. But not one of these seemed even to have dreamed that there was any occasion to explain the existence of matter. . . . When we ask why beings exist as such, matter and form and accidents included, there is but one possible answer—God's creative act.'

In what follows, I will begin with the Presocratics (Section 1) and then will move onto Plato and Aristotle, determining whether or not they did in Thomas's view arrive at an appreciation of creation (Section 2); finally I will consider the *aliqui* who according to Thomas certainly understood the meaning of creation (Section 3).

1 THE PRESOCRATICS

Both of the aforementioned texts locate the beginning of philosophical reflection on creation in the beginnings of philosophy itself in the thinking of the Presocratic philosophers. Thomas holds that these philosophers were focussed on material sensible bodies and that such focus impacted on their ability to arrive at a proper account of the being of things.[5]

Aquinas claims elsewhere that some of the Presocratics in focussing on the materiality of things posited a single material principle of things; for example, Thales posited water, Heraclitus and Hippasus posited fire, and Anaximenes posited air. On the other hand, other Presocratics posited multiple material principles; for example, Empedocles posited earth, air, fire, and water, and Anaxagoras posited fundamental homogenous particles. Accordingly, these ancient materialists held that some material reality, suitably construed, is responsible for all things such that everything derives from it.[6]

Reasoning on behalf of the Presocratics, Thomas maintains that they focussed on four conditions of matter that make it fit to be considered a principle or cause: (i) a principle is that of which something is composed, (ii) a principle is that from which a thing

---

5. For a historical account of the theological thought of the Presocratics see Werner Jaeger, *The Theology of the Early Greek Philosophers* (Oxford: Clarendon Press, 1947).
6. For Aquinas's understanding of these positions see *In Metaphysicam Aristotelis Commentaria* (Turin: Marietti, 1935), Lib. 1, lect. 4.

comes to be, (iii) a principle is that into which a thing is ultimately dissolved, and (iv) a principle remains in existence throughout generation. Thomas maintains that matter meets these conditions, in which case matter is suitably taken to be a principle.[7] Hence, in his view it was on this basis that the Presocratics took matter to be the principle of all things.

Concerning those who posited a single material principle (Thales, Heraclitus, Hippasus, and Anaximenes), Aquinas maintains that they were concerned only with accidental form. This is because any modifications of the underlying material substrate (water, fire, air) will be accidental modifications thereof. So the form that a thing takes will only be a modification of some material substance already underlying it. As is clear from the *De Potentia Dei* text, Thomas maintains that these philosophers did not move beyond sensation in their consideration of beings; for sensation perceives only accidental and not substantial form. On the other hand, those who posited several material principles (Empedocles and Anaxagoras) arrived at some consideration of substantial form, since on their understanding the form of things is not simply a modification of some underlying substance, but the formation of the various elements/particles into one substance rather than another, which form is distinct from the matter that it informs. Hence, Aquinas believes that these philosophers did move beyond sensation. However, such a move does not signify a discovery of universals under which many singulars are unified as of a single kind, which is the thinking represented by the Platonic and Aristotelian traditions; for according to Thomas, Empedocles and Anaxagoras were still tied down to matter and did not fully envisage the distinction between matter and substantial form.[8]

Given these considerations of the form(s) that the material principle takes, we can consider the causality involved in the change of

---

7. Ibid., n. 74.
8. *De Potentia Dei*, qu. 3, art. 5: 'Posteriores vero philosophi, substantiales formas aliquatenus considerare coeperunt; non tamen pervenerunt ad cognitionem universalium, sed tota eorum intentio circa speciales versabatur.'

form. As Aquinas understands them, some of the Presocratics held that not only is there a material cause from which all things come to be but also there is some kind of efficient or agent cause, which suitably forms the underlying material substrate.[9] Historically speaking, Anaximenes seems to have been the first to have held this view; for he held that it is through condensation and rarefaction that air is made into bodies and fire, respectively. Nevertheless, in his commentaries on the *Physics* and *Metaphysics*, Thomas attributes this view not only to Anaximenes, but to Thales, Heraclitus, and Hippasus as well.[10]

On the other hand, the philosophers who posited multiple material principles—Empedocles and Anaxagoras—were led to consider that the elements/particles are re-formed into different kinds of things by means of some cause(s) independent of the material principles themselves. Thus, Empedocles held that there are four unchanging elements (earth, air, fire, and water) and these are brought together or separated in a continuing cycle through love and hate; and somewhat similarly, Anaxagoras held that there are ultimate homogenous unchanging particles and they are brought together through intellect or mind (*intellectum*).[11] Despite their differences, in Thomas's eyes all these thinkers held that beyond the material principle(s) there is some kind of efficient causality at

9. *In I Met.*, lect. 5, n. 93: 'Sed ponentes causam materialem unam vel plures, dicebant ex ea sicut ex subiecto fieri generationem et corruptionem rerum: ergo oportet quod sit aliqua alia causa mutationis; et hoc est quaerere aliud genus principii et causae, quod nominatur, unde principium motus.'
10. See *In Octo Libros Physicorum Aristotelis Expositio* (Turin: Marietti, 1954), Lib. 2, lect. 2, n. 13: 'Nullus vero eorum qui posuerunt principium unum tantum, dixit illud esse terram, propter eius grossitiem. Huiusmodi autem principia mobilia dicebant, quia per horum alicuius rarefactionem et condensationem alia fieri dicebant'; *In I Met.*, lect. 5, n. 95: 'In quo differebant a primis naturalibus, qui dicebant unam causam esse omnium rerum substantiam, quae tamen movetur per rarefactionem et condensationem.'
11. *Summa Theologiae*, Ia, qu. 44, art. 2: 'Quorum qui ponebant in eis motum, non considerabant motum nisi secundum aliqua accidentia ut puta secundum raritatem et densitatem, per congregationem et segregationem. Et supponentes ipsam substantiam corporum increatam, assignabant aliquas causas huiusmodi accidentalium transmutationum; ut puta amicitiam, litem, intellectum, aut aliquid huiusmodi'; see also *In I Met.*, lect. 5.

work which modifies material reality. Nevertheless, Thomas holds that these thinkers remained committed to some uncreated material reality.[12]

So, in light of this, what appears to be the common failing of the Presocratics in Thomas's eyes is that all being is ultimately rooted in some material principle(s), and the only things that exist are certain modifications thereof brought about by some efficient cause. In that context, nothing is either absolutely produced or destroyed; all 'creation' is relative to some uncreated material reality. There is no creation proper, only transmutation. On this account nothing comes into being, but everything merely undergoes a change in being. There is no room for a cause of all that is precisely because all causality must ultimately presuppose a material substrate that is uncaused.[13]

What we can see here is that there is a strict contrast between Aquinas and the Presocratics in their appreciation of the nature of reality, and this contrast produces the divergence in their respective philosophies of creation. The Presocratics as Aquinas understands them could not see beyond a material principle of things; for them there is always a permanent and uncreated material reality simply worked upon by some sort of efficient cause. The contrast for these Presocratics was never between being and nonbeing; rather it was a contrast between being this and not being that; efficient causality has a role, but only insofar as it is exercised on something already existing. The idea of some cause bringing something into being out of nothing would have been alien to the Presocratic mind as understood by St Thomas,

12. Speaking of Empedocles and Anaxagoras, Aquinas writes, *De Potentia Dei*, qu. 3, art. 5: 'Posuerunt quidam aliquas causas agentes, non tamen quae universaliter rebus conferrent, sed quae ad hanc vel ad illam formam, materiam permutarent; sicut intellectum et amicitiam et litem, quorum actionem ponebant in segregando et congregando; et ideo etiam secundum ipsos non omnia entia a causa efficiente procedebant, sed materia actioni causae agentis praesupponebatur.'

13. *In I Met.*, Lect. 4, n. 75: 'Materia autem quae est rerum substantia secundum eos semper manet. Omnis autem mutatio fit circa aliqua quae adveniunt ei, ut passiones. Et ex hoc concludebant quod nihil generatur vel corrumpitur simpliciter, sed solum secundum quid.'

because their metaphysical categories were not sufficiently developed to consider the very being of things. Thus in Thomas's eyes, whilst the Presocratics did begin the metaphysical reflection on being and even came upon some kind of efficient causality independent of matter, they failed to consider the being of things in any universal fashion, and so could not come upon a cause of all things tout court. Hence, there will be a significant advance in the metaphysical discussion when one comes to consider being in a more universal fashion and not as tied down to this or that but as independent of the beings that share in it.

2 PLATO AND ARISTOTLE

One would think that if there was any advance beyond the consideration of individual beings to a consideration of universal being, it occurred in the thinking of Plato and Aristotle. However, as has been shown above, the two texts detailing the history of thinking on creation appear to place Plato and Aristotle on the one hand as having arrived at a consideration of the very being of things and thus at a satisfactory philosophy of creation (*De Potentia Dei*) and on the other hand as indeed going further than the earlier Presocratics but yet remaining with beings and their determinations rather than progressing to the being that all things have in common (*Summa Theologiae*). So what are we to make of this? In order to untangle this interpretative web, I will consider Aquinas's understanding of Plato and Aristotle specifically with regard to their philosophies of creation. Having done so, I will then address the question of whether Thomas does change his mind between the *De Potentia Dei* and *Summa Theologiae* texts.

2.1 Plato

Aquinas had next to no direct knowledge of Plato's thought; rather his knowledge of Plato was diffused through the lenses of various historical authors, notably Aristotle, Dionysius, Boethius, and

Augustine.[14] Nevertheless, whilst ignorant of Plato's own writings, Thomas does have a somewhat accurate generic knowledge of Platonic thought. Accordingly, he sees Plato as having inherited the traditional metaphysical problem of squaring the one and the many.[15] He notes that Plato adopted the Socratic approach when considering natural things, so that when Plato engages with the things that we see around us he looks for the universal definitions of those things. However, such definitions cannot be given in sensibility, because sensible things are always changing; hence, according to Thomas, Plato assigned such definitions to certain entities that are universal and separated from material things, which entities he named 'ideas' or 'species'.[16] It is through participation in these ideas that sensible things exist.[17]

Now, in this context, Thomas understands participation in the following way. When something possesses the nature of the species totally and without addition it exists per se or *per essentiam*. However, when something possesses the essence of the species not totally but in an individual respect through some addition, e.g. through matter, then it only participates in the nature of the species.[18] Participation then is the possession in an individual fashion of what is in itself universal.[19]

14. For a brief survey of Aquinas's knowledge of the historical Plato see Wayne Hankey, 'Aquinas, Plato, and Neoplatonism', in *The Oxford Handbook of Aquinas*, ed. by Eleonore Stump and Brian Davies, (Oxford: Oxford University Press, 2012), Chapter 4.

15. *In I Met.*, lect. 10, n. 152.

16. Ibid., n. 153.

17. Ibid.: 'Per earum participationem esse substantiale habebant. . . . Unde et sensibilia omnia habent esse propter pradictas et secundum eas.'

18. Ibid., n. 154: 'Individuum autem est homo per participationem, inquantum natura specie in hac materia designata participatur. Quod enim totaliter est aliquid, non participat illud, sed est per essentiam idem illi. Quod vero non totaliter est aliquid habens aliquid aliud adiunctum, proprie participare dicitur.'

19. Aquinas, *Super Boethium De Trinitate et Expositio Librii De Ebdomadibus* (Rome: Commissio Leonina, 1992), *Expositio De Ebdomadibus*, lect. 2, p. 271: 70–73: 'Est autem participare quasi partem capere; et ideo quando aliquid particulariter recipit id quod ad alterum pertinet universaliter, dicitur participare illud.'

It is notable that in the commentary on the *Metaphysics* and elsewhere Aquinas draws out his understanding of the meaning of participation. Such a definition of participation cannot be found in the text of the *Metaphysics* on which Thomas comments, nor did the historical Plato offer any such definition. Furthermore, Aristotle's impatience with the notion of participation was well known, and indeed that impatience shines through in the very text on which Thomas is commenting.[20] Despite all this, Thomas undertakes to provide Plato with a definition of participation which while it may not be historically accurate in fact coincides quite neatly with Plato's thought. Evidently, Aquinas thought this aspect of Plato's thinking was worth salvaging even though with Aristotle he rejected Plato's commitment to separately existing universals. The reason why Thomas salvaged the Platonic notion of participation is because he utilizes it in his account of how essence is related to the act of existence, the *esse*, in existing things, and how created *esse* is related to divine *esse* in creation; these are themes that will reappear later in this current book.[21]

Turning then to the Platonic thinking itself and its contribution to the historical development of reflection on creation, one of the core differences between the Presocratics and Plato is that

20. Aristotle, *Metaphysics*, Bk. 1, Chapter 6, 987b10–13: 'Only the name "participation" was new; for the Pythagoreans say that things exist by imitation of numbers, and Plato says they exist by participation, changing the name. But what the participation or the imitation of the Forms could be they left an open question'; as found in *The Complete Works of Aristotle*, ed. by Jonathan Barnes (Princeton: Princeton University Press, 1984).

21. Probably one of the most significant fruits of the Thomistic revival of the twentieth century was the rediscovery of the Platonic heritage of Thomism and in particular the doctrine of participation; for details of this see Cornelio Fabro, *La nozione metafisica di partecipazione scondo s. Tommaso d'Aquino* (Turin: Società Editrice Internazionale, 1950), *Participation et Causalité* (Louvain: Publications Universitaires de Louvain; Paris: Éditions Béatrice-Nauwelaerts, 1961); Louis-Bertrand Geiger, *La participation dans la philosophie de s. Thomas d'Aquin* (Paris: Librairie Philosophique J. Vrin, 1942); and more recently Rudi te Velde, *Participation and Substantiality in Thomas Aquinas* (Leiden: Brill, 1995). For discussion see Wippel, *The Metaphysical Thought of Thomas Aquinas*, Chapter 4.

Plato recognizes some immaterial reality on which all of material reality depends. Without the ideas to give it structure and stability, there would be no sensible reality. The principle of things and their unity is nothing material on the Platonic account but is immaterial. By contrast things are for the Presocratics on account of their matter, and multiplicity arises based on the various forms that such matter takes.[22]

So much for Aquinas's understanding of Plato's general metaphysical views; how does Aquinas evaluate them with regard to creation?

On this issue it would appear that Aquinas's attitude evolved. For a certain period at the beginning of his career, Aquinas lumped Plato together with Anaxagoras, and held that they both took the world to be made by God out of some preexistent matter, but what is novel on the Platonic account is the introduction of universal forms, which are absent in Anaxagoras's thought as Aquinas understands him. Such a view fails to arrive at creation since it envisages God merely working to transform something that already exists, not to bring it to be. Hence, early in his career Aquinas saw Plato's thinking on creation as being more in line with that of the Presocratics.[23]

---

22. *In I Phy.*, lect. 8, n. 55: 'Plato posuit magnum et parvum ex parte materiae, quia ponebat unum principium formale, quod est quaedam idea participata a diversis secundum diversitatem materiae: antiqui vero naturales ponebant contrarietatem ex parte formae, quia ponebant primum principium unam materiam, ex qua multa constituuntur secundum diversas formas'; see also *In I Met.*, lect. 10, n. 166, for the same.

23. See *Scriptum Super Libros Sententiarum* (Paris: Lethielleux, 1929), Lib. 2, dist. 1, art. 1: 'Tertius error fuit eorum qui posuerunt agens et materiam, sed agens non esse principium materiae, quamvis sit unum tantum agens: et haec est opinio Anaxagorae et Platonis: nisi quod Plato superaddidit tertium principium, scilicet ideas separatas a rebus, quas exemplaria dicebat; et nullam esse causam alterius; sed per haec tria causari mundum, et res ex quibus mundus constat'; *De Articulis Fidei* (Turin: Marietti, 1954): 'Secundus est error Platonis et Anaxagorae, qui posuerunt mundum factum a Deo, sed ex materia praeiacenti.' However, beginning with the *Expositio Super Primam Decretalem* Aquinas attributes this error solely to Anaxagoras and no longer includes Plato, even though he had the opportunity to do so. It would appear that from this point onwards Aquinas's appreciation of Plato

Nevertheless, given that the principle of things for Plato is not material but immaterial, the way is open in Plato's thinking to affirm that matter is created and hence in need of a creator. Later in his career, Aquinas ceases to associate Plato with Anaxagoras and the general Presocratic view regarding the uncreatedness of matter, and in fact, as is clear from the *De Potentia Dei* text, he credits Plato with having arrived at a philosophical vision which is in accord with the Catholic faith in this regard.[24]

Mark Johnson credits Aquinas's shift in opinion here to his deepening appreciation of St Augustine's *City of God* and Augustine's sympathetic treatment of the teachings of the Platonists therein; it is also worth pointing out, as Johnson does, that in the *De Potentia Dei* text Aquinas explicitly refers to St Augustine as an authority on the Catholicity of the doctrines of both Plato and Aristotle.[25] Be that as it may, the more interesting issue (at least from a purely philosophical perspective) is why Aquinas in his mature thinking held that Plato reached so far as to have arrived at a philosophically acceptable account of creation. What interpretation of Plato's thought could Aquinas offer that would see Plato hold that there is some single principle from which all that is comes to be?

---

as a thinker of being *qua* being deepened. For discussion of these and related texts see Mark Johnson, 'Aquinas's Changing Evaluation of Plato on Creation', *American Catholic Philosophical Quarterly*, 66:1 (1992), 81–88.

24. Aquinas also displays some hesitation in reporting Plato's views in later texts. Notice for instance that in *Summa Theologiae*, Ia, qu. 15, art. 3, ad. 3, he states: 'Dicendum quod Plato, *secundum quosdam*, posuit materiam non creatam', and in ad. 4: 'Individua vero, secundum Platonem, non habebant aliam ideam quam ideam speciei, tum quia singularia individuantur per materiam, quam ponebat esse increatam, *ut quidam dicunt*'. Evidently, at least in these instances, Aquinas wishes to qualify that it is only certain people who say that Plato took matter to be uncreated but does not have the confidence himself to say that Plato held this view.

25. See Johnson, 'Aquinas's Changing Evaluation of Plato on Creation', p. 88: 'A possibility may be that Thomas, early in his Italian sojourn, was able to read the relevant passages in Augustine's *De civitate dei*, where the latter speaks so highly of Plato, and his teaching regarding what Augustine took to be a creator God. It was in Italy, and in a text from his disputed question *De Potentia Dei* (1265), one notes, that Thomas invokes the authority of Augustine after discussing Plato and creation.'

In order to answer this question, we can return to the *De Potentia Dei*, wherein Aquinas reconstructs Plato's thought so as to furnish Plato with a suitable account of creation. In the *De Potentia Dei*, qu. 3, art. 5, just after the text quoted at the beginning of this chapter, Aquinas offers the following argument on Plato's behalf.

If something that is one is common to many distinct things, it is necessary that it be caused in each of them by some single cause. It cannot belong essentially to those individual things themselves since they are distinct from each other, and given that a diversity of causes produces a diversity of effects, if the common feature were essential to diverse things, it would no longer be common. So should some common feature belong essentially to individual things and not be derived from a single common cause, it would no longer be one. Now, *esse* is found to be common in all distinct things and so belongs to them not essentially (*non ex se ipsis*) but is derived from some single cause.[26] Aquinas immediately attributes this argumentation to Plato, stating that his way of proceeding was to some unity that preceded all multiplicity in things.[27]

---

26. *De Potentia Dei*, qu. 3, art. 5: 'Oportet enim, si aliquid unum communiter in pluribus invenitur, quod ab aliqua una causa in illis causetur; non enim potest esse quod illud commune utrique ex se ipso conveniat, cum utrumque, secundum quod ipsum est, ab altero distinguatur; et diversitas causarum diversos effectus producit. Cum ergo esse inveniatur omnibus rebus commune, quae secundum illud quod sunt, ad invicem distinctae sunt, oportet quod de necessitate eis non ex se ipsis, sed ab aliqua una causa esse attribuatur.'

27. Ibid.: 'Et ista videtur ratio Platonis, qui voluit, quod ante omnem multitudinem esset aliqua unitas non solum in numeris, sed etiam in rerum naturis.' The same argument can be found substantially, without the attribution to Plato, in *Summa Theologiae*, Ia, qu. 65, art. 1. Note also the following assertions by Thomas that Plato did attribute the creation of all things to God: *Lectura Romana in Primum Sententiarum Petri Lombardi*, ed. by Leonard Boyle and John Boyle (Toronto: Pontifical Institute of Mediaeval Studies, 2006), dist. 3, qu. 1, art. 3, ad. 1: 'Plato non habet ita in libris suis sicut nos habemus. Ipse enim posuit unum primum ens, quod est causa omnibus rebus, esse Deum et Patrem totius universitatis rerum; et posuit mentem divinam sub ipso et dixit eam creaturam Dei, et in ipsa mente posuit ideas'; *In Aristotelis Libros De Caelo et Mundo* (Turin: Marietti, 1952), Lib. 1, n. 61: 'Plato posuit caelum genitum, non intellexit ex hoc quod est generationi subiectum, quod Aristoteles hic negare intendit: sed quod necesse est

The Platonic nature of this argumentation is indisputable, and indeed it utilizes Aquinas's understanding of the Platonic doctrine of participation; for in accord with the latter if something possesses some feature non-essentially it possesses it through participation in what does so possess that feature per se. Hence, once we have reached some common feature of all things, a feature such things possess through participation, we can infer the dependence of such things on that which possesses that feature essentially. Here that feature is *esse*, the act of existence. Hence all things that simply have *esse*, but are not identical with the *esse* they have, derive it from what does have it essentially, i.e. something whose essence is its *esse*. So this is how Aquinas envisages Plato as having arrived at an account of creation.

Despite all this, historically speaking it is not the case that Plato ever arrived at a consideration of what Thomas understood *esse* to be, i.e. the act of existence correlative to the essence of a creature.[28] So in this context Aquinas is reading Plato in a highly sympathetic light and is even willing to attribute his own metaphysical views on *esse* to Plato. This would tie in with Johnson's point about the authority of Augustine leading Aquinas to reevaluate his views on Plato such that Aquinas attributes to Plato views that Plato never held yet Thomas did hold and that to his

ipsum habere esse ab aliqua superiori causa, utpote multitudinem et distensionem in suis partibus habens; per quod significatur esse eius a primo uno causari, a quo oportet omnem multitudinem causari.'

28. See Charles Kahn, 'Why Existence Does Not Emerge as a Distinct Concept in Greek Philosophy', in *Philosophies of Existence*, ed. Parviz Morewedge (New York: Fordham University Press, 1982), pp. 7–18, for a discussion of the lack of recognition of the act of existence in the classical period of ancient Greek philosophy terminating with Aristotle. Kahn is explicit in his general view that 'existence' only emerges as a distinct philosophical concept when Greek philosophy is interpreted in light of biblical creation, since the focus of the latter is on being and nothing. Hence, as with Aquinas, Kahn holds that the concept of existence is necessary for a genuine philosophical account of creation, though Kahn does not think such a concept emerges in ancient philosophy. See also Paul Seligman, 'Being and Forms in Plato', in *Philosophies of Existence*, ed. by Morewedge, pp. 18–33, for an account of Plato's notion of being.

mind justified a sympathetic reading. This reading is not out of sync with the general tendency of Plato's thought but is certainly historically inaccurate.

2.2 Aristotle

Central to the Aristotelian notion of being is that it is said neither univocally nor equivocally but proportionately, depending on the being under consideration. Thus within the Aristotelian framework, being is said primarily of substance and secondarily of accidents whose being depends on the substance of which they are the accidents. Moreover, change is possible precisely because substances have some element of potency (matter in the case of material substances), which is actualized, thereby bringing to completion the process of change. Hence, Aristotle is able to say, against Parmenides, that change need not imply an illegitimate move from nonbeing to being, since potency is a legitimate though secondary feature of being, whilst at the same time holding, against the Heraclitean doctrine, that being is not primarily in flux, since the primary signification of being is substance which exists in act. In order to grant the intelligibility of this notion of being, Aristotle had to introduce potency into his metaphysics and contrast this with act, so that potency stands to be actualized whereas the principle of actuality actualizes some potency. This framework is in turn applicable to Aristotle's theory of forms.

It is well known that Aristotle rejects the Platonic theory of forms but does not abandon the forms completely; rather he situates them within the context of his own notion of being. Accordingly, insofar as substance is the primary signification of being, and, following Plato, forms are the principles of reality in an important respect, Aristotle holds that form is the principle of actuality of the substance, but given his rejection of separately existing universals, Aristotle holds that form is immanent in the substance. Hence form is the form of the individual substance, and its ontological coprinciple (for material things at least) is matter. Form then informs matter, and given that form is the principle of act, matter is the respective principle of potency. Form actualizes the potentiality of matter, which in itself is unformed. Given that matter in itself is unformed, such unformed or prime matter is pure potency, whereas given that form in itself is without matter, immaterial form is pure act. When form comes to inform prime matter, a substance is produced, so that the form informing the matter is the substantial form. Such a substance can admit of accidental variations in accord with the categories of accident that Aristotle recognizes, and the forms of such variations are accidental forms which accrue to the matter of an already existing substance.

Reality is made up of individual substances, and these substances are composites of potency and act. Governing these substances are certain causal processes which relate to the metaphysical components involved. In the substance itself the form actuates the matter, giving it some sort of structure; so that there is a kind of causality that the form exercises over the matter such that the matter would be unformed without it, and this is formal causality. Not only that, the matter itself exercises a kind of causality insofar as the form is not Platonic and does not exist independently of that of which it is the form, hence the matter is that within which the form comes to be, and this is material causality. But forms do not just come and go in the thing, there is a cause independent of the thing that brings about the change of form, and this is the efficient cause. But the efficient cause does not act for no reason at all; it always acts for a purpose, and the goal towards which the efficient cause acts is the final cause. There are thus four kinds of causality: material, formal, efficient, and final, and the being of a thing cannot be explained without these.

Overall then Aristotle has a very generous notion of being centred on substance and accident and their ontological principles governed by the different kinds of causality that he recognizes.[29] So

29. This reading of Aristotelian metaphysics runs throughout Aquinas's work, and various details of it are continually brought to bear on his thinking on a number of issues. A good central text in which Aquinas treats of these issues is the commentary

I will now consider Aquinas's evaluation of Aristotle with regard to creation.

It has already been observed that in the *De Potentia Dei* text, Aquinas singled out Plato and Aristotle as having arrived at some sort of legitimate account of creation; I have outlined how Aquinas justifies this with regard to Plato; I will now consider how he does so with Aristotle.[30] In the same place, *De Potentia Dei* , qu. 3, art. 5, Aquinas offers the following reasoning on Aristotle's behalf.

When something is found participated in by many things in a diverse way it must be attributed to those things in which it is found imperfectly in a way different from that in which it is found perfectly; for those things that are said to be in varying degrees (*secundum magis et minus*) are so in virtue of their degree of remoteness or closeness in approach to that which is one. If a perfection were found to be in individual things essentially (*ex se ipso*), there would be no reason why the same perfection would be in one more perfectly than in another. We must then posit a single being which is most perfect and true, which is proved from the fact that there is a mover which is wholly immobile and most perfect, as proved by the philosophers. All other less perfect things receive their *esse* from this.[31]

---

on the *Metaphysics*, in particular Books 7–9; see also the youthful *De Principiis Naturae* for Aquinas's own résumé of Aristotelian metaphysics. For an account of Aristotelian metaphysics free from any Thomist glosses see Terence Irwin, *Aristotle's First Principles* (Oxford: Clarendon Press, 1988).

30. For further texts in which Aquinas attributes a doctrine of creation to Aristotle see Steven Baldner and William Carroll, trans., *Aquinas on Creation: Writings on the 'Sentences' of Peter Lombard Book 2, Distinction 1, Question 1* (Toronto: Pontifical Institute of Mediaeval Studies, 1997), Appendix D.

31. *De Potentia Dei*, qu. 3, art. 5: 'Secunda ratio est, quia, cum aliquid invenitur a pluribus diversimode participatum oportet quod ab eo in quo perfectissime invenitur, attribuatur omnibus illis in quibus imperfectius invenitur. Nam ea quae positive secundum magis et minus dicuntur, hoc habent ex accessu remotiori vel propinquiori ad aliquid unum: si enim unicuique eorum ex se ipso illud conveniret, non esset ratio cur perfectius in uno quam in alio inveniretur. . . . Est autem ponere unum ens, quod est perfectissimum et verissimum ens: quod ex hoc probatur, quia est aliquid movens omnino immobile et perfectissimum, ut a philosophis est

There is a similarity between this demonstration and the previous one attributed to Plato such that there is a doctrine of participation at work in both. Notice that the reasoning begins with a consideration of perfections possessed in diverse ways through participation. The greater or lesser degree of participation in perfection itself is precisely the mark of something's existing not absolutely but in a dependent way. In the Platonic argument Aquinas sees Plato as reasoning from the *esse* that is held in common to some source on which all such possessors of *esse* depend. In the current argument attributed to Aristotle, we are asked to consider the diverse participations in some perfection and their unified dependence on what is perfection itself. It is from this that all things derive their *esse*. Hence Thomas reads the trajectory of Aristotelian metaphysics as pointing towards some source or principle of actuality that in itself can account for the diversity of individual things. That source can only be a cause of *esse*, because *esse* is the only metaphysical principle that all things share.

So as with the Platonic argument so too with this one, the universality of *esse* and its possession non-essentially, i.e. through participation, are key notions for arriving at a sound metaphysics of creation. Again, as with Plato so too with Aristotle; we see Aquinas attributing to him a metaphysical doctrine that the historical Aristotle would not have recognized: the dependence of things on *esse* for their being.[32] Not only that, the argument offered here on Aristotle's behalf bears a striking similarity to the fourth way of *Summa Theologiae*, Ia, qu. 2, art. 3, which further buttresses the impression that Aquinas is reading something of his own thought into Aristotle's here. So, again, Aquinas is reading an ancient philosopher, Aristotle, in a highly sympathetic light in order that

---

probatum. Oportet ergo quod omnia alia minus perfecta ab ipso esse recipiant. Et haec est probatio philosophi.' The most likely textual source that Thomas has in mind for this demonstration is *Metaphysics*, Bk. 2.

32. See Kahn, 'Why Existence Does Not Emerge as a Distinct Concept in Greek Philosophy.'

his thinking (Aristotle's) may yield a legitimate metaphysics of creation.

Notwithstanding all that, Aquinas does maintain that Aristotle erred somewhat when it came to creation. Aquinas is clear in most of the texts (aside from the *Summa Theologiae* one quoted above) that Aristotle taught that the *esse* of things depends on some single principle so that without the causal activity of that principle there would be nothing; hence even matter requires a cause for its being. However, Aquinas maintains that Aristotle erred in thinking that the universe is without a beginning, so that whilst the universe depends on God and is thereby created, it did not have a beginning in time (an issue I shall consider in Chapter 6).[33] Thus whilst Aquinas thinks Aristotle correctly located the being of all things in a single source, Aquinas nevertheless maintains that Aristotle erred when it came to his affirmation of the beginninglessness of creation. Yet at least for the plain fact of affirming the dependency of all things on God, Aquinas holds that Aristotle did come to an understanding of creation.

2.3 *De Potentia Dei* versus *Summa Theologiae*

We now turn to the vexed issue of what appears to be Aquinas's changing evaluation of Plato and Aristotle across the texts in *De Potentia Dei* and *Summa Theologiae*. The tricky text is *Summa Theologiae*, Ia, qu. 44, art. 2, for therein he seems to diverge from other instances wherein he attributes to Plato and Aristotle a universal consideration of being permitting them to arrive at an

---

33. *In II Sent.*, dist. 1, qu. 2, art. 5, expositio textus: 'Aristoteles non erravit in ponendo plura principia: quia posuit esse omnium tantum a primo principio dependere; et ita relinquitur unum esse primum principium. Erravit autem in positione aeternitatis mundi'; *Expositio Super Primam Decretalem* (Rome: Leonine, 1968), E35: 432–437: 'Alius error fuit Aristotilis ponentis quidem omnia a Deo esse producta sed ab aeterno, et nullum fuisse principium temporis, cum tamen scriptum sit Gen. 1:1: "In principio creavit Deus caelum et terram"; et ad hoc excludendum addit *ab initio temporis*.'

acceptable account of creation. Let us just recall the movement of thought in the *Summa* text. Aquinas begins with the Presocratic materialists, whom he says focussed on sensible things and so were constrained to consider only accidental forms and the transmutation of some underlying material principle. Then there were those who came to an understanding of the distinction between substantial form and matter, the latter of which they took to be uncreated; and so they took the change of forms in things to be in accord with certain essential forms whose causes were more universal, such as the oblique circle in Aristotle or the ideas in Plato. However, Thomas points out that matter is contracted to a certain species by form, and so too a substance is contracted to a certain mode of being by the accidents which accrue to it. It is at this point where the disputed text comes in which I shall present in the Latin so as to be clear on Thomas's meaning; he says:

> Utrique igitur consideraverunt ens particulari quadam consideratione, vel inquantum est hoc ens, vel inquantum est tale ens. Et sic rebus causas agentes particulares assignaverunt.

The evaluative content of this is clear, the positions under consideration considered being either in an individual sense, i.e. as this or that being, or in terms of being such and such, i.e. in terms of its essence. Both stop short of a consideration of being in itself and hence of a universal cause of being. Hence the need to go further.

Now the question is, where do Plato and Aristotle fit in? Are they envisaged by this negative evaluation such that they stopped short of a universal consideration of being and hence short of a cause of all that is?

On one translation this text may read as follows: 'Both considered being under a particular consideration, either insofar as it is this or insofar as it is such. And thus they assigned particular agent causes for things.' Given what has come before in the text, under this translation Aquinas has in mind Plato and Aristotle, and he holds that they offered only a particular consideration of being, in which case we move onto the later *aliqui* who offered a universal consideration of being. This is the translation (or something like it) favoured by Gilson and Pegis, both of whom take this to indicate that Aquinas never attributed a doctrine of creation to either Plato or Aristotle.[34]

The latter position seems odd, not to mention excessive, given that we have already observed Aquinas attributing to Plato and Aristotle the view that all things come from some primary source and hence are created. The only way to downplay the latter would be to hold that the *Summa* text, under the interpretation that Aquinas does have Plato and Aristotle in his sights, is to be taken as representative of Aquinas's considered view of the matter. And this is precisely what Gilson does. He takes the *Summa* as the proof text by which all others are to be evaluated. So that when Aquinas appears to attribute a doctrine of creation or a consideration of the cause of *esse* to Plato or Aristotle in other texts, Gilson holds that the *esse* taken in those texts is not actually Thomist *esse*, i.e. the actuating coprinciple of essence, but, for Aristotle at least, the substantial *esse* of the thing not signifying its 'to be' but its 'to be this such and such'. So elsewhere, such as the commentary on Aristotle's *Physics* (*In VIII Phy.*, lect. 2, n. 975), when Aquinas says that Plato and Aristotle arrived at the knowledge of the *principium totius esse*, for Gilson he really only means that they arrived at the principles of the substance of the thing, i.e. matter and form; this is not to say that they arrived at a knowledge of *esse* as the coprinciple of essence and caused by God the creator of all. Hence, for Gilson Plato and Aristotle could not have arrived at a doctrine of creation precisely because they did not arrive at a consideration of *esse*

---

34. Étienne Gilson, *The Spirit of Medieval Philosophy* (New York: Scribner, 1940), pp. 438–441, n. 4; Anton Pegis, 'A Note on St. Thomas, *Summa Theologica*, I, 44, 1–2', *Mediaeval Studies*, 8 (1946), 159–168; *St. Thomas and the Greeks* (Milwaukee: Marquette University Press, 1939), p. 67, pp. 101–104, n. 64. Fabro also holds that Aquinas denies a doctrine of creation to Plato and Aristotle in this text; see *Participation et Causalité*, p. 368.

as that without which nothing would be, and the text from the *Summa* confirms this.[35]

On the other hand Mark Johnson and following him Lawrence Dewan have pointed out that *utrique* in the foregoing text does not mean to refer to 'both' Plato and Aristotle, but to 'each' position advocated by a certain group of philosophers. Note that before Aquinas mentions Plato and Aristotle in the text he has already delineated the positions of two groups of philosophers. For the first group (i)—i.e. Thales, Heraclitus, and Anaximenes—there were only accidental transmutations of a single underlying uncreated material substrate. For the second group (ii) there is still an underlying uncreated material substrate, but that substrate is made up of many elements/particles which stand to be formed in a certain way by more universal causes—i.e. the positions of Empedocles and Anaxagoras. On Johnson's reading, *utrique* refers to each of these groups but not to Plato and Aristotle. This interpretation is buttressed by the fact that in the text *utrique* takes the plural of the verb: *consideraverunt*, because it refers to two groups of thinkers, whereas if it were referring to two individuals (Plato and Aristotle) it would have taken the singular of the verb: *consideravit*.[36] Given this reading, Aquinas does not envisage Plato and Aristotle as amongst those who only considered being in a particular fashion; rather he has in mind the Presocratics, most notably Anaxagoras and Empedocles, who held that the underlying elements/particles stand to undergo some formal reconstitution, and that the cause of such change is more universal than the matter that is changed, nevertheless stopping just short of a universal consideration of

---

35. See Gilson, *The Christian Philosophy of St Thomas Aquinas*, pp. 130–132, in particular note 6.

36. Mark Johnson, 'Did St Thomas Attribute a Doctrine of Creation to Aristotle', *New Scholasticism*, 63:2 (1989), 144–145: 'What emerges is that the *utrique* refers not to two individuals taken separately, but to two groups taken separately, and the shift from individuals to groups, from the singular *uterque* to the plural *utrique* explains why the verb here is in the plural: "utrique . . . consideraverunt".

being. Thus, on this interpretation Aquinas does not deny Plato and Aristotle their place as defenders of creation.[37]

Yet the association of Plato and Aristotle with the second, less than universal, consideration of being is troubling. Johnson himself concedes this point and recognizes that in the *Summa Theologiae* Plato and Aristotle are not explicitly mentioned as being members of the third group, the *aliqui*, who did reach a consideration of the very being of things. Wippel sees this as an indication that Aquinas did locate Plato and Aristotle in the second group and that he simply changed his mind from his earlier discussion in the *De Potentia Dei*. Nevertheless, Wippel notes that after writing this part of the *Summa* (1266–68), Aquinas quickly changed his mind back to the *De Potentia Dei* view, which places Plato and Aristotle in the third group. So that in the commentary on the *Physics* (1268–69) Aquinas once again attributes to Plato and Aristotle the privilege of having arrived at a knowledge of a cause of *esse* and thus a creator.[38]

Johnson however makes the important point that in the *Summa* the second group of philosophers held that matter is uncreated, in which case they could not have arrived at the notion of a creator responsible for all things.[39] The uncreatedness of matter is a view that Aquinas *never* attributed to Aristotle (and it is a view he was unwilling even to attribute to Plato later in his career); rather Aquinas on a number of occasions takes Aristotle to be committed to the dependence of all things on some single absolute cause, and this presumably also includes the existence of matter.[40] Hence, Plato and Aristotle should be naturally excluded

37. Ibid., p. 145.
38. John Wippel, 'Aquinas on Creation and the Preambles of Faith', *The Thomist*, 78:1 (2014), 22–23. For the commentary on the *Physics* see *In VIII Phy.*, lect. 2, n. 975: 'Postremi vero, ut Plato et Aristoteles, pervenerunt ad cognoscendum principium totius esse.'
39. *Summa Theologiae*, Ia, qu. 44, art. 2: 'Ulterius vero procedentes distinxerunt per intellectum inter formam substantialem et materiam, quam ponebant increatam.'
40. The most explicit text in this regard is *In II Sent.*, dist. 1, *expositio textus*: 'Ad quod dicendum quod Aristoteles non erravit in ponendo plura principia, qua posuit esse

from this second group on Aquinas's view, in which case they belong with the *aliqui*.

So, what do I say on this matter?

Johnson has some compelling reasons for reading the text as he does, and it does indeed seem clear that Gilson is taking the *Summa* text and forcing the interpretation of others in light of it. Could it be that Thomas simply changed his mind when it came to the *Summa Theologiae*? The short time between the *De Potentia Dei* (1265–66) and the *Summa Theologiae* (1266–68) would indicate that his change in mind was quite abrupt, and that his reversion back to the *De Potentia Dei* mindset was just as abrupt. The *Summa* then would represent a blip in his reading of Plato and Aristotle and their respective philosophies of creation. Not only that, if in the *Summa Theologiae* Plato and Aristotle are to be located in the second group, then we have to contend with the fact that he attributes to members of this group the view that matter is uncreated, a view that he nowhere attributes to Aristotle and that by the time of the *Summa* (and even in the *Summa* itself; see note 24) he is unwilling to ascribe to Plato. These facts would be enough to warrant a certain degree of scepticism in regard to the view that he did change his evaluation of Plato and Aristotle in the *Summa* text. Nevertheless, in the *Summa Theologiae* Plato and Aristotle are not explicitly referred to as being amongst the *aliqui* but are at least associated with those who only reached a particular consideration of being. So we cannot rule out a change of mind on Aquinas's part.

I think the safest option is the following. If Aquinas did change his mind in the *Summa Theologiae*, he quickly changed it back again, and so overall his considered opinion appears to be

omnium tantum a primo principio dependere, et ita relinquitur unum esse primum principium. Erravit autem in positione aeternitatis mundi'; see also Johnson, 'Did St Thomas Attribute a Doctrine of Creation to Aristotle, texts 1–4, for a discussion of texts, including this one, in which Aquinas thinks that Aristotle holds that all created things, including their matter, depend on some single principle for their being.

that Plato and Aristotle arrived at the knowledge of a cause of the *esse* of things and so at the doctrine of creation. Setting aside these hermeneutical issues, Aquinas is generally of the view that Plato and Aristotle went beyond the limits of Presocratic philosophy by advocating for some universal cause on which all things depend and on which even matter depends for its being.

3 THE *ALIQUI*

In Thomas's eyes Plato and Aristotle arrived at an understanding of God as a primary principle from which all things come to be. That should give us an indication then of who exactly the *aliqui* are. Simply speaking the *aliqui* are those authoritative philosophers and theologians from whatever background who posited a primary cause of all things without which there would be nothing. Thus, included in the *aliqui* will be representative thinkers from the Christian, Jewish, and Islamic philosophical traditions along with various Neoplatonic sources, in particular the *De Causis*, that attribute all of reality to a single primary source. We are now in the domain of philosophical monotheism.[41]

Having named earlier thinkers, Aquinas does not specifically name those he considers to have arrived at a satisfactory understanding of creation. This is not surprising if one remembers that philosophers moving in the regions of philosophical monotheism all generally held that there is nothing in reality that is not

---

41. For some details of the influence of philosophical monotheism on Aquinas on creation see Baldner and Carroll, *Aquinas on Creation*, pp. 12–22. Also worth consulting for the thinking of some of these philosophers in themselves is Herbert Davidson, *Proofs for Eternity, Creation and the Existence of God in Medieval Islamic and Jewish Philosophy* (New York: Caravan Books, 1982). Fabro believes that the *aliqui* are the *Platonici*, i.e. the Neoplatonists, and he is probably correct in this view; however, that should not exclude other philosophical monotheists whose philosophical teachings had an impact on Aquinas's thinking; see *Participation et Causalité*, p. 368, n. 13.

dependent on God for its being. Where they differ is in the ways they account for this; yet all are committed to the same truth and can be lumped together in the same group.

In the *De Potentia Dei* Aquinas gives us an indication of the reasoning of the *aliqui*, wherein he presents the following argument, which he attributes to Avicenna.

What is through another is reduced to a cause that is through itself. So for instance if there were a single heat existing through itself it would have to be the cause of heat for all other heats, which have heat through participation. The reduction of what is through another to what is through itself results in the positing of something that is itself *esse*, because there must be a primary being that is pure act and in which there is no composition. It follows then that from this one being all others come to be and they have being through participation but not in themselves.[42]

This philosophical reasoning moves in the immediate vicinity of Aquinas's own most cherished thinking on the existence of God and the nature of creatures. Typically in demonstrating God's existence, Aquinas argues that the *esse* that creatures have as distinct from their essences leads us to a causal regress whose termination is in something that is simply pure *esse* and on which all things depend for their existing. This is a position on God as primary cause that Thomas retains throughout his writing career, and never repudiated.

Now, given the arguments that Thomas advances on behalf of Plato and Aristotle, we notice again some degree of commonality

---

42. *De Potentia Dei*, qu. 3, art. 5: 'Tertio ratio est, quia illud quod est per alterum, reducitur sicut in causam ad illud quod est per se. Unde si esset unus calor per se existens, oporteret ipsum esse causam omnium calidorum, quae per modum participationis calorem habent. Est autem ponere aliquod ens quod est ipsum suum esse: quod ex hoc probatur, quia oportet esse aliquod primum ens quod sit actus purus, in quo nulla sit compositio. Unde oportet quod ab uno illo ente omnia alia sint, quaecumque non sunt suum esse, sed habent esse per modum participationis. Haec est ratio Avicennae [*Metaphysica*, Lib. 8, Cap. 7, and Lib. 9, Cap. 4].' Aquinas attributes more or less the same argument to Avicenna in *In II Sent.*,dist. 1, qu. 1, art. 1.

between them and this one. This is to the effect that what exists through another is dependent on what exists in itself. Things that exist do not do so of themselves; they are dependent on something for their *esse,* and this dependence ultimately terminates in God. Aquinas sees both Plato and Aristotle as having arrived in their respective ways at the same truth, and now he attributes the same reasoning to the philosophical monotheism of the *aliqui.* This tells us that in Aquinas's eyes what is needed for a suitable doctrine of creation is a position that has God as the primary source of all things without Whose creative activity there would be nothing. Only when this position has been established is it possible to affirm creation.

So what is at stake in the metaphysics of creation is establishing an account of things that exhibits the complete and utter dependence of them on God. This is what Aquinas sees the philosophical tradition, beginning with the Presocratics, as having been slowly moving towards, and it is this insight that he strives to preserve throughout his own discussions of creation. Aquinas's metaphysics of *esse,* a metaphysical view that I have shown him attributing several times to historical philosophers, is uniquely placed to allow him to develop a systematic metaphysics of creation; for once one has latched onto *esse* as the very principle by means of which anything at all exists, one has arrived at what all existing things have in common and the cause of which possesses it essentially.[43] With that

---

43. I should point out here that the role of *esse* in the metaphysical constitution of a creature precisely as something created was also the dominant focus of discussions of essence and *esse* in the aftermath of Aquinas's death. Indeed, James of Viterbo launches his discussion of essence and *esse* with the question: can creation be maintained if *esse* and essence do not really differ in creatures? This indicates that the essence/*esse* distinction was by now thought to be crucial to determining the notion of creation, so much so that a denial or qualification of the distinction could be seen to undermine creation. For details see Wippel, 'The Relationship Between Essence and Existence in Late Thirteenth Century Thought: Giles of Rome, Henry of Ghent, Godfrey of Fontaines, and James of Viterbo', in *Philosophies of Existence,* ed. by Morewedge, pp. 131–165.

in mind, I shall now proceed to a consideration of Aquinas's own philosophy of creation and observe how throughout he preserves the key insight which is essential to his concept of creation: that all things that exist in whatever way they exist are dependent on God for their existence. The next chapter thus considers God as the agent of creation from Whom all things come to be.

2

THE AGENT OF CREATION

AQUINAS IS CLEARLY COMMITTED TO a primary cause of all things, and throughout his writings he offers demonstrations for the existence of such a being. I will not consider those demonstrations here because I wish to articulate Aquinas's metaphysics of creation, i.e. what creation involves given that God exists. Nevertheless, the primary cause Whose existence Thomas establishes elsewhere is the agent of creation; it is because of this agent's causality that anything exists at all. Hence all things derive their existence from this cause. Such a commitment to an agent of creation does not tell us much about creation itself. Nevertheless, in order to consider what is involved in creation, it is necessary to consider what kind of being the agent of creation is.

The goal of this chapter is to consider what God must be like in order to be the agent of creation. That will involve a consideration of God's power, since it is by it that God creates; but God's power is an activity that proceeds from Himself to an external effect, and according to Thomas it is not exercised without two internal activities: intellect and will. All of these must be considered in order to consider Aquinas's metaphysics of creation. However, in numerous places Aquinas maintains that we cannot know the essence of God by means of philosophy and that natural reason only provides us with a pale indirect knowledge thereof. Doesn't the claim to treat philosophically of God's activity in creating stand in tension with such agnosticism about the divine essence? If it does, then we face a problem before our consideration of creation even begins. Thus, I will consider first how it is that we can treat philosophically of the divine essence at all, and second, the nature of God's creative attributes of intellect, will, and power. Whilst not an exhaustive treatment of Aquinas's philosophy of God, the treatment here will be sufficient for my consideration of the metaphysics of creation.

1 OUR KNOWLEDGE OF GOD

We are material beings and our knowledge begins in the senses. Hence, Aquinas holds that we arrive at knowledge of the immaterial by means of the material. We have no direct epistemic contact with immaterial things; indeed when we try to think about such things for ourselves it is like the eye of an owl trying to look at the sun; such luminosity is overpowering to the eye, hence the owl must look away from the sun and is only aware of it indirectly. Similarly with God, we cannot think directly about God in Himself, we can only know Him in Himself as He reveals Himself to us.[1] Such revelation cannot furnish philosophy with a set of principles for consideration of divine things, and this is because philosophy must proceed on the basis of natural reason; it cannot proceed by taking for granted what has been supernaturally revealed. Hence, for Aquinas, we have an indirect knowledge of God in philosophy, which knowledge is attained through inference from created material things.[2]

---

1. *Super Boethium De Trinitate*, p. 154: 149–154: 'Quia autem huiusmodi prima principia quamuis sint in se maxime nota, tamen intellectus noster se habet ad ea ut oculus noctue ad lucem solis, ut dicitur in II Metaphisice, per lumen naturalis rationis peruenire non possumus in ea nisi secundum quod per effectus in ea ducimur'; and a little further Aquinas tells us that theology proper deals with these divine beings and depends on revelation, p. 154: 175–182: 'Sic ergo theologia siue scientia diuina est duplex: una in qua considerantur res diuine non tamquam subiectum scientie, set tamquam principia subiecti, et talis est theologia quam philosophi prosequuntur, que alio nomine metaphisica dicitur; alia uero que ipsas res diuinas considerat propter se ipsas ut subiectum scientie, et hec est theologia que in sacra Scriptura traditur.'
2. *Summa Theologiae*, Ia, qu. 12, art. 12: 'quia sunt eius effectus a causa dependentes, ex eis in hoc perduci possumus, ut cognoscamus de Deo an est; et ut cognoscamus

For Aquinas, the highest degree of knowledge we can attain of created things is to be found in metaphysics; for metaphysics considers beings in their very being. Thus, we begin to approach the divine from metaphysics; but this is not to say that Thomistic metaphysics is primarily about God. Rather for Aquinas metaphysics considers being, and it does so through looking at the everyday beings we see around us; it is these beings which disclose to us the nature of being, for our encounter with being is through these. It is from a consideration of these beings that we proceed to a consideration of God as the cause of such beings, in which case God is the goal of metaphysics, not its starting point.

A number of dyadic structures are to be found in Aquinas's metaphysical thought: substance and accident, matter and form, act and potency, essence and *esse*.[3] By far the most important is the distinction and composition of essence and *esse* whereby these are correlated with potency and act respectively. It has been noted by a number of scholars that *esse* is Aquinas's unique contribution to the metaphysical heritage that he adopted, and I have already adverted to instances where he imposes it on his reading of earlier thinkers. It was through his insight that there is a principle of actuality without which nothing would be that Aquinas was able to integrate the Platonic notion of participation with the Aristotelian doctrine of act/potency composition.[4]

de ipso ea quae necesse est ei convenire secundum quod est prima omnium causa, excedens omnia sua causata. Unde cognoscimus de ipso habitudinem ipsius ad creaturas, quod scilicet omnium est causa; et differentiam creaturarum ab ipso, quod scilicet ipse non est aliquid eorum quae ab eo causantur'; see also *In I Sent.*, dist. 3, qu. 1, art. 1, ad. 5; *Super De Trinitate*, qu. 1, art. 2.

3. This interpretation of Thomist metaphysics in terms of the dyadic structures of being is from William Norris Clarke, *The One and the Many* (Notre Dame: University of Notre Dame Press, 2001). What it envisions is the fundamental compositional structure of the being that is the subject matter of metaphysics, as opposed to the simplicity of God, Who is treated as the subject of theology proper.

4. The neo-Thomist literature on this area is vast, but the following works are highly recommended: Fabro, *La Nozione Metafisica di Partecipazione secondo S. Tommaso d'Aquino, Participation et causalité selon s. Thomas d'Aquin*; Geiger, *La Participation dans la philosophie de s. Thomas d'Aquin*; Gilson, *Being and Some Philosophers*

Effectively Aquinas argued first that all creatures are composites of essence and *esse*, with essence being in potency to the *esse* by which they actually exist. Now in accord with the definition of participation offered by Aquinas when discussing Plato, an essence participates in its *esse* in order to be. This is because the essence, which is distinct from the *esse*, does not possess the actuality of *esse* in its fullness; rather the *esse* is the *esse* of that essence and in actuating the essence is limited to the contours of it. It follows then that no essence/*esse* composite realizes *esse* in its fullness, since the *esse* of every such composite is limited to the essence that is actuated.[5] Hence every such composite exists only insofar as it participates in the *esse* that it has. Not only that, insofar as no such composite is *esse per essentiam* but only *per participationem*, the *esse* of all such composites is a limited, finite, individual *esse*, what Thomas labels elsewhere *esse commune*. Being only a limited and derived *esse*, *esse commune* participates in that which is pure *esse*, or *esse per essentiam*, and this is the divine *esse*. Thus, there is a dual participation scheme in Aquinas's thought: (i) that of essences participating in their respective *esse*, and (ii) such *esse commune* itself participating in God's *esse*.[6] Given that essence and *esse* are

(Toronto: Pontifical Institute of Medieval Studies, 1952); Joseph de Finance, *Être et agir dans la philosophie de Saint Thomas* (Rome: Librairie Éditrice de l'Université Grégorienne, 1960); Rudi te Velde, *Participation and Substantiality in Thomas Aquinas* (Leiden: Brill, 1995). In addition to these important book-length studies, a plethora of articles has been published on the centrality of *esse* and its role in participation in Aquinas's thought; for further details see the relevant chapters of Wippel, *The Metaphysical Thought of Thomas Aquinas*. My own contribution to this aspect of Thomist scholarship can be found in 'Thomist *Esse* and Analytical Philosophy', *International Philosophical Quarterly*, 55:1 (2015), 25–47, and *Aquinas's Way to God*, Chapters 1–3.

5. *Summa Contra Gentiles*, Lib. 2, Cap. 52: 'Esse autem, in quantum est esse, non potest esse diversum: potest autem diversificari per aliquid quod est praeter esse; sicut esse lapidis est aliud ab esse hominis'; *De Potentia Dei*, qu. 1, art. 2: 'Esse enim hominis terminatum est ad hominis speciem, quia est receptum in natura speciei humanae; et simile est de esse equi, vel cuiuslibet creaturae.'

6. *In Librum Beati Dionysii De Divinis Nominibus Expositio* (Turin: Marietti, 1950), Cap. 5, lect. 2, n. 660: 'Alia existentia dependent ab esse communi, non autem Deus, sed magis esse commune dependet a Deo. . . . Omnia existentia continentur sub

related not only as potency and act but through participation, Aquinas unites the Aristotelian composition structure of act and potency with the Platonic participation scheme. We can thus see why Aquinas was keen to protect Plato from Aristotle's attacks on the notion of participation: because the notion of participation is essential to Aquinas's own characteristic thinking.[7]

In focussing on *esse* Thomas is the first to take note of the centrality of the actual existence of things as a metaphysically significant feature of them, rather than simply a general fact about them. Thomas's focus on the actuality of existence is so stressed that unless there is some ontological principle at the heart of being without which there would be nothing, one's metaphysics remains incomplete; no principle of actuality other than the act of existence could account for the reality of things. Thus for Thomas *esse* is a metaphysical principle of things without which they literally would not be. All other metaphysical components such as matter and form are subject to *esse*, so that without *esse* there would be

---

ipso esse communi, non autem Deus, sed magis esse commune continetur sub eius virtute, quia virtus divina plus extenditur quam ipsum esse creatum. . . . Omnia alia existentia participant eo quod est esse, non autem Deus, sed magis ipsum esse creatum est quaedam participatio Dei et similitudo Ipsius'. For a helpful overview of these two themes in Aquinas's thought, (i) essence/*esse* composition, and (ii) participation in *esse*, see Wippel, *The Metaphysical Thought of Thomas Aquinas*, Chapters 4–5.

7. As a textual reinforcement of this observation see *Tractatus De Substantis Separatis* (West Hartford: St Joseph College, 1962), Cap. 3, p. 46: 26–35: 'Omne participans oportet esse compositum ex potentia et actu, id enim quod recipitur ut participatum oportet esse actum ipsius substantiae participantis; et sic cum omnes substantiae praeter supremam quae est per se unum et per se bonum sint participantes secundum Platonem, necesse est quod omnes sint compositae ex potentia et actu. Quod etiam necesse est dicere secundum sententiam Aristotelis', and also Fabro, *La Nozione Metafisica di Partecipazione*, p. 5: 'In questo "sviluppo" dell'Aristotelismo S. Tommaso giunge all'*assimilazione*, non obbligata o fittizia, ma naturale per lui e reale del midollo speculativo, cioè dell'aspetto perenne, del Platonismo che è fatto convivere assieme all'Aristotelismo e, quello che più conta anche se può sorprendere, che questo fondo speculativo neoplatonico si sistiene quasi sempre nel Tomismo per principî aristotelici.'

no actuality. *Esse* then is the act of all acts, and in being so it is the perfection of all perfections.[8]

Accordingly, without *esse* there would be nothing. Either a thing is *esse* itself, in which case it is God, or it merely has *esse* but is not identical with the *esse* it has. The latter is a composite of essence and *esse* and does not exist unless it participates in the *esse* caused in it by God. Things then are creatures insofar as they have *esse*, and God is considered creator insofar as He gives *esse*. This leaves much to be unpacked, but what it primarily tells us is that God as the agent of creation is metaphysically quite unlike anything that has been created. He is *per essentiam*: there is no composition of essence and *esse* in Him; whereas creatures are *per participationem*: they are composites of essence and *esse*.[9]

---

8. For some representative texts see: *In I Sent.,* dist. 19, qu. 2, art. 2: 'Esse est actus existentis, inquantum ens est'; *De Ente et Essentia* (Rome: Editori di San Tommaso, 1976), p. 377: 147–152: 'Omne autem quod recipit aliquid ab alio est in potentia respectu illius, et hoc quod receptum est in eo est actus eius; ergo oportet quod ipsa quiditas uel forma que est intelligentia sit in potentia respectu esse quod a Deo recipit, et illud esse receptum est per modum actus'; *Summa Theologiae*, Ia, qu. 76, art. 6: 'Primum autem inter omnes actus est esse', and qu. 3, art. 4: 'Esse est actualitas omnis formae vel naturae'; *De Potentia Dei*, qu. 7, art. 2, ad. 9: 'Hoc quod dico esse est actualitas omnium actuum, et propter hoc est perfectio omnium perfectionum.'

9. *Summa Theologiae*, Ia, qu. 3, art. 4. The view that God is simply pure *esse* itself existing *per essentiam* is found throughout Aquinas's work; here are some instances: *Summa Contra Gentiles*, Lib. 3, Cap. 19: 'Esse habent omnia quod Deo assimilantur, qui est ipsum esse subsistens'; *Summa Theologiae*, Ia, qu. 4, art. 2: 'Cum Deus sit ipsum esse subsistens, nihil de perfectione essendi potest ei deesse'; qu. 11, art. 4: 'Est enim maxime ens, inquantum est non habens aliquod esse determinatum per aliquam naturam cui adveniat, sed est ipsum esse subsistens'; *Quaestio Disputata De Anima* (Turin: Marietti, 1927), art. 6, ad. 2: 'Si sit aliquid quod sit ipsum esse subsistens, sicut de Deo dicimus, nihil participare dicimus'; *Quaestio Disputata De Spiritualibus Creaturis* (Turin: Marietti, 1927), art. 1: 'Unde dicimus, quod Deus est ipsum suum esse'; *Quaestiones Disputatae De Malo* (Turin: Marietti, 1927), qu. 16, art. 3: 'Deus enim per suam essentiam est ipsum esse subsistens'; *Quaestiones Quodlibetales* (Turin: Marietti, 1927), Quod. 3, qu. 1, art. 1: 'Cum autem Deus sit ipsum esse subsistens, manifestum est quod natura essendi convenit Deo infinite absque omni limitatione et contractione'; *De Divinis Nominibus*, Cap. 5, lect. 1: 'Sed solus Deus, qui est ipsum esse subsistens, secundum totam virtutem essendi, esse habet'; *In Librum De Causis Expositio* (Turin: Marietti, 1955), lect. 7, n. 182: 'Causa

As composites of essence and *esse*, creatures are caused in their *esse*; this is because nothing can be without *esse*, and since *esse* is not identical with the essence of any creature, no creature would be unless it received *esse* from some cause. God is the cause from Whom all creatures receive their *esse*, since He is *esse* itself, not dependent on anything for His *esse* but capable of originating *esse* in other things. Hence God is the cause of *esse* for all things.

The otherness of God from creatures is important to bear in mind, for frequently unreflective depictions of God as creator portray Him as just another albeit significantly more powerful being existing alongside creatures. Accordingly, God is thought of as a being different in degree but not in kind from creatures. For Thomas, God is wholly different in kind from creatures, and this is because of the identity of essence and *esse* in Him. No creature could be identical with its *esse*, since all such things are caused in their *esse*. God completely transcends creatures.

Nevertheless, God is not so other from creatures as to be metaphysically distant. Both God and creatures are beings; and even though God is not just any other being and there is a significant difference between Him and creatures, it is true to say that both God and creatures are beings, and so they are alike in some way. (Aquinas in fact states that 'He Who is' is the most proper name of God, even more proper than the name 'God' itself.)[10] The likeness between God and creatures resides in their *esse*. But whereas God is His very *esse*, creatures are beings because they have *esse*. Thus whilst they are alike, there is no identity between God and creatures. It is this likeness but not altogether identity

autem prima non est natura subsistens in suo esse quasi participato, sed potius est ipsum esse subsistens.'

10. *Summa Theologiae*, Ia, qu. 13, art. 7: 'Hoc nomine, *qui est* . . . est maxime proprium nomen Dei. Primo propter sui significationem. Non enim significat formam aliquam, sed ipsum esse. Unde cum esse Dei sit ipsa ejus essentia, et hoc nulli alii conveniat . . . manifestum est quod inter alia nomina hoc maxime proprie nominat Deum'; and ad. 1: 'Hoc nomen, *qui est*, est magis proprium nomen Dei, quam hoc nomen, *Deus*, quantum ad id a quo imponitur, scilicet ab esse.'

that underlines Aquinas's doctrine of the analogical nature of the predications obtaining between God and creatures.[11]

Attributes that are commonly applied to both God and creatures are predicated primarily (*per prius*) of God and secondarily of creatures; this is because God possesses these attributes in a much more eminent fashion than do creatures. The mode of God's possession of any attribute is the mode of full and complete actuality with no admixture of potency. This is because God is pure *esse* and hence pure actuality. So whatever attribute we can apply to God, it will be applied in such a way as to admit of no admixture of potency. In that case, God possesses all attributes that He has perfectly. Creatures on the other hand are not pure act, they admit of an admixture of potency, and so they do not possess their attributes in a perfect mode but in an imperfect mode. Given the difference in mode of possession, the mode of signifying common attributes in God and creatures must accord with the degree of perfection by which such attributes are possessed. Despite the difference in mode of possession, God and creatures do share some attributes in common such as knowledge, goodness, life, etc.[12] On the basis of all this Aquinas can say that common names of God

11. A good treatment of Thomas's doctrine of analogy not restricted to the analogical predication of names of God is Bernard Montagnes, *The Doctrine of the Analogy of Being According to Thomas Aquinas*, trans. by E. M. Macierowski (Milwaukee: Marquette University Press, 2004); see also: Wippel, *The Metaphysical Thought of Thomas Aquinas*, pp. 73–94 (for analogy in general) and pp. 543–72 (for analogical knowledge of God); Gyula Klima, 'Theory of Language', in *The Oxford Handbook of Aquinas*, ed. by Stump and Davies, pp. 371–90, and 'Aquinas's Theory of the Copula and the Analogy of Being', *Logical Analysis and History of Phliosophy*, 5 (2002), 159–176; Brian Davies, 'The Limits of Language and the Notion of Analogy', in *The Oxford Handbook of Aquinas*, ed. by Stump and Davies, pp. 390–401.
12. *Summa Theologiae*, Ia, qu. 13, art. 3: 'In nominibus igitur quae Deo attribuimus, est duo considerare, scilicet, perfectiones ipsas significatas, ut bonitatem, vitam, et huiusmodi; et modum significandi. Quantum igitur ad id quod significant huiusmodi nomina, proprie competunt Deo, et magis proprie quam ipsis creaturis, et per prius dicuntur de eo. Quantum vero ad modum significandi, non proprie dicuntur de Deo, habent enim modum significandi qui creaturis competit.'

and creatures when applied to God are applied neither univocally (given the difference in mode of possession) nor equivocally (given the agreement in the attribute possessed), but analogically. Hence, true affirmations can be made about God by reasoning from creatures.[13]

It has already been observed that because God is pure *esse*, He cannot be subject to any potency and so His possession of any attribute must be perfect. But not only that, if there is no potency in God, there can be no composition in Him, because the possession of some potency which stands to be actualized is a *sine qua non* of composition; for composition involves the actualization of some potency (e.g. matter) by some principle of act (e.g. form). If God is composite in no way, then God is utterly simple—there is no division in Him whatsoever.[14] It follows then that not only are attributes attributed to God in a perfect manner, but they are attributed to Him in a simple manner as well. The divine attributes cannot be thought to be distinct from the divine essence, since that would entail composition. Hence the divine attributes must be identical with the divine essence. This can be summed up in the expression: 'whatever is in God is God'. Other than those signifying some negation or relation, the divine attributes that we apply to God are in one way or another identical with God and apply to Him substantially.[15] We creatures divide up and enumerate these attributes because our being is so limited that we cannot comprehend the divine essence in its fullness; we must make use of multiple concepts so as to signify all those divine attributes which to us are distinct in sense but identical in reference. The division and multiplicity of attributes does not signify divisions in God but in the concepts that we use in thinking of God in an affirmative manner.[16]

---

13. Ibid., qu. 13, art. 5; see also *Summa Contra Gentiles*, Lib. 1, Cap. 34.
14. *Summa Theologiae*, Ia, qu. 3, art. 7; *Summa Contra Gentiles*, Lib. 1, Cap. 18.
15. *Summa Theologiae*, Ia, qu. 13, art. 2; *De Potentia Dei*, qu. 7, art. 5.
16. *Summa Theologiae*, Ia, qu. 13, art. 4: 'Intellectus autem noster, cum cognoscat Deum ex creaturis, format ad intelligendum Deum conceptiones proportionatas perfectionibus procedentibus a Deo in creaturas. Quae quidem perfectiones

Furthermore, given God's simplicity, God cannot change in any way; this is because change requires the actualization of some potency, but insofar as God is not subject to any potency, He lacks that necessary condition for change. Hence God is immutable. Not only that, things that are composite are limited in some respect. I have already adverted to this when discussing essence/*esse* composition. The *esse* as principle of act is limited to the confines of the corresponding potency, the essence, that it actuates; the *esse* is the *esse* of that essence. Similarly, whilst form in itself is universal, form when composed with matter is limited to the conditions of the matter with which it is composed. Accordingly, a principle of act is limited by the corresponding potency that it actuates. But God is wholly simple, pure *esse* and hence pure act, in which case there is no potency in God for His actuality to actuate, in which case He is limited by nothing—there is no distinct limiting principle by which God's being is limited. Hence, God's being is infinite.[17]

Now given that God is immutable, His being is not subject to succession, in which case there is no before and after in His being. Furthermore, given that God is infinite, there is no beginning or end to His being. Accordingly, insofar as God's being is not subject to succession and is without beginning or end, God's being is wholly timeless, in which case it is eternal.[18] And He alone is

in Deo praeexistunt unite et simpliciter, in creaturis vero recipiuntur divise et multipliciter. Sicut igitur diversis perfectionibus creaturarum respondet unum simplex principium, repraesentatum per diversas perfectiones creaturarum varie et multipliciter; ita variis et multiplicibus conceptibus intellectus nostri respondet unum omnino simplex, secundum huiusmodi conceptiones imperfecte intellectum. Et ideo nomina Deo attributa, licet significent unam rem, tamen, quia significant eam sub rationibus multis et diversis, non sunt synonyma'; see also *Summa Contra Gentiles*, Lib. 1, Cap. 35.

17. *Summa Theologiae*, Ia, qq. 8–9. For details of Aquinas's endorsement of the principle that act is limited by a distinct potency that receives it, see Wippel, 'Thomas Aquinas and the Axiom That Unreceived Act Is Unlimited', in *Metaphysical Themes in Thomas Aquinas II* (Washington, DC: Catholic University of America, 2007), pp. 123–152.

18. *Summa Theologiae*, Ia, qu. 10, and *Summa Contra Gentiles*, Lib. 1, Cap. 15. For a defence of the classical notion of God's eternity, one which stresses the independence of

essentially eternal given that He is pure *esse*, and thus simple, immutable, and infinite; all else is composite in some fashion, and thus subject to change and finitude, in which case the being of such things is temporal.

I noted above that Aquinas compares our thinking about God to the eye of an owl attempting to look at the sun, in which case God can be known only indirectly. Nonetheless, it would appear that in dealing with the divine attributes we have conceded that the divine essence is after all knowable by us and that certain properties can be applied to God substantially. In order to avoid any charge of inconsistency it should be noted that when Thomas comes to deal with the divine attributes he has already established that there is a primary cause of all things in Whom essence and *esse* are identical, and this we call God. When it comes to establishing something about God and thereby making attributions to Him, we must do so in light of the unity of essence and *esse* in Him, i.e. we must respect this fundamental conclusion of the proof of God. The identity of essence and *esse* in God is not known as the result of any direct insight into the divine essence itself but is derived through the causal argumentation used to establish that there is a primary source of *esse* for all things, i.e. pure *esse* itself. So much is clear from the demonstration of God's existence. With that understanding in place we can then go on to infer what God must be like given that He is *esse* itself. And it is in doing this that we can make positive affirmations of God without denying a certain degree of ignorance of the divine essence.[19]

God has His attributes then in virtue of His being pure *esse*; they are significations of the *esse* of God not originally contained in the notion of *esse* itself; and they are attributes that are held by God in a wholly simple, changeless, and infinite fashion, from all

God's being from temporal creatures, see Eleonore Stump and Norman Kretzmann, 'Eternity', *Journal of Philosophy*, 78 (1981), 429–458.
19. See note 2 above for textual reinforcement of this point.

eternity.[20] I shall now consider those divine attributes that are most pertinent to my investigation into Aquinas's metaphysics of creation: intellect, will, and power.

2 CREATIVE ATTRIBUTES: INTELLECT, WILL, AND POWER

Aquinas does not conceive of God's creating as an activity of blind necessity which he cannot control. There is no nature, no power, no compulsion independent of God that makes God do anything; to affirm so would be to affirm that there is some potency in God that is actuated by a distinct principle. So God's creating involves only Himself. Nevertheless, whilst creation is an exercise of power into an outward effect, it is dependent on two inward operations by which (i) God envisages all that He could create, and (ii) chooses both to create and what to create.[21] So in light of this we must deal with the creative attributes of God, two of which, intellect and will, are inward, and one of which is outward, so called because it passes into an outward effect: power.

20. For more details on this way of thinking in Aquinas's thought see my article 'Aquinas, Stump, and the Nature of a Simple God', *American Catholic Philosophical Quarterly*, 90:3 (2016), 441–454.
21. *De Potentia Dei*, qu. 1, art. 5: 'Impossibile est autem, id quod agit ex naturae necessitate, sibi ipsi determinare finem: quia quod est tale, est ex se agens; et quod est agens vel motum ex se ipso, in ipso est agere vel non agere, moveri vel non moveri . . . et hoc non potest competere ei quod ex necessitate movetur, cum sit determinatum ad unum. Unde oportet quod omni ei quod agit ex necessitate naturae, determinetur finis ab aliquo quod sit intelligens. . . . [I]d quod ex necessitate naturae agit, impossibile est esse principium agens, cum determinetur sibi finis ab alio. Et sic patet quod impossibile est Deum agere ex necessitate naturae'; see also *Summa Theologiae*, Ia, qu. 19, art. 4 (first and second arguments) and *Summa Contra Gentiles*, Lib. 1, Cap. 44, n. 7 'Item.'

2.1 Intellect

God's complete independence in His being provides Thomas with a way into considering His intellect and will. As the *De Potentia Dei*, n. 21, makes clear, what is not independent in its being, i.e. what is dependent on another, does not wholly determine its end for itself but has its end determined by another (at the very least by some nature with which it is not identical). God on the other hand is determined by nothing outside Himself, and so the determination of His action in creating must come from Himself alone. This then implies that as self-determining God not only knows all the possible determinations of His power to create but also that He chooses from amongst those possibilities when He creates; otherwise God would not be free from determination in His being. Hence, intellect and will are at work in God's creative activity.

Now elsewhere Aquinas argues that God is intelligent, i.e. that He has an intellect, precisely because of His immateriality. Immateriality points towards intelligence because what is material can possess only its own form; if the material thing comes to possess the form of another, its matter comes to be informed by that form and so it takes on the form of that thing in a material way. What is intelligent on the other hand not only possesses its own form, say a rational soul, but also possesses the forms of things other than itself without thereby becoming those things. And this is what is involved in knowing, the possession of the forms of things distinct from oneself without thereby becoming those things.

On the basis of this reasoning, nonintelligent things are taken to be more limited in their being since they cannot take on the forms of other things without thereby becoming informed by the very forms that they receive. Contrariwise, intelligent things are not so limited since they can take on the forms of other things without becoming those things. Limitation comes through potency, which limits its correlative actuality; I already showed this principle at work above when I considered the limitation of *esse* by essence and the participation framework that ensues. In material things, matter is a principle of limitation since it is the principle of individuation contracting the nature of the species to this or that individual. Hence what is not limited through matter is not so limited in its being, in which case its being is more extended than that of material things. The extension in being which results from a lack of matter in turn is what permits the reception of forms from distinct things without thereby becoming those things. Hence, immaterial things are intelligent, since they can receive the forms of things distinct from themselves without thereby becoming those things. But God is infinite, limited neither by materiality nor by being composed of essence and *esse*. As wholly unlimited then, God's being can extend to the forms of things distinct from Himself without Himself becoming those things, and this is the being of intelligent things, in which case God is Himself intelligent.[22]

Now, nondivine intelligent things do not come fully furnished with a set of forms in their intellects depicting the range of what could be known. Rather they come to know things distinct from themselves through the forms of such things. Hence the knowledge possessed by nondivine things is dependent on the actuality of other things and not the actuality of the intelligent things themselves (though of course the intelligent thing must be actual and have the use of its epistemic faculties). Hence the knowledge that nondivine things have is dependent on the actuality of things distinct from themselves.[23]

God on the other hand is pure act, and so His knowledge cannot be dependent on things other than Himself; there is nothing that

---

22. *Summa Contra Gentiles*, Lib. 1, Cap. 44, n. 5 'Item'; *Summa Theologiae*, Ia, qu. 14, art. 1.

23. I here gloss over the dynamics of cognition as understood by Aquinas in terms of, for man at least, possible intellect, abstraction of species by agent intellect, and deposition of form in the possible intellect. What I'm focussed on is the more general issue that for intelligent things that are not God their knowledge is dependent on the actuality of objects distinct from them. For an account of Aquinas's thought on the cognitional process see Bernard Lonergan, *Verbum: Word and Idea in Aquinas* (Toronto: University of Toronto Press, 1997).

can actualize God's intellect. Not only that, given that whatever is in God is identical with God, it must be that God's understanding and what He understands are identical in Him. What God understands then is His own divine essence and not anything distinct therefrom; God understands Himself through Himself.[24] But the divine essence is *esse* itself, that without which nothing would be. In understanding His being *esse* itself, God understands everything that could be as a result of His *esse*. Thus, unlike nondivine intelligent things, God's intellect is indeed fully furnished with the forms of things, and these forms signify all the possibilities of being; these forms in God's intellect are what are called the divine ideas.[25]

The divine ideas do not signify several distinct accidents in the mind of God, the way various conceptual contents exist in our minds. Rather, the divine ideas signify the various possibilities to which God's power extends. Hence by a single act of understanding His essence, God understands all these possibilities, but that does not entail that all these possibilities exist as diverse mental contents in the divine intellect. The divine intellect understands the divine essence, and in so understanding the divine essence understands all that could possibly be understood.

In saying this, one is not committed to the view that God understands *only* His essence, and nothing other than Himself, i.e. that God does not understand creatures. God knows Himself perfectly given the identity of that knowing with His essence. But to know something perfectly is not only to know it in itself but also to know that to which its power extends. Hence God knows perfectly that to which His power extends, which includes but is not limited to creatures.[26] This knowledge of creatures is not some vague foreshadowing of an effect in its cause. Rather it must include a

---

24. *Summa Theologiae*, Ia, qu. 14, art. 2.
25. For an extended treatment of the divine ideas in Aquinas's thought see Vivian Boland, *Ideas in God According to Saint Thomas Aquinas: Sources and Synthesis* (New York: Brill, 1996).
26. *Summa Theologiae*, Ia, qu. 14, art. 5.

proper knowledge of creatures in themselves and in their singularity; for without such knowledge of singulars in themselves, God would not perfectly know Himself and to what His power extends, i.e. particular things.[27]

When it comes to the application of God's knowledge in bringing things to be, Aquinas argues that God's knowledge relates to things as that of an artist to his work of art. The artist's knowledge has a causal influence on the artwork such that the form in his intellect is the principle by which the artist produces his work and signifies his vision for it. The artist undoubtedly has other forms in his mind that he could bring about but none of which, in this case, he wills himself to bring about. The artist simply understands these forms, but in the creation of his work of art he doesn't envision bringing any of them into being. Similarly, for God, creatures are modelled after the knowledge that God has of Himself. In knowing Himself God knows all the possibilities of being, the divine ideas. In creating, God grants *esse* to some of these ideas, thereby bringing about creatures. Those ideas that God intends to bring into existence are known to Him by a knowledge of vision; like the artist, He envisions bringing them into being. However, those ideas that God has no intention of bringing into being are known to Him by a knowledge of simple intelligence.[28]

Given that God's intellect extends to many and diverse possibilities of being, not all of which are created or even must be created, the divine ideas, God's understanding of His divine essence, are not enough to determine which if any of the possibilities of being will be created; for this God has to make a choice, and it is the will that so chooses. So to return to the artist metaphor, the artist having undertaken to produce a work of art has many ideas of what he would like his work to resemble, but he settles on one of them and endeavours to bring it about. This settling on one is an act of the will determining the artist's action to bring about

27. Ibid., aa. 6 and 11.
28. Ibid., art. 9.

one work of art rather than another. Similarly in God, should He choose to create, He chooses some determinate possibilities of being, and in doing so He brings them about through the exercise of His power. Consequently, in creating things God uses not only His intellect but also His will.[29] Hence, whereas God's intellect provides the formal principles of creation, i.e. it determines what exactly He will create, His will provides what could be called the final or motivating principle of creation. So I shall now turn to God's will.

2.2 Will

Thomas attributes will to God through consideration of the nature of the good. The good is that which all desire, that is to say, the good is such that it draws all things to it. Now this magnetic attraction of the good applies to both intelligent and unintelligent things. Unintelligent things are drawn to the good on the basis of natural disposition—they seek out the good and rest therein, e.g. an irrational animal seeks food or shelter and, once found, comes to rest in what it has been seeking. On the other hand intelligent things seek out the good not through some natural disposition but through coming to know the good and in so knowing the good seeking it and resting in it in an intellectual manner. This intellectual appetite for the good is the will, so that the will is the intellectual manifestation of the universal attraction of the good.[30]

---

29. *Summa Theologiae*, Ia, qu. 14, art 8: 'forma intelligibilis non nominat principium actionis secundum quod est tantum in intelligente, nisi adiungatur ei inclinatio ad effectum, quae est per voluntatem. Cum enim forma intelligibilis ad opposita se habeat (cum sit eadem scientia oppositorum), non produceret determinatum effectum, nisi determinaretur ad unum per appetitum. . . . Manifestum est autem quod Deus per intellectum suum causat res, cum suum esse sit suum intelligere. Unde necesse est quod sua scientia sit causa rerum, secundum quod habet voluntatem coniunctam.' See also *De Potentia Dei*, qu. 1, art. 7, ad. 5.

30. *Summa Contra Gentiles*, Lib. 2, Cap. 47: 'Inest enim omnibus appetitus boni: cum bonum sit quod omnia appetunt, ut philosophi tradunt. Huiusmodi autem appetitus in his quidem quae cognitione carent, dicitur naturalis appetitus: sicut

God is intelligent, and as intelligent He reflects back upon His own essence such that He knows Himself through Himself. I have already said that in knowing Himself He knows every possibility of being, but it should be said that in knowing Himself God also knows the good itself. This is because insofar as God is pure act, there is nothing independent of Him that can be good for Him, yet as the source of actuality of all other things, God is that by which all other things are brought to completion or perfected. Hence God is the good of all things, but nothing is good for Him. God then is the good itself.[31] So in understanding His divine essence, God knows Himself as good and in so knowing Himself as good, God's intellect is drawn to that good, and this is His will.[32]

Just as God's intellect is identical with His essence so too is His will; for His will is nothing more than His intellectual appetite for the good that He Himself is. Moreover, insofar as the object of God's will is nothing other than the divine essence itself, God's will is not moved by anything outside of Himself, but by the very good that He is essentially.[33] Nevertheless Aquinas maintains that

dicitur quod lapis appetit esse deorsum. In his autem quae cognitionem sensitivam habent, dicitur appetitus animalis, qui dividitur in concupiscibilem et irascibilem. In his vero quae intelligunt, dicitur appetitus intellectualis seu rationalis, qui est voluntas.' For a discussion of this general outlook see Norman Kretzmann, *The Metaphysics of Theism: Aquinas's Natural Theology in Summa Contra Gentiles I* (Oxford: Clarendon Press, 1997), pp. 199–203.

31. *De Divinis Nominibus*, Cap. 4, lect. 1, n. 269: 'ipsa divina Essentia est ipsa bonitas, quod in aliis rebus non contingit: Deus enim est bonus per suam essentiam, omnia vero alia per participationem; unumquodque enim bonum est, secundum quod est res actu; Deo autem proprium est quod sit suum esse, unde ipse solus est sua bonitas.' See also *Summa Contra Gentiles*, Lib. 1, Cap. 38.

32. *Summa Contra Gentiles*, Lib. 1, Cap. 72: 'Cum enim bonum intellectum sit obiectum proprium voluntatis, oportet quod bonum intellectum, inquantum huiusmodi, sit volitum. Intellectum autem dicitur ad intelligentem. Necesse est igitur quod intelligens bonum, inquantum huiusmodi, sit volens. Deus autem intelligit bonum: cum enim sit perfecte intelligens, ut ex supra dictis patet, intelligit ens simul cum ratione boni. Est igitur volens.'

33. *Summa Theologiae*, Ia, qu. 19, art. 1, ad. 3: 'voluntas cuius obiectum principale est bonum quod est extra voluntatem, oportet quod sit mota ab aliquo. Sed obiectum divinae voluntatis est bonitas sua, quae est eius essentia. Unde, cum voluntas Dei

God wills things other than Himself, not because He is moved by such things but because of a feature of the good itself, namely its self-diffusiveness such that what is genuinely good seeks to diffuse its goodness to others.[34] Aquinas accordingly holds that in being the good itself God seeks to diffuse His goodness. God thus always wills His goodness, and to diffuse it He wills other things, i.e. creatures, for that end. God thus wills that creatures be in order that they be for the end which is the divine goodness itself.[35]

Does all of this mean that God was helpless in creating, i.e. that He was constrained by His own goodness to create others? Like the light of the sun, could God not help diffusing the rays of His goodness on others so that creation was somewhat necessary?

If one were to interpret the self-diffusiveness of the good as a principle pertaining to efficient causality, it would appear that in being self-diffusive, whatever is good has to spread out that goodness like light emanating from the sun. Indeed on this view Aquinas would have to say that the self-diffusiveness of God's goodness determines Him to create things other than Himself which can enjoy that goodness. Yet this stands in tension with the *De Potentia Dei* text which I cited at the beginning of this section to the effect that there is nothing independent of God that necessitates His action. So we have a problem.

To resolve this problem, Aquinas does not interpret the self-diffusiveness principle as pertaining to efficient causality, as something constraining God and forcing Him to create; rather, he sees it as pertaining to final causality. The good is self-diffusive insofar as

---

sit eius essentia, non movetur ab alio a se, sed a se tantum, eo modo loquendi quo intelligere et velle dicitur motus.'

34. See Julien Peghaire, 'L'Axiome "Bonum est diffusivum sui" dans le néo-platonisme et le thomisme', *Revue de l'Université d'Ottawa*, I (1932), Parts 1–2, for details of this principle in general, and Part 3 for its adoption by Aquinas in particular.

35. *Summa Theologiae*, Ia, qu. 19, art. 2. See also *De Divinis Nominibus*, Cap. 3, lect. 1, n. 228: 'quidquid Deus facit creaturis, sive esse sive vivere et quodcumque aliud totum ex bonitate divina procedit et totum ad bonitatem pertinent creaturae', and Cap. 4, lect. 1, n. 261: 'quidquid in creaturas procedit, hoc creaturae suae propter suam bonitatem communicat.'

it is the end towards which all are drawn.[36] Hence, Aquinas holds that God must necessarily will His own goodness as an end, but this does not entail that God must will the existence of creatures. Creatures are only willed as ordered to the end which is God's goodness. Now, things ordered to an end are not necessary for that end unless the end cannot be willed without them, e.g. willing the consumption of food is only necessary if one's end is the preservation of one's life. On the other hand, we will without necessity those things without which the end can be attained, e.g. I can will to walk to work or cycle to work—the end can be attained by either means, so neither is willed necessarily. God's goodness is perfect, nothing can add to it, and it can be without the aid of others; this is because God stands in potency to nothing, so nothing can be good for God. Given the latter, it is not necessary for God to will others so that He may will His own good.[37] Hence God wills others as ordered to the good out of sheer gratuity, i.e. He wills others to exist as ordered to the good that He is because He wants to, not because He has to. So unlike light from the sun, the good that God diffuses over creatures in creating them does not necessarily emanate from Him but has been willed to do so.[38]

Whilst otherwise favourable to Aquinas's philosophy of God, Norman Kretzmann finds this particular conclusion repugnant, and he sees in it an affirmation of the uselessness of creatures. The charge of uselessness stems from the lack of necessity involved in God's willing of creatures, so that God has no use, no need for them; He can will His own goodness without creatures. Worse, on Kretzmann's reading, is that creatures are only willed to be because

---

36. Peghaire, 'L'Axiome "Bonum est diffusivum sui" dans le néo-platonisme et le thomisme', stresses that the interpretation of the self-diffusiveness principle in terms of final causality was a key feature in Thomas's adoption of this principle.
37. *Summa Theologiae*, Ia, qu. 19, art. 3.
38. See *De Divinis Nominibus*, Cap. 4, lect. 1, nn. 270–271, for explicit rejection by Thomas of the view that goodness diffuses over creation like rays of the sun; rather, here Thomas quite clearly affirms that when God creates by diffusing His goodness He does so in an intelligent and volitional manner.

they manifest certain likenesses of God which in turn permit God to enjoy His own goodness; they do not appear to have a value in themselves.[39] As an alternative Kretzmann attempts to justify a necessitarian reading of Aquinas, and holds that there is some degree of necessity to God's creating, a necessity that Kretzmann derives from reading the good as self-diffusive in terms of efficient causality, so that God cannot but bring about creatures.[40] Needless to say the latter goes against Aquinas's typical reading of the good's self-diffusiveness in terms of final causality; indeed Kretzmann's reading of the self-diffusiveness of the good is surprising, given that he cites the article in which Peghaire stresses that Aquinas in particular was a defender of this principle in terms of final as opposed to efficient causality.[41]

Setting aside Kretzmann's interpretation of Aquinas's texts and focussing on the more philosophical issue, I would like to ask: why should our being willed to manifest God's goodness and

39. Kretzmann, *The Metaphysics of Theism*, p. 223: 'I get the idea that it's supposed to be *suitable* to God's eternal, perfect pleasure in, and love of, perfect goodness that perfect goodness be surrounded by uncountably many variously incomplete *likenesses* of itself, and I find that idea repugnant.'

40. Arthur Lovejoy raises a similar issue not only for Aquinas but for Western philosophy in general going right back to Plato. He argues that if the creator is self-sufficient yet wholly good, He has no need of creatures and yet cannot help but bring them about; see *The Great Chain of Being: A Study of the History of an Idea* (New York: Harper and Row, 1960), p. 54: 'The goodness of God . . . is a constraining goodness; he is not, in Milton's phrase, "free to create or not", nor free to choose some possible kinds of beings as the recipients of the privilege of existence, while denying it to others. For details of the Thomist reaction to Lovejoy and Lovejoy's reaction to the Thomist reaction see Edward Mahoney, 'Metaphysical Foundations of the Hierarchy of Being According to Some Late-Medieval and Renaissance Philosophers', in *Philosophies of Existence*, ed. by Morewedge, pp. 212–213.

41. See the overall discussion in *The Metaphysics of Theism*, Chapter 7, Sections 7–9. For critical reaction which to my mind establishes decisively Kretzmann's misreading of Aquinas see Wippel, 'Norman Kretzmann on Aquinas's Attribution of Will and Freedom to Create to God', *Religious Studies*, 39:3 (2003), 287–298, and 'Thomas Aquinas on the Ultimate Why Question: Why Is There Anything At All Rather Than Nothing Whatsoever', in *The Ultimate Why Question: Why Is There Anything At All Rather Than Nothing Whatsoever?*), ed. by John Wippel (Washington, DC: Catholic University of America Press, 2011).

the attendant uselessness of creatures give us cause for concern? Emotional reactions aside, our being useless for God's happiness in willing His own good does not entail that we are valueless; for all creatures are participations in God's being and so are goods in themselves, albeit finite and limited. The latter is not removed through affirming that creatures are not absolutely necessary. In fact, the lack of necessity in God's willing of creatures illuminates something of their value, and this precisely because without having to will that creatures exist and so being able to enjoy His divine goodness quite easily without creatures, God nevertheless chooses to bring things into existence so that they can enjoy something of the goodness that He enjoys. That confers a special significance on creatures despite their lack of necessity, precisely because God chooses to create them when He doesn't have to, thereby raising the possibility that Christianity affirms to the effect that God has a particular concern for creatures precisely because of His love for them. On the other hand if creation was some necessary emanation from God, as Kretzmann appears to wish it to be, it would be difficult to embrace some of the more compelling religious conceptions of God as being worthy of worship (not to mention love and devotion); for necessitarianism would imply that God is indifferent to creatures. Thus, I don't see the same problem that Kretzmann sees with Thomas's lack of necessitarianism.

God is the cause of things other than Himself by means of His intellect and will. God's intellect provides Him with a set of possibilities; but it is His will that determines (i) what He will create and (ii) that He will create. Creation then involves a formal principle in God's intellect providing God with all the possibilities of being; but it also involves a final or motivating principle in God's will by which He chooses both to create and what to create.

These formal and final principles remain within God. I shall now move on to consider another principle of creation aside from the formal and final, and this is the efficient principle, i.e. that by which God actually brings things into existence other than Himself. This is God's power.

2.3 Power

Thomas divides power (*potentia*) into active and passive. Active power is the power to act, whereas passive power is the power to undergo some action. In order to have active power one must be in act, whereas in order to have passive power one must be in potency in some respect. Hence that which is in act has power to act. Above I have alluded to the fact that for Thomas *esse* is the act of all acts; there would be no actuality without *esse*, for without *esse* there would be nothing. It follows then that whatever has *esse* is in act in some way, and so is able to act. Hence whatever has *esse* has active power, and the limitations of that power will be the limitations of the *esse* whence that power is derived. God is pure *esse* and thus pure actuality. It follows then that in God there is power to act.[42]

Now as being in act and thus with active power, creatures exercise their active power in action. For instance, I have the active power to write a book and in writing a book I exercise that power. There is a real distinction in me between my power to write a book and my actual writing of the book; when I am not writing my book, I still have power to write it, but only when I write it am I exercising that power. The same cannot be said for God, since God's power is rooted in His being pure *esse*, and as is clear there is no composition in God, in which case there is no real distinction between His active power and His exercise of that power, only a distinction of reason.[43] In creatures power is a principle of action

---

42. *Summa Theologiae*, Ia, qu. 25, art. 1; *De Potentia Dei*, qu. 1, art. 1; *Summa Contra Gentiles*, Lib. 2, Cap. 7; note in particular the second argument in the latter: 'Sicut potentia passiva sequitur ens in potentia, ita potentia activa sequitur ens in actu: unumquodque enim ex hoc agit quod est actu, patitur vero ex hoc quod est potentia. Sed Deo convenit esse actu. Igitur convenit sibi potentia activa.'

43. *Summa Theologiae*, Ia, qu. 25, art. 1, ad. 3; *De Potentia*, qu. 1, art. 1, ad. 8; *Summa Contra Gentiles*, Lib. 2, Cap. 9. For discussion of the *Summa Contra Gentiles* text see Kretzmann, *The Metaphysics of Creation*, Chapter 2, Section 5, and note in particular p. 46: 'since in God there is no real (but only a conceptual) distinction between his power (to produce other things) and his activity (of producing other things),

distinct from that action, whereas in God power is the principle of action not distinct from the action. The unity of power to act and action in God does not entail that for as long as God is there are creatures; for this would entail that creatures are from God by means of natural necessity, which overlooks God's absolute independence and in turn dismisses the presence of intellect and will in Him. So creatures come to be as and when God wills them to be, yet the power by which they come to be and the exercise of that power in bringing them to be are not distinct in God.

Whilst there is no real distinction between the power to create and the act of creating, there is such a distinction between the act of creating and the product of that act, i.e. the effect that God brings about. This is because God's power, whilst not the principle of God's action (for in Him power and action are identical), is a principle of the thing made.[44] Thus, there is a real distinction between God and creatures and the ground of this real distinction is that of the distinction between essence and *esse* in creatures. In being composed of essence and *esse*, creatures are wholly other than God yet dependent on Him, in which case they would not be without Him.

An interesting corollary follows from the identity of power to act and acting in God. This is to the effect that there are no intermediaries of which God makes use when He creates; He creates simply by means of His own power and nothing else. God is completely independent in creating and has need of nothing in order to create. Consequently, God's act of creating is from nothing but His own resources, in which case God creates out of nothing; I shall delve into this issue more thoroughly in the next chapter but for now I shall consider the limits of God's power.

---

power is attributable to him not as the immediate source of his activity (and thereby the more remote source of its effects) but simply as the source of the effects.'

44. *Summa Contra Gentiles*, Lib. 2, Cap. 10: 'potentia non dicitur in Deo sicut principium actionis, sed sicut principium facti.'

God's *esse* is not limited through being conjoined to some essence distinct from it (in God essence and *esse* are identical), it is infinite, in which case there is nothing other than God that limits His power. Hence God's power is also infinite. Not only that, insofar as there is no limit on His power, God is omnipotent; for there is nothing to which God's power does not extend. In saying that, we must be careful in articulating this notion of omnipotence because it has a very technical sense in Aquinas's metaphysics. For Thomas possibility is a necessary but not sufficient condition for actuality. So nothing that is impossible is possible, and some possibilities are present actualities. God's power is rooted in His actuality, which is His *esse*, hence God's power to act is a power to bring about anything that may be. But what may be is precisely what is possible as opposed to what is impossible. What is possible is that whose conceptual formulation does not imply a contradiction, in which case God can bring about any possibility of being. An impossibility is precisely nothing, since it is lacking in that necessary condition—possibility—by which anything could be. God cannot bring about such an impossibility, not because His power is deficient or the task is too hard but because the thing itself cannot be done, which is to say that the thing itself is precisely nothing; and this is the limit of God's power.[45]

I have labelled intellect, will, and power the creative attributes of God. This is because these attributes are involved in creating. God understands every possibility of being, selects from those possibilities, and brings them into existence; these are the formal, final, and efficient principles of creation. Whilst I distinguish them here, they are united in God given His simplicity. Thus, God as pure *esse* itself is pure understanding itself and as such by a single act of understanding understands all that could be understood. That same understanding understands the divine goodness which God

45. *Summa Theologiae*, Ia, qu. 25, aa. 2–3; *De Potentia Dei*, qu. 1, aa. 2–3.

is as pure *esse*, which understanding of the divine goodness draws God's will to Himself as the good which He is. His will cannot but will that divine goodness, He cannot deny Himself, but He can go without bringing about creatures. He however chooses to create and what to create and in order to bring that about He grants *esse* to the things He so chooses.

In the previous chapter we observed that Aquinas was dissatisfied with philosophical reflections on creation that did not account for the very being of things. Any account which stopped short of the being of things merely accounting for this or that or such a being was deemed inappropriate. So far in this chapter I have considered the source of all things as Thomas conceives of Him. I have not covered everything that Aquinas has to say about God, nor have I dealt with the nuances of his thought in this regard in any significant degree; I have only dealt with those aspects of his philosophy of God relevant to exploring Aquinas's metaphysics of creation. What is important to point out is that Aquinas's characteristic conception of God as pure *esse* itself and the source of *esse* in others preserves Aquinas's insight that only when we account for the very being of things can we say that we have an account of creation. God as pure *esse* itself accounts for the being of things, since God originates *esse* in all things, so that there is nothing in the creature that escapes the actuality of its *esse*, and no created *esse* escapes the power of God's causing things to be. All actuality then is rooted in God's causal activity, activity which embraces the formal (intellect), final (will), and efficient (power) aspects of causality.

Aquinas has not abandoned the insight by which he was able to criticize the earlier philosophers who had not considered the very being of things. By thinking of God as pure *esse* and originating *esse* in all else, Aquinas is thinking of creatures in terms of their being, not in terms of their matter, form, essence, etc. (though of course these do have their rightful place in a consideration of creation). The contrast is between being and nonbeing, between having *esse*, and thereby actually existing, and not having *esse*, literally nothing. Aquinas is thinking precisely of what it is to be, and so he is considering being universally. Thus, by his own standards he is engaged in a level of philosophical thinking that is adequate for drawing out the metaphysics of creation. The next chapter then will consider the meaning of creation in Aquinas's thought.

3

THE MEANING OF CREATION

IN THE PREVIOUS CHAPTER I CONSIDERED God as the agent of creation, and therein I distinguished between His intellect, will, and power, all of which are necessary for His act of creating. I correlated these with the formal, final, and efficient principles of creation and observed that it is God's power, the efficient principle, by which He actually produces something in being other than Himself. So a consideration of God's power in creating will be the entryway into the meaning of creation.

Before doing that however I should like to point out that it is well known that Aquinas adopted a highly cautious attitude when it came to the issue of creation and indeed its meaning. His attitude was so cautious that when it came to the issue of the temporal beginning of the universe, he affirmed neither the arguments for nor the arguments against its being created at some point in time, maintaining that neither set of arguments were demonstrative. Ultimately belief in the temporal beginning of creation was an article of faith for Thomas. He gives us reason for such caution in the *Summa Contra Gentiles* where he states that insofar as the temporal beginning of creatures is an article of faith, we ought to adopt a high level of critical resistance thereto so that we do not admit as a reason for faith something that may turn out later to be false, thereby subjecting faith to ridicule.[1]

---

1. Aquinas, *Summa Contra Gentiles*, Lib. 2, Cap. 38: 'Ne videatur fides Catholica in vanis rationibus constituta, et non potius in solidissima Dei doctrina.'; see also *Summa Theologiae*, Ia, q. 46, art. 2: 'Et hoc utile est ut consideretur, ne forte aliquis,

Thomas was true to his word, even going so far as to uphold the possibility of an eternally created universe. Evidently for Thomas, the universe's being created is one thing, whereas its being created in time, i.e. its having a temporal beginning, is another. The two are separable for Aquinas, so much so that one requires an act of faith whereas the other can be established demonstratively. So in what follows I will be considering what we can know philosophically about the meaning of creation; I pass over here the issues concerning the temporal beginning of things for when I come to consider the history of creation in Chapter 6.

1 THE MEANING OF CREATION

In the previous chapter I noted that God's power is rooted in His *esse* so that God is powerful precisely because He is pure *esse*. It is God's power which represents the efficient principle in creating, and this is to say that it is by means of His power that God produces something other than Himself. But if this is the case, then the exercise of that power, being an exercise of God's *esse*, will entail a communication of *esse* to the thing brought to be. The communication of *esse* will in turn set up the participation structure between created *esse* (*commune*) and God, as well as the distinction of essence and *esse* in the creature (and the ensuing participation structure involved in their composition). So whatever meaning is attached to creation, it will have to involve the communication or originating of *esse* in creatures.

There are four instances wherein Aquinas offers us a sustained treatment of creation: (i) the commentary on the *Sentences* of Peter Lombard, Lib. 2, dist. 1, qu. 1; (ii) *Summa Contra Gentiles*, Lib. 2, Cap. 6–38; (iii) *Quaestiones Disputatae De Potentia Dei*,

quod fidei est demonstrare praesumens, rationes non necessarias inducat, quae praebeant materiam irridendi infidelibus, existimantibus nos propter huiusmodi rationes credere quae fidei sunt.'

qu. 3; (iv) *Summa Theologiae*, Ia, qq. 44–49.[2] All of them revolve around the notion that in creating God originates *esse* in things. Accordingly, as a concise definition of creation Thomas offers us the following: to create something is to produce it in being (*esse*) according to its total substance.[3] This is a definition that Thomas affirmed throughout his career.

What is significant about this definition serving to tie it in with Aquinas's more general thought is that to create is to produce something in being, in its *esse*, and so an essential feature of creation as the exercise of God's power is the origin of *esse* in things. Not only that, it is the total substance that is brought into being in the act of creation; nothing is left out. So with the production of the total substance in being, whatever is actual in the substance is produced in creation; nothing escapes the actualizing power of *esse*, in which case nothing escapes God's creative power in originating *esse*. The production then of the total substance is the granting of *esse* to some potentially existing essence, since that to which *esse* is not granted is precisely nothing, in which case what is produced through the granting of *esse* is the total substance whole and complete. To create then is to grant *esse* to some potentially existing essence, so that when God creates He grants *esse* to things, or better, He is the source of their *esse*.

Given this understanding, Thomas can avoid the association of creation with change. Accordingly, he distinguishes between

---

2. For translation of and/or commentary on these treatments of creation see the following: for the *Sentences* commentary see Baldner and Carroll, *Aquinas on Creation: Writings on the 'Sentences' of Peter Lombard 2.1.1*; for the *Summa Contra Gentiles* see Kretzmann, *The Metaphysics of Creation*; for the *De Potentia Dei* see *On Creation: Quaestiones De Potentia Dei Qu. 3*, trans. with introduction and notes by S. C. Selner-Wright (Washington, DC: Catholic University of America Press, 2011); for the *Summa Theologiae* see Reginald Garrigou-Lagrange, *De Deo Trino et Creatore* (Turin: Marietti, 1943).

3. Aquinas, *In II Sent.*, dist. 1, qu. 1, art. 2: 'Hoc autem creare dicimus, scilicet producere rem in esse secundum totam suam substantiam'. The same definition can be found in *Summa Contra Gentiles*, Lib 2, Cap. 17; *De Potentia Dei*, qu. 3, art. 1; *Summa Theologiae*, Ia, qu. 45, art. 1; *Tractatus De Substantiis Separatis*, Cap. 10, n. 56.

creation and (i) change, (ii) making, and (iii) natural generation; none of these involves the granting of *esse* to things, but they all presuppose the existence, and hence the *esse*, of something already in being.

Change is a movement from potency to act, because for change to occur, some potentiality has to be actualized. In that case, an underlying potency exists prior to the change thereby making it possible; the preexistence of potency then is a necessary condition for change. Creation is the granting of *esse* to essence, which does not preexist its creation. Unless a thing is created, it does not have *esse* and is thus nothing. It follows then that nothing preexists the granting of *esse*; but if that is the case, then creation cannot be change, since all change, precisely as change, requires as a necessary condition some preexisting potency.

Similar reasons militate against envisaging creation as a kind of making. Such a view is a familiar one classically articulated in the *Timaeus,* wherein Plato sets aside three precreation realities: matter, Forms, and the Demiurge. Creation is envisaged as the Demiurge taking the preexistent matter and forming it after the model of the Forms. But in Thomas's thought, it cannot be the case that matter preexists creation, for then it would be uncreated and without *esse*, in which case it would not exist; and if matter cannot exist prior to creation, then creation cannot be the making of things from matter. Hence creation is not making.

Finally, creation cannot be anything like natural generation. In generation, it is not the case that nothing would exist if the generation had not taken place; for in generation, something of the potential offspring would still remain in the matter of the generator(s) had generation not occurred. But in the case of creation, had not the act of creating occurred, nothing (other than God) would be. Furthermore, natural generation is akin to a kind of making, which is itself a kind of change, since it occurs through the manipulation of pre-existing materials, which signifies the formation of a new life; and just as such cannot be the case for creation in relation to change and making, so too it cannot be in relation to natural generation.[4]

Effectively, in denying that creation is change/making/generation, Aquinas is avoiding any kind of charge of the thinking for which he criticized the Presocratics. Recall that in their thinking the Presocratics failed to reach a level of reflection whereby the very being of things is considered. Hence, all causality involves some kind of change of an underlying material reality; it does not involve the bringing into being of that reality itself. In considering the *esse* of things Thomas does indeed consider the very being of things, because *esse* is the fundamental principle without which such things would not be. Following on from that, insofar as creation is the granting of *esse* to things, such creating cannot presuppose what is without *esse*, for that would be nothing. Hence, nothing can be supposed by creation. This accords well with the general definition offered earlier, to wit, that creation is the production of the total substance in being. Given the latter, nothing is left out in the act of creation; everything in the substance is brought about in creation. By disassociating creation from change, Thomas then distinguishes creation as a special kind of action, one that can presuppose nothing, whereas all other kinds of action presuppose *esse*, they do not grant it. Therefore, creation uniquely involves the origination of *esse* in things.

---

4. *Summa Contra Gentiles*, Lib. 2, Cap. 17: 'Ubi autem tota substantia rei in esse producitur, non potest esse aliquod idem aliter et aliter se habens: quia illud esset non productum, sed productioni praesuppositum. Non est ergo creatio mutatio'; Cap. 21: 'Creatio autem est prima actio: eo quod nullam aliam praesupponit, omnes autem aliae praesupponunt eam. Est igitur creatio propria Dei solius actio, qui est agens primum'; *De Potentia Dei*, qu. 3, art. 1: 'Per suam actionem [Deus] producit totum ens subsistens, nullo praesupposito'; *Summa Theologiae*, Ia, qu. 45, art. 1: 'Non solum oportet considerare emanationem alicuius entis particularis ab aliquo particulari agente, sed etiam emanationem totius entis a causa universali, quae est Deus, et hanc quidem emanationem designamus nomine creationis'; art. 5: 'Illud autem quod est proprius effectus Dei creantis, est illud quod praesupponitur omnibus aliis, scilicet esse absolute.'

Given all of this, there are two commitments to Aquinas's notion of creation: (i) creation presupposes nothing of the thing created, but rather the thing created is brought into being whole and complete, and (ii) nonbeing precedes the being of the creature, since prior to its being the creature was nothing. Point (i) is sufficiently clear given Aquinas's understanding of *esse*: there is nothing to the thing that is not produced by the granting of *esse* to it, since whatever is without *esse* is nothing. Point (ii) however bears some reflection. Clearly before a thing receives *esse* it is nothing, but this seems to imply a temporal dimension to being created such that to be created is to begin to be, and that appears to entail a beginning of creation, something that I noted Thomas is keen to withhold from the demonstrative abilities of philosophy. So I will consider the priority of nonbeing in creatures.

The priority of nonbeing to the creature in creation can be taken in a twofold way: (i) in a temporal sense, and (ii) in an analytical sense. The temporal priority of nonbeing over the being of creatures signifies creatures' coming into being in time such that there was a beginning of their creation. Given such a beginning, we can conceivably think back in time to the point at which things began to be and thereby affirm a beginning. The analytical priority of nonbeing over being in creatures signifies that their very being created is impossible without the activity of the creator. Thomas holds that (ii) need not imply (i), though often enough (i) implies (ii). To draw this out further, consider an example offered by Richard Taylor.[5]

Imagine both the sun and the moon have existed eternally, so that without beginning the sun has been illuminating the surface of the moon. The sun is thus the cause of the moon's illumination such that without the sun the moon would not be

---

5. Richard Taylor, 'The Metaphysics of Causation', in *Causation and Conditionals* (Oxford: Oxford University Press, 1975), ed. by Ernest Sosa, p. 44. I make much use of this example in 'A Thomistic Metaphysics of Creation', *Religious Studies*, 48 (2012), 337–356, and *Aquinas's Way to God*, Chapter 7.

illuminated. But, as noted, the illumination of the moon never had a beginning, yet the sun is still the cause of the moon's illumination. Accordingly, we have a case of causality whereby we are able to affirm a dependency relation without thereby affirming a temporal beginning. The sun has causal priority over the moon since the sun is the cause of the illumination of the moon, yet both being eternal, the sun is not prior to the moon in time. It is this nontemporal yet genuinely causal priority that is involved in the priority of creator to the creature, and it in turn allows us to clarify how nonbeing can be nontemporally prior to the being of creatures.

Nonbeing precedes the being of the creature in a way similar to the darkness of the moon preceding its illumination; like the illumination of the moon, the being of the creature is not something that the creature has of itself but requires a cause, hence the creature is naturally nothing, just as the moon is not naturally illuminated. Whilst the creature is in fact existing and the moon is in fact being illuminated, they are not existing/illuminated of themselves, in which case that which exists/illuminates of itself provides the existence/illumination of the other. Causality is present so long as there is dependence, whether that is dependence for *esse* in the case of creation or dependence for illumination in the sun and moon example; but such causality need not imply temporal priority, since, as the sun and moon example shows, the cause can be eternally causing the effect without the effect's ever having had a beginning, yet the effect remains dependent on the cause. The same goes for creation. The creature need only depend on God for its being, but such dependence need not entail temporal priority, since the dependency can exist without a temporal beginning.

Given all of this, it is clear that for Thomas in being created a creature is created from nothing but God's own resources and emerges out of a state of nothingness. In other words, Aquinas takes creation to be *ex nihilo*. But how does he understand this?

In holding that creation is *ex nihilo*, it should be clear that Aquinas does not mean that nothingness is the stuff out of which God makes everything; for if we can make any sense of nothingness being a kind of stuff, creation out of that would be mere transformation of something already preexisting, hence not creation defined as the production of the total substance in being. So consider a more philosophically correct approach to the meaning of creation *ex nihilo*.

When we take the expression *ex nihilo*, the negation that *nihilo* specifies either negates (i) the preposition *ex*, or (ii) falls under the preposition, i.e. is subject to, *ex*. If (i), then the preposition is negated in either of two ways: (i.i) the preposition is negated and also what is prior to it, so that to say that something is *ex nihilo* is to say that there is nothing from which that thing came to be, i.e. it has no cause—and this is applicable to God alone, God comes to be from nothing at all;[6] (i.ii) on the other hand only the preposition is negated but not what comes before it, so that when we say that something comes to be *ex nihilo*, we mean that nothing preexists that thing from which it comes to be, i.e. there is nothing that is matter, the stuff, from which creatures come to be—and Thomas does think this is what creation involves, since he holds that creatures are not the result of a transformation of some preexisting potency. So this is one way in which creation is *ex nihilo*.

Now consider (ii) when the negation falls under the preposition. This may occur in a twofold manner. On the one hand is (ii.i) when the negation is taken to be the cause of things, so creation is *ex nihilo* such that the nothing is the cause of creation; but this is absurd since in any genuine causal context something actually existing must be the cause of what exists. On the other hand is (ii.ii) when the *nihilo* signifies some sort of order such that something follows after it; and in this case creation *ex nihilo* signifies that the

---

6. Just as in English, so too in Latin, this is taken to be an odd kind of expression, and Aquinas readily admits that we do not usually speak like this; see *De Potentia Dei*, qu. 3, art. 1, ad. 7: 'Iste modus loquendi non sit consuetus.'

creature comes to be *after* its being nothing. And this is the second way in which creation is *ex nihilo*.[7]

We thus have two senses in which *ex nihilo* is applicable to creation: (i.ii) nothing is presupposed for the act of creation, and (ii. ii) the being of a creature follows its own nothingness; the specification of *ex nihilo* is thus applied to God's side of creation as well as to that of creatures. In accord with (i.ii), God makes use of nothing in bringing creatures into existence, that is, there is nothing that He needs such as matter in order to create. In accord with (ii.ii), creatures come into being from a prior state of nonbeing, such that the act of creation is what draws creatures from a state of nonbeing into a state of being; the act of creation crosses the most extreme ontological divide and makes creatures stand out as beings from their own nothingness. Now how this can be is an issue that I shall deal with in the next chapter, because obviously creatures cannot preexist their existence, so it is right and just that we interrogate Aquinas's doctrine of creation as to exactly whence creatures are coming when they are brought into creation. Nevertheless, for the purposes of offering an understanding of what creation *ex nihilo* signifies with respect to creatures it can truthfully be said that the nonbeing of creatures is prior to their being; they do not naturally exist.

The *ex nihilo* character of creation follows readily from the metaphysical framework that Aquinas draws on in order to articulate it. Recall that creatures are composites of essence and *esse* whereas God is pure *esse* itself. As such nothing exists other than God, from which creatures come, in which case God makes use of nothing in creating. Furthermore, creatures do not exist in virtue of what they are; it is not within their natures to exist; their existence (their *esse*) is distinct from what they are, in which case prior to their being created, all creatures are nothing.

With the foregoing understanding of creation in place, I proceed to deepen the furrow by considering creation as a relation.

---

7. See James Anderson, *The Cause of Being: The Philosophy of Creation in St Thomas* (London: Herder, 1952), pp. 7–9.

2 THE RELATION OF CREATION

It is clear that creation involves some sort of causal relationship; for in granting *esse* God is the cause of all things such that without God there would be nothing. A relationship is thereby set up between God and creatures, and indeed creation is signified by this relationship. Creation then is not an entity in the way a creature can be said to be but is just the causal relation that obtains between God and creatures. The act of creation is God's making use of His power to grant *esse* to things; what is created, what one could call the product, are the creatures we see all around us.

Relation is one of Aristotle's nine categories of accident, and as is clear from the Aristotelian doctrine, accidents are dependent on substances in some way.[8] Now, whereas accidents typically depend on a substance in which they inhere, for example, the accidents of quantity or quality depend on the substance whose quantity and quality they are, relation requires at least two substances that are related. In the relation the two substances are said to have a certain bearing to one another, and this bearing is the basis for the relation; this is so even in the case of a substance's relation to itself, since in such a relation we represent to ourselves the one substance in a twofold manner and predicate the relation accordingly.[9] Hence, there are always at least two extremes to a relation. Not only that, some relations are so because there is some real foundation in the substances by which they are related, some relations are so not because of a real foundation in the substances but because of how we conceive of them, and some relations are a mixture of both. I will now consider these relations.[10]

---

8. See Aristotle, *Categories*, Chapters 1–5, for the categories in general and for the category of substance, and Chapter 7 for the category of relation.
9. Aquinas, *Summa Theologiae*, Ia, qu. 13, art. 7: 'ratio apprehendit bis aliquod unum, statuit illud ut duo; et sic apprehendit quandam habitudinem ipsius ad seipsum.'
10. See Mark Gerald Henninger, 'Aquinas on the Ontological Status of Relations', *Journal of the History of Philosophy*, 25:4 (1987), 491–515, for Aquinas's account of relations, focussing in particular on real relations.

First, the two extremes can be related merely by reason such that the order obtaining between them is one apprehended by reason alone; this is a 'relation of reason' or a 'rational relation'. Thomas gives three examples of this. The first is where the terms of the relation are not themselves real substances, for instance the concepts of man and animal are related as species and genus; such is a relation of reason because the genus and species do not exist as substances themselves but are abstracted from individual substances and hence entertained as being so related by our reason. The second is where the terms are not really distinct from each other but reason treats them as if they were really distinct, as in self-identity, where we consider the substance as standing in relation to itself. The third is when there is no real foundation in the substance for the relation (so-called Cambridge relations) as when a column has the relation of being to the right of something. What is common to all these relations is that they depend on the intellect to form the relation and are not founded on some real feature of the substances that are taken to be so related.[11]

Second, the two extremes can be really related to each other such that there is something in the things themselves by which they are so related. The typical example here is a relation based on quantity (though Aquinas also sees relations based on action and passion as being real relations), since quantity is a real feature of substances, which in turn permits a comparative relation between two substances. Hence X will be taller that Y given the appropriate quantities of each. If this relation were taken away from X and Y, they would have to change in some way so that X would no longer be taller than Y. Hence, there is something about the substances themselves that permits their relation, in which case such relations

---

11. *Summa Theologiae*, Ia, qu. 13, art. 7; for discussion see Henninger, 'Aquinas on the Ontological Status of Relations', *Journal of the History of Philosophy*, 25:4 (1987), 491–515.

do not require an act of reason and subsist independently of our understanding them.[12]

Third, the two extremes can be related such that at one extreme there is a real relation whilst at the other there is a relation of reason only. For example, in knowing, the object of knowledge is related to the intellect as known, whereas the intellect is related to the object of knowledge as being caused and measured thereby. The intellect is really related to its object since it would not know were it not for the object. However, the object of knowledge is only related by a relation of reason, since it can go on being the object that it is without being so related to the intellect.[13]

Now consider the relation of creation, what kind of relation is this? In order to consider it we must consider the extremes. At one extreme we have God, Who grants *esse* to creatures; at the other extreme we have creatures who receive their *esse* from God. Is this a relation of reason, a real relation, or a mixture of both?

Clearly if we were to remove the relation of creation from creatures they themselves would be fundamentally altered since were it not for being created they would not be. Hence creation is something real in creatures by which they are related to God; and this is because creatures are causally dependent on God. Yet this causal dependency is asymmetric; God is not causally dependent on creatures. He is wholly independent in His being, even independent of creation, such that in creating there is no change in Him, and even with creation God is not altered in any way in His being. God remains the same whether He creates or not. Had God not chosen to create, He would still be Who He is; hence remove the relation of creation and you do nothing to alter God. This follows from what was observed about God's action in the previous chapter such that God is not necessitated to create but chooses to; if He were so necessitated His being would be altered

---

12. *Summa Theologiae*, Ia, qu. 13, art. 7, *De Potentia Dei*, qu. 7, art. 9, and *In V Met.*, nn. 1001–1005.
13. *Summa Theologiae*, Ia, qu. 13, art. 7.

in some way by creating since He would have been moved to do so. Consequently, the relation of creation is nothing real in God, in which case it is a relation of reason. Hence, God is not really related to creatures through being their creator. This does not make God indifferent to creation, since God does indeed choose to create, but it does indicate that God's being is unaffected by creation.

Accordingly, creation is a relation of the third kind outlined above, i.e. one wherein it is real at one extreme (creatures) and of reason at another extreme (God).[14] Insofar as God is the cause of creatures, the relation pertains to God in an active sense, that is, God is the active party in creation.[15] Insofar as creatures are the recipients of God's action the relation is in creatures in a passive sense: they undergo (they suffer) the activity of God's granting *esse* to them. Insofar as this passive relation is predicated on the basis of the origin of the creature's being, passive creation signifies a real relation to God with the newness or origination of being.[16]

Now two problems immediately present themselves to this view of creation as a relation. Resolving these will give us greater insight into Aquinas's notion of creation.

First, insofar as creation is a real relation in creatures, it itself must be something created; otherwise it would be uncreated and thus identical with God. But creation is nothing real in God, in which case the relation of creation must itself be a creature. If

14. *De Potentia Dei*, qu. 3, art. 3: 'Creatura autem secundum nomen refertur ad creatorem. Dependet autem creatura a creatore, et non e converso. Unde oportet quod relatio qua creatura ad creatorem refertur, sit realis; sed in Deo est relatio secundum rationem tantum.'
15. Ibid.: 'Si sumatur active, sic designat Dei actionem, quae est eius essentia, cum relatione ad creaturam; quae non est realis relatio, sed secundum rationem tantum.'
16. Ibid.: 'unde in ipsa creatione non importatur aliquis accessus ad esse, nec transmutatio a creante, sed solummodo inceptio essendi, et relatio ad creatorem a quo esse habet; et sic creatio nihil est aliud realiter quam relatio quaedam ad Deum cum novitate essendi.' Above I have spoken of the 'origin' of being, and this refers to Thomas's use of 'inceptio' in this quote. I have not referred to the 'beginning of being' because of Thomas's subtle views on this matter, which I will explore in Chapter 6.

creation is a relation that is created, then the creation of that creation is something created also, and the creation of that must also created, and so on. Hence, we have an infinite regress of relations of creation.[17]

Second, an accident is ontologically dependent on its substance. Hence creation as a relation must be ontologically dependent on the substances in which it is found. But creation is the production of the total substance in being, in which case creation can't be ontologically posterior to and dependent on created substances but must be prior to all substances; for without creation there would be no substance in which the relation exists. Thus, thinking of creation as a relation is absurd.[18]

To the first objection, if we take creation in an active sense it simply signifies the divine action with the rational relation in God—God chooses to create and so creates. In this sense creation is uncreated since it signifies the power of God in relation to creatures, yet it is nothing real in God. Taken passively, creation is the real relation that creatures have to God as their creator, which relation includes the origin of their being. This relation is something created in a very general sense because it is from God, but it is not created in the way that substances are created: i.e. *esse* is not granted to that relation but to the substances that bear that relation. The relation comes about through such substances coming to be, and in so coming to be they are related to their cause, which is God. Hence creation as a real relation in creatures is just that ontological dependence of creatures on their creator; this relation of dependence is derivable from God because He is the cause of creatures, but it is not some third thing independently created by God binding creatures to Him; rather it is simply the passive reception of *esse* in creatures, thereby setting them up as effects related to their cause.

---

17. Ibid., obj. 2.
18. Ibid., obj. 3.

Accordingly, there is not an infinity of created creations, and this is because creation is not a substance that is created thereby calling for another substance as its cause creating it and another and so on. Rather, creation is a relation that refers to two extremes: God and creatures; and that relation itself does not require a further relation in order to be; the relation simply comes about, or is cocreated, when God causes creatures to be.[19]

I will turn now to the second objection, which concerns the ontological dependence of the relation on the substance in which it inheres. As a relation, creation is an accident inhering in a created substance, but it is not such that it is constituted out of the principles of the substance of which it is an accident in the way that quantity and quality are. Rather the relation comes to be through the action of God in creating, and the act of creation thereby brings about the relation of creatures to creator. The relation exists prior to creatures in God, Who chooses to create and then comes to exist in creatures when they are created. Thus it is not absurd to think of creation as a relation because of its ontological posteriority; for whilst it is posterior in created substances, it is prior in God. Hence the relation exists prior to all creatures as God's choice to bring about beings known to Him by His intellect.

A corollary to all of this is that all real change implied in the notion of creation is really applied to creatures but not to God, and this because creation is a real relation in creatures only. This then allows for the possibility of creation's having had a beginning without thereby attributing some change to God; for the newness of being implied in the beginning of creation does not entail a newness in God, since the relation is only rational and not real in Him. Hence, God can will that creation have a beginning and that it be subject to temporal succession without His being altered in any

---

19. Ibid., ad. 2: 'Si vero nomen creaturae accipiamus magis stricte pro eo tantum quod subsistit (quod proprie fit et creatur, sicut proprie habet esse), tunc relatio praedicta non est quoddam creatum, sed concreatum, sicut nec est ens proprie loquendo, sed inhaerens. Et simile est de omnibus accidentibus.'

way. The change and multiplicity of creatures therefore does not affect the being of God, since God is not really related to creatures.

Having considered the meaning of creation and its nature as a relation, I will now consider whether or not creatures can create.

3 CREATURELY CREATION

In addressing creaturely creation I am considering whether or not God is the only agent of creation. And it would seem from what I have said that there can be no other agent of creation. This is because no creature exists essentially, since no creature's essence is identical with its *esse*. Only in God are essence and *esse* identical, and such identity equips God to be the creator, for only that which is *esse* itself can originate *esse*. Thus, the ability to create, properly so-called, is an ability that only God possesses.[20] Every creature presupposes its being for its action, in which case any action it undertakes presupposes something. So no action of a creature could be *ex nihilo*, and hence no creaturely action could be creation. Thus, all actions of creatures are mere changes not to be identified with creation. Creatures can only bring about changes in being, they cannot originate it.

Nevertheless, even granting that creatures cannot originate being, some have argued that creatures can participate in God's creative activity in some way. What I mean here is that some have thought that creatures can actually co-operate with God and assist Him in His creating. There are two forms this position takes,

---

20. *Summa Theologiae*, Ia, qu. 45, art. 5: 'Producere autem esse absolute, non inquantum est hoc, vel tale, pertinet ad rationem creationis. Unde manifestum est quod creatio est propria actio ipsius Dei'; *De Potentia Dei*, qu. 3, art. 4: 'Dicitur enim creari quod ex nihilo fit. Quod etiam non praesupponat aliquam priorem causam agentem. . . . Si igitur sic stricte creatio accipitur, constat quod creatio non potest nisi primo agenti convenire, nam causa secunda non agit nisi ex influentia causae primae; et sic omnis actio causae secundae est ex praesuppositione causae agentis.'

a strong one and a weak one; Aquinas denies the cogency of both and holds that no creature can assist God in His creating.

The strong view is to be found in the Islamic philosophers, particularly Avicenna, and the *Liber De Causis*, and it turns on the belief that the closer a creature is to God the one unified primary cause, the more unified that creature is, and the further one moves away from the primary cause, the more multiple and diverse the creature is. Creation on this account is the necessary emanation and diversification of creatures from the creator, and because it is a necessary emanation it is not freely chosen but results out of a necessity of nature. Thus, the one unified primary cause necessarily emanates something that is itself one and simple but not as simple as the primary cause, and that emanates something one and simple, and that emanates something, and so on; this emanation proceeds until we have the diverse multiplicity of things that we see around us.[21]

On this account it is evident that God is not the direct and immediate creator of all things but creates what immediately succeeds Him, and in so creating bestows on His successor a certain power to create but not as much as He has in Himself; this process then continues all the way down. Thus, secondary causes assist in the creative work of the primary cause, whereas the latter's activity

---

21. Aquinas, *De Potentia Dei*, qu. 3, art. 4: 'quorumdam philosophorum fuit positio, quod Deus creavit creaturas inferiores mediantibus superioribus, ut patet in Lib. de causis; et in Metaphys. Avicennae, et Algazelis, et movebantur ad hoc opinandum propter quod credebant quod ab uno simplici non posset immediate nisi unum provenire, et illo mediante ex uno primo multitudo procedebat. Hoc autem dicebant, ac si Deus ageret per necessitatem naturae, per quem modum ex uno simplici non fit nisi unum.' It should be noted that in his commentary on the *De Causis* Aquinas gives this position a rather benign interpretation such that the author is not referring to the co-operation of inferior beings in the creative activity of superior beings but to the intellectual illumination of inferior beings by superior ones. For an independent presentation of Avicenna's account of creation see Rahim Acar, 'Creation: Avicenna's Metaphysical Account', in *Creation and the God of Abraham* (Cambridge: Cambridge University Press, 2010), ed. by David Burrell, Carlo Cogliati, Janet M. Soskice, and William R. Stoeger, pp. 77–91; note in particular pp. 80–83 for Avicenna's emanationism.

terminates in its immediately succeeding effect, which carries the work forward.

Aquinas undoubtedly denies this strong position because it entails that God in creating does not act with intelligence and will but is necessitated to create by His nature. For Thomas, whilst God is essentially good and wants to create, He nevertheless makes a choice to create and does not work out of the necessity of nature. This is because if God were not free to create, He would be subject to something distinct from Himself; but God is not so subject given that He is pure *esse*, so He freely creates. All creatures then are willed to be by God, no matter their ontological distance from Him. Consequently, all creatures, from the lowest to the highest, are created directly by God.

So much for the stronger position; I will now turn to a weaker position. Aquinas attributes the weaker position to Peter Lombard: whilst God directly wills all that He creates, He establishes secondary causes as ministers of creation.[22] We can see even in created things that this can occur since a superior cause can pass on its causality to an inferior cause such that the inferior cause is the minister of the causality of its superior. Aquinas offers the example of air being heated and in turn heating other things.[23] Thus, the sun can heat the atmosphere, and those in the atmosphere can enjoy the heat of the sun through the ministry of the air. The air of itself cannot heat, indeed should the heat be too stifling one can go to a place where the air is not so heated by the sun and is thus cooler. Nevertheless, the air can act as the minister for the heat of the sun. So it is suggested that secondary causes act as ministers causing other beings and passing on the *esse* received from God to them.

---

22. *De Potentia Dei,* qu. 3, art. 4: 'Quidam tamen Catholici tractatores dixerunt quod, etsi nulla creatura possit aliquid creare, communicari tamen potuit creaturae ut per eius ministerium Deus aliquid crearet. Et hoc ponit Magister in 5 dist., IV libro Sentent.'

23. See *Summa Theologiae,* Ia, qu. 45, art. 5.

This position is somewhat weaker because it does not deny that God acts by intellect and will; whereas for the stronger position there is a trickle-down effect from the primary cause to the production of all creatures. On the Lombardian view then all creatures are directly willed to be by God, just as things which stand in the sun are enjoying the heat *of* the sun, yet God can make use of secondary causes in granting being to things, making them genuine causes of being, just as the heat from the sun is mediated through the atmosphere.

Aquinas rejects this position, and he does so precisely because to create is to grant being to things, which granting of being presupposes nothing. Nothing but God can act as such, because everything other than God presupposes the being that it receives from God. Thus, because creatures are not identical with their *esse*, they cannot grant *esse* to others and so cannot create. All creatures can do is modify being in some way. But modifications of being are simply changes, they are not acts of creation, and creatures which modify being do not act as ministers of creation. Thus, for Aquinas, God creates all things directly, from the highest angel to the lowest substance, whereas creatures can only act to change being and cannot originate it. This is not to say that creatures do not have a genuine causal role in creation, only that that causal role is not to be identified with creation.

We can relate this to what was observed about God in the previous chapter. Therein I highlighted that God's power is identical with His essence and that it is not exercised by the mediation of anything other than God; rather God's power and His exercise of that power are identical in Him. Thus, when God uses His power to bring anything into being, that is, to create, He does so completely of Himself and makes use of nothing other than Himself. Hence, God does not make use of any creature in using His power to give *esse*, but all creatures, of whatever grade, are caused directly and immediately by God.

Nevertheless, two problems can be raised against this position. The first is a scholarly issue to the effect that there are important texts in which Aquinas seems to endorse the Lombardian position. The second is a philosophical problem to the effect that insistence on God as the only cause of *esse* undermines the efficient causality of material substances.

To begin with the scholarly issue, Wippel has pointed out occasions where Aquinas does seem to argue that creatures are somewhat inferior ministers of creation, in spite of what I have said above.[24] What is common to these texts is that Aquinas affirms that creatures act to cause being in some way through the power granted them by God to do so, and that seems to be the Lombardian position. However, on these occasions Aquinas is not dealing with the creation of beings, that is, he is not dealing with the origin of *esse* in things; rather he is dealing with the preservation of things in being. Now, as will be seen in the next chapter, it is the case that by one and the same act God both creates and preserves creatures in being, and it can be the case that created things can be involved in the preservation of things yet excluded from their origination. Hence, whilst creatures can be involved in the preservation of beings and indeed in God's providential ordering of things, they cannot play a role in the act of creation itself as the origination of being; this is because no creature is per se but always *per participationem*, in which no creature can be the source of *esse* for any other, even though a creature can be instrumental in the preservation of such being. Thus, whilst Aquinas may endorse something like the Lombardian position in the texts that Wippel mentions, Aquinas is not speaking of creation proper, i.e. the origin of *esse*, but of the preservation of things in *esse*.

The second issue is more problematic. It can be argued that reserving creation to God alone undermines the efficient causality of material substances. This is because it seems clearly to be the case that material substances bring about the *esse* of other material

---

24. For details see Wippel, 'Aquinas on Creation and Preambles of Faith', *The Thomist*, 78:1 (2014), Section 5. Wippel focuses on *Summa Contra Gentiles*, Lib. 3, Cap. 66, *De Potentia Dei*, qu. 3, art. 7, and *Summa Theologiae*, Ia, qu. 104, aa. 1–2.

substances, and this is nowhere more apparent than in the case of natural generation; for when such generation occurs a complete entity is newly formed, in which case we have a newly existing substance. On Aquinas's account as I have articulated it above, God is responsible for causing the *esse* of this substance, whereas all we can say about its material generators is that they co-operated somewhat in causing that substance. Hence their act of generation was nothing more than the occasion for God to act to bring about the new substance, in which case God is really the cause of the thing, and secondary causes have no causality of their own. Thus we descend into a kind of occasionalism whereby all secondary causality is really only the occasion for God's acting in creation, and this is a view which Aquinas rejects.[25] The Lombardian position of creatures as co-operative ministers in creation now seems very appealing, lest we end up affirming occasionalism.[26]

As a way of resolving this problem, I'd like to begin by distinguishing, as Thomas does, between a cause of becoming and a cause of being. A cause of becoming is a cause that engages in certain actions whose result is the coming to be of some new substance; such causality evidently presupposes the existence of materials at hand on which the cause works so that the new

---

25. *De Potentia Dei*, qu. 3, art. 7.
26. Wippel highlights this issue in 'Thomas Aquinas on Creatures as Causes of *Esse*', in *Metaphysical Themes in Thomas Aquinas II*, p. 174. See also Alfred Freddoso, 'God's Concurrence with Secondary Causes: Why Conservation Is Not Enough', *Philosophical Perspectives*, 5 (1991), 553–585, in which he outlines the extremes of occasionalism and mere conservation, with the latter being akin to the Lombardian position. Freddoso makes use of the thinking of Aquinas, Suarez, and indeed Molina to navigate, successfully to my mind, the middle path of concurrentism, wherein creatures do have genuine causality (*pace* occasionalism) but a causality which also requires co-operation with God's primary causality (*pace* mere conservation). For a discussion of occasionalism itself and the Aristotelian case against it as presented by Aquinas, Molina, and Suarez see Freddoso, 'Medieval Aristotelianism and the Case against Secondary Causation in Nature', in *Divine and Human Action: Essays in the Metaphysics of Theism*, ed. by Thomas Morris (Ithaca, NY: Cornell University Press, 1988), pp. 74–118, especially Sections 2–4 for occasionalism and Section 5 for the objections.

substance can come to be. A cause of being originates the *esse* of a thing and clearly does not presuppose any materials on which to work; such a cause is a creator.[27] Now what is significant here is that if you remove the cause of becoming, the presupposed materials that would have otherwise been transformed by the cause (of becoming) remain in being, but they are simply not transformed. On the other hand removal of a cause of being entails that there would be nothing simpliciter, since whatever exists depends on that cause in order to be. This fact is implicit in the examples Thomas uses of each kind of causality; for the cause of becoming he offers the example of a smith making a knife, and for the cause of *esse* he offers the example of the sun's illumination of the atmosphere. In the former case, should the smith not produce the knife, the materials for the production of the knife remain, whereas in the latter case, removal of the sun entails the removal of all illumination from the atmosphere.

With the foregoing distinction in mind, we can say that material creatures can be the causes of becoming of other material creatures, but we cannot say that they are the causes of *esse* such that they originate the *esse* of others. This is because all creatures presuppose something in their causality whereas the cause of *esse*

---

27. For some texts in which Aquinas makes this distinction see *De Veritate*, qu. 5, art. 8, ad. 8: 'Sed in causis inferioribus quaedam sunt causae fiendi, quaedam vero essendi: et dicitur causa fiendi quod educit formam de potentia materiae per motum, sicut faber est causa efficiens cultelli; causa vero essendi rem est illud a quo per se esse rei dependet, sicut esse luminis in aere dependet a sole'; *De Potentia Dei*, qu. 5, art. 1: 'formae generatorum dependent a generantibus naturaliter, quod educuntur de potentia materiae, non autem quantum ad esse absolutum. Unde et remota actione generantis, cessat eductio de potentia in actum quod est fieri generatorum; non autem cessant ipsae formae, secundum quas generata habent esse. Et inde est quod esse rerum generatarum manet, sed non fieri, cessante actione generantis'; *Summa Theologiae*, Ia, qu. 104, art. 1: 'aliquod agens est causa sui effectus secundum fieri tantum, et non directe secundum esse eius. . . . [S]i aliquod agens non est causa formae inquantum huiusmodi, non erit per se causa esse quod consequitur ad talem formam, sed erit causa effectus secundum fieri tantum.' For a discussion of these and other texts see Wippel, 'Thomas Aquinas on Creatures as Causes of *Esse*', Section 2.

presupposes nothing. Hence, even if the creaturely cause does not act, what it would have presupposed for its causal activity would still be in existence, whereas if the cause of *esse* were not to act, nothing would be.

Now undoubtedly creaturely causes can act as causes only insofar as they are in act, and they are in act through their participating in the existence granted to them by God. Hence creaturely causes act through the power of the primary cause, as Thomas explicitly affirms.[28] But acting through the power of the primary cause is not the same as causing the *esse* of a thing, as the Lombardian position would suggest. A secondary cause acts through the power of the primary cause through utilizing its own actuality, its own *esse*, in order to act as a cause in the world; it is in this way that it is a cause of becoming, and since its *esse* is individual to it, it exercises a genuine causality. But this does not make it a cause of *esse*, since it must presuppose *esse* in order to act, in which case it cannot originate it. Hence, no creature can confer *esse* on another creature, but through its own actuality (dependent on the primary cause) a creature can act so as to bring about a substance, which depends on the creaturely cause(s) for its particular determination, e.g. as a dog or cat or whatever, yet in order to be, that effect must participate in its own act of being, which it can get from nowhere else but the primary cause. Hence it can be denied that creatures are causes of *esse* whilst at the same time the genuine causality of creatures can be affirmed.

The upshot of all this is that creatures are directly caused to be by God; there is nothing that exists which is not caused by God. God then does not simply get the ball rolling and leave creatures to themselves (a parody of the Islamic and *Liber De Causis* position), nor does He make creatures ministers of the *esse* that He grants. God directly creates everything from the highest to the

---

28. *De Potentia Dei*, qu. 3, art. 7, and qu. 5, art. 1, and *Summa Theologiae*, Ia, qu. 104, art. 1. For discussion see Wippel, 'Thomas Aquinas on Creatures as Causes of *Esse*', Section 3.

lowest. And this brings us back to the fact that God's creating is His granting of *esse* to things. Temporally speaking, a creature such as a rabbit may come very late after the beginning of the universe, but God grants existence to it just as much as He grants existence to every creature that came before it and every creature that comes after it; for that rabbit would not be had God not willed it to be and thereby granted *esse* to it (the same for all other creatures). This certainly does raise questions for the role of natural processes in the physical evolution of creatures from an initial starting point, and I shall deal with those questions in Chapter 6 where I deal with the history of creation, but for now it suffices to say that Aquinas's metaphysics of creation commits him to the view that whatever role such physical processes play, the *esse* of creatures is not a result of those physical processes; for that would be something like the Lombardian approach, whereby creatures (or in this case physical processes) are ministers of God's creative activity and not simply its recipients.

4 CONCLUSION

What is clear from all this is that Aquinas's metaphysics of creation centres on his characteristic understanding of *esse* as the metaphysical principle without which there would be nothing. *Esse* replaces form as the supreme principle of act, so that form only tells us what kind of being we are dealing with, whereas *esse* is the reason for there being anything at all. It is natural that such a metaphysical principle should play a fundamental role in Aquinas's metaphysics of creation, since without *esse* there would be nothing, in which case in order for there to be something, i.e. creatures, *esse* must be originated in some way, and that origination is creation. In creating things then God grants *esse* to things, and on the basis of this characterization of creation Aquinas can proceed to argue that creation is *ex nihilo*, presupposing nothing, that it signifies a relation between God and creatures, and that only what is *esse* itself, i.e. God, can properly speaking create. *Esse* then will be the touchstone for any Thomist metaphysics of creation.

The Presocratics failed to develop a notion of creation precisely because they failed to grasp the complete origination of being in things; and they failed in the latter because they failed to grasp that things have a principle without which they are nothing. Given the latter, the Presocratics could not envisage the crossing of the most extreme ontological divide, that of being and nothingness, because they could not envisage an agent of creation that was in Himself the principle without which nothing would be. Thus, they had to presuppose many preexistent principles which coalesced to bring about creatures.

Plato and Aristotle certainly represent an advance in the philosophical thinking on creation, and whilst Aquinas does attribute a doctrine of creation to both, it is undoubtedly the case that neither would have recognized Aquinas's metaphysical principle of *esse* nor his conception of God as pure *esse*, despite Aquinas's moulding of their thought into his own. Thus, whilst a case can be made for Plato and Aristotle's recognition that there is a supreme primary cause for all things, it is only by attributing to them an understanding of *esse* that Aquinas can hold that they arrived at a notion of creation.

Turning to the monotheistic inheritance, Aquinas clearly does think that we have arrived at a level of philosophical reflection wherein the very being of things is considered, and it was observed in Chapter 1 that he attributes an understanding of *esse* to at least one representative monotheistic philosopher, Avicenna. Hence, once again, only when a philosopher or philosophical tradition comes to an understanding of *esse* does that philosopher or tradition arrive at a notion of creation; for in considering that without which a thing would not be, one is inevitably led to consider the origin of the thing's being and hence its creation.

So far in this chapter I have been concerned with definitional matters, and they have revolved around determining what creation actually means and whether or not it can be applied to creatures.

We now know that for Aquinas creation is God's granting of *esse*, thereby constituting a relation between God and creatures, and that whilst creatures may play a role in the preservation of things, they certainly cannot be said to create things. What is immediately evident in my investigations in this chapter is that creation is inextricably linked with causality, and so the next chapter will consider the causality of creation.

4

THE CAUSALITY

OF CREATION

I NOTED IN CHAPTER 1 THAT Thomas found fault with the thought of earlier thinkers for not fully grasping the causality involved in creation; this is to say, they had appreciated, to some degree or other, aspects of the causal relations amongst beings, but none of them save Plato and Aristotle (to Thomas's mind) had come to appreciate what could be called absolute or universal causality without which nothing would be. Thus, one way or another the Presocratics all presupposed being and considered the causality that obtains amongst beings without considering a cause for being itself.

It was this shortcoming that prevented such philosophers from coming to terms with the metaphysics of creation, since it requires that one push the notion of causality to the limit and countenance a cause of *esse*. A genuine philosophy of creation seeks to think through the absolute cause of being, because that's what it is to create: to bring into being from nothing what does not naturally have being.

Aquinas's metaphysics of *esse* is well suited to the articulation of such a creationist metaphysics; this is because *esse* is a component of the creature without which the creature would not be. All creatures then must have *esse* in order to be, in which case *esse* will be involved in the causality of creation. In effect if we articulate the causality involved in the causality of *esse*, we can articulate the causality of creation.

Esse is typically thought of in terms of efficient causality given that it is the act of all acts. So the reasoning goes that insofar as *esse* is that without which nothing would be, the cause of *esse* is an originating primary cause; and this would be an efficient cause. However, Thomas also conceives *esse* as the perfection of all perfections. Not only is it the act by which anything at all is in act, it is also that by which all that is in the creature (and hence all that is in creation) is perfected and brought to completion. There is a finality then to *esse* as a causal principle, in which case an adequate account of the causality of creation must address not only the efficient causal aspect of *esse* but also its finality.

So, in considering the causality of creation, we must consider the causality of *esse* in terms of efficient causality (its being the act of all acts), and then consider it in terms of final causality (its being the perfection of all perfections). The remainder of this book is devoted to these tasks. This chapter will consider the causality of creation in terms of God as the originating primary cause of *esse*. The next two chapters will consider the things that are so originated by God. Hence Chapter 5 will consider the object of creation and its metaphysical constitution, focussing on its being subject to *esse*; Chapter 6 will consider the history of things that are so subject. Finally Chapter 7 will consider the ultimate end of creation, wherein I will consider the causality of creation in terms of final causality.

This chapter begins by looking at causality in general (Section 1) and then moving on to consider God's primary causality as bringing all things into existence (Section 2). Having done that, I consider whether or not Aquinas is committed to any preexisting potential essences of which God makes use in creating (Section 3). The summary (Section 4) anticipates future chapters.

1 CAUSALITY IN GENERAL

Causality is a kind of relationship relating one thing as cause to another thing as effect. The relationship itself involves act and potency, such that the effect is in potency in some respect to the cause, which is actual in that respect.[1] This then permits Thomas quite a generous notion of causality since there are as many causal contexts as there are kinds of act/potency relationship. They have traditionally been divided into four: (i) material, (ii) formal, (iii) efficient, and (iv) final.

The material and formal causes can be called the intrinsic causal principles of a thing, since they serve to constitute the thing. The efficient and final causes can be called extrinsic causal principles since they are not intrinsic to the thing. The material cause is that by which the form is present in material things; the form has no existence other than as the form of some material thing so that the material cause, the matter, instances the form. The formal cause is the form by which the matter is formed in some way. The efficient cause is the first source of motion, such that it is that by which the form of the thing is informed in the matter. The final cause is the cause motivating the efficient cause.

These different causes are related hierarchically. The material cause has the least causal scope since it only instantiates the form and in doing so allows for change. The formal cause has greater causal scope since it informs matter and can do so many times over. The efficient cause has even greater scope precisely because it is what introduces the form to matter. But the final cause has the greatest causal scope since it is what motivates the efficient cause to introduce form to matter. Thus, Aquinas calls the final cause the cause of causes.[2]

Now, it has been seen that in Aquinas's view creation is a relation and involves act and potency such that the creature is brought

---

1. Aquinas, *In V Met.*, lect. 1, n. 751: 'Hoc nomen causa, importat influxum quemdam ad esse causati', and lect. 3, n. 794: 'Potentia et actus diversificant habitudinem causae ad effectum'; *In II Phy.*, lect. 5, n. 183: 'Omnia ista habent unam rationem causae, prout dicitur causa id ex quo fit aliquid.'

2. *De Principiis Naturae* (Rome: Editori di San Tommasso, 1976), Cap. 4: 'finis est causa causalitatis efficientis, quia facit efficiens esse efficiens: similiter facit materiam esse materiam, et formam esse formam, cum materia non suscipiat formam nisi per finem, et forma non perficiat materiam nisi per finem. Unde dicitur quod finis est causa causarum, quia est causa causalitatis in omnibus causis.'

to act by the creator, Who grants *esse* to it. Hence creation is a kind of causal relation. Now, when it comes to the causality of creation, I will be focussing especially on (i) the efficient (this chapter) and final (Chapter 7) causal activity of God; this is because God exercises His power in granting *esse* to things (and that would be to signify efficient causality), but He only does so because He wills to do so (and that would be to signify final causality). But we must not overlook His role as a formal principle of things (nor His role in causing the matter of things), since as was observed in Chapter 2, God's intellect provides Him with an inventory of possibilities that He could create, and these divine ideas, signify the formal elements of creation; I will consider the latter in Section 3 of this chapter.

Returning to the general account of causality, it should be evident that something can be a cause in one respect because it is actual in that respect whilst being in potency and hence an effect in another respect. So for instance, a form can be actual with respect to the matter it informs but in potency to the agency of the efficient cause without which it would not inform matter. The distinctions of causal contexts allow for this, since they allow us to distinguish the different respects in which things can be in potency and act. It is only when we have a being on Whom all things depend for actuality that we have a cause that is in potency in no respect.

Now creatures are effects of the creator, and so they are in potency in some respect and, having been created, actualized in that respect. The potency that all creatures are in is the potency to existence; and in Thomas's metaphysics that is the potency exhibited by the essence of the thing in relation to *esse*. Hence essence is related to *esse* as potency to act, and the *esse* that a creature possesses is in turn dependent on God's *esse*. A creature thus depends on God as cause for its existence.

Automatically this framework raises a critical issue, and it concerns the metaphysical significance of essence as standing in potency to *esse*. Usually when we say something stands in potency as an effect to something else as its cause, the thing standing in potency already exists and in its existence there are certain potencies that can be actualized. So for instance the marble of a statue already exists, and it stands to be informed (formal cause) by the artist (efficient cause) for some reason or other (final cause). But with regard to creation, prior to creating there is nothing; so nothing exists which is in potency to *esse*, yet I have just affirmed that on the Thomist view to create is to grant *esse* to essence. The essence to which the *esse* is granted and which is actualized would appear to require some kind of existence prior to being created; and that would undermine Aquinas's determination of creation *ex nihilo* as intelligible only in terms of *esse* being granted to the thing.

The issue of the preexistence of the essence to which *esse* is granted pertains to the potency of creatures, and as such cannot be considered until their actuality is considered, and in particular their actuality with respect of their cause. To this task I now turn.

2 GOD'S PRIMARY CAUSALITY

In demonstrating God's existence, Aquinas establishes that God is the primary cause of all that is; but in order to do so, Aquinas must establish that God is the primary cause of some causal series which includes all existing things. This will involve Aquinas in a consideration of the infinity of causal series and whether or not one can reasonably affirm there to be some series that includes all that is and so is subject to the causality of God. Accordingly, Aquinas's thought on God as primary cause is tied up with his denial of an infinite regress of causes and the metaphysics associated therewith.

Now, in considering causal series, Aquinas makes a distinction between two kinds of series: (i) the per se and (ii) the *per accidens*.[3]

---

3. I consider each of these series at length in 'Essentially Ordered Series Reconsidered', *American Catholic Philosophical Quarterly*, 86:4 (2012), 155–174, and in *Aquinas's Way to God*, Chapter 5. For instances wherein Aquinas makes this distinction see *De Veritate*, qu. 2, art. 10, *Quodlibet IX*, qu. 1, *Summa Theologiae*, Ia, qu. 7, art. 4, *Quodlibet XII*, qu. 2, art. 2.

In per se causal series the posterior causal relata require a cause of their causality. The cause of their causality is the primary cause precisely because it is the cause of the causality of the series yet not itself needing a cause for the causality that it causes. The posterior causal relata are posterior because they are dependent for their causality. They do not possess such causality in themselves; it is distinct from what they are, distinct from their essences. Hence the effects of such series, i.e. things dependent on the primary cause, do not possess the causality of the series essentially, whereas the primary cause does.

In *per accidens* series on the other hand the posterior causal relata don't require a cause for their causality; they are linked together, but each one possesses the causality of the series in itself and not independently of itself. Hence in such a series each member is capable of exercising its causality without dependence on some primary cause that grants causality to the series.

With these characterizations in mind, consider an example of each series.[4]

(i) *Per se*: a stone (z) is moved by a stick (y), which is moved by a hand (x), which is moved by the mind (w). Hence: $w \rightarrow (x \rightarrow (y \rightarrow z))$.

(ii) *Per accidens*: a son, z, is begotten by his father, y, who is begotten by his father, x, who is begotten by his father, w, and so on. Hence: $(\ldots) \rightarrow (w \rightarrow x) \rightarrow (x \rightarrow y) \rightarrow (y \rightarrow z)$.

In accord with the characterization offered above, notice that in the per se series there is a cause for the causality of the series, i.e. the mind (or mental agent, or subject of experience, or whatever one takes to be responsible for intentional action), whereas in the *per accidens* series there is no such cause. Hence the per se series is represented as having a primary cause whose causal scope

4. These examples are taken from *Summa Theologiae*, Ia, qu. 46, art. 2, ad. 7.

dominates everything in the series, whereas in the *per accidens* series there is no primary cause with causal scope ranging over everything in the series.

In the per se series the hand, stick, and stone are in themselves causally inefficacious with respect to the causality of the series (motion) and so depend on what is not so inefficacious (the mind) but is capable of bringing about the causality of the series in question. The hand, stick, and stone are posterior precisely because they do not possess the causality of the series themselves but are dependent on another for such causality.

Contrast that with the *per accidens* series. In the series of fathers and sons, none of the members of the series are dependent on any other for the causality of the series (begetting, paternity, reproducing, etc.). Each member possesses the causality of the series in himself and so does not depend on any other for the causality in question. A father brings about a son, but the father does not bring about the son's ability to procreate; the son can do that on his own without his father's help. Hence the grandfather's son is the father of the grandfather's grandson; the grandfather is not.

Now in the per se series the mind brings about the motion of the hand, and the hand's thus depending on the mind permits the hand to bring about motion in the stick, which depending on the hand's depending on the mind brings about motion in the stone. Hence the hand cannot be without the influence of the mind in order to bring about its own motion in the stick and similarly with the stick to the stone. Accordingly, in the per se series the effects all participate in the causality imparted to the series by the primary cause such that without the primary cause there would be no causality in the series. And this notion of participation is in accord with that offered by Thomas on behalf of Platonism, outlined in Chapter 1, and his own view of participation, outlined in Chapter 2: that a participant possesses some actuality in a derived and limited fashion. In this case, the posterior causal relata all possess the causality of the mind in a derived and limited fashion, and not of themselves.

On the other hand in the *per accidens* series the father simply brings about his son, but not in the sense that the son must always participate in the causality of begetting imparted to it by something that essentially begets. Rather, the son can be without his father and yet able to produce his own son in virtue of being a biologically functioning male. So for instance, a man can produce a son and having done so go off and die. Effectively the father drops out of the series. But the son he generated can go on to produce his own son; he is not dependent on his father's causality in order to exercise his own reproductive causality. Accordingly, in *per accidens* series some previous cause can drop out and the causality of the series will not cease. Contrast that with the per se series, where there is need of a primary cause from which causality is derived, and one can conclude that in such a series if the primary cause (the mind) dropped out of the per se series, causality would cease, and the series would collapse precisely as a causal series.

Consequently, a per se series is such that without a primary cause granting causal efficacy to it, there would be no causal series in question (although of course with respect to the example, there would be hands, sticks, and stones; they would just be immobile without anything moving them). On the other hand *per accidens* series do not need a primary cause in such a fashion.

We can derive the same conclusion in a much more general form if we focus on the symbolic formulation above for representing these series.

In the per se series w exercises causal efficacy over every member of the series, and its causal input descends down to the ultimate effect. Thus w is responsible for the causality of x, y, and z, so that w is the cause not only of x (the hand) but also of y and z (the stick and stone). Nevertheless, x and y (the hand and stick) do indeed exercise causality insofar as they determine the causality (the motion) brought about in them by w; they focus such causality to a determined effect—the hand determines the mobility given to it so as to produce motion in the stick, and the stick determines such mobility to produce motion in the stone. Hence their causality is not as extensive as that of w but still has its own extent to produce their own effects.

Posterior or secondary causes act to exercise genuine causality, for y would have no motion were it not for x, and z would have no motion were it not for y. Yet this is only a secondary kind of causality dependent on the primary causality of w, which has causal scope over all such secondary causes in the series. None of this could occur unless the actuality of the causality of the series were independent of the natures of the effects in the series. Hence, x, y, and z (the hand, stick, and stone) do not of themselves possess causal efficacy but participate in the causal efficacy granted to them by the primary cause, and in so participating they delimit that efficacy to their own uses thereof.

Secondary causes have real causal efficacy, though it is not identical to the nature of the things which act as causes; what secondary causes produce then exceeds their own capacity but not that of the primary cause. Hence the hand-stick-stone of themselves cannot move without the mind, yet the hand, through participation in the causal activity of the mind, genuinely moves the stick, and similarly the stick moves the stone. So secondary causes themselves produce some effect proportionate to them but exceeding their capacity, thereby requiring the causal influence of the primary cause.[5]

This account of causality in per se series sits nicely with Aquinas's metaphysics of *esse*, since a creature can act as a cause

---

5. *Summa Theologiae*, Ia, qu. 104, art. 2: 'Cum enim sunt multae causae ordinatae, necesse est quod effectus dependeat primo quidem et principaliter a causa prima; secundario vero ab omnibus causis mediis'; *De Causis*, lect. 1, n. 23: 'operatio, qua secunda causa causat effectum, causatur a causa prima; nam causa prima adiuvat causam secundam faciens eam operari', and n. 28: 'Causa secunda non agit in causatum suum nisi virtute causae primae. Ergo et causatum non procedit a causa secunda nisi per virtutem causae primae.' For the same see *Summa Theologiae*, Ia, qu. 21, art. 4, qu. 65, art. 3, and *De Potentia Dei*, qu. 3, art. 4; see also James Alberston, 'Instrumental Causality in St Thomas', *New Scholasticism*, 28 (1954), 409–443; Armand Maurer, 'Darwin, Thomists, and Secondary Causality', *Review of Metaphysics*, 57 (2004), 491–514.

precisely because it has *esse*; but the *esse* that it has is not identical with its essence but distinct therefrom, so that *esse* is individuated to the thing whose *esse* it is. It follows then that the causality of creatures is an individuated causality, and whilst it is proper to the individual creature itself as flowing from that creature's *esse*, it is nevertheless dependent on the primary cause (of *esse*), i.e. God, without Whom there would be no *esse* in question. Hence just as a creature's *esse* is really its own yet distinct from it and derived from God, so too is a creature's causality (in respect of per se series) really its own yet distinct from it and derived from the primary cause.

Not only does this division of primary and secondary causality help to characterize the metaphysics of the per se series, it also avoids any sort of occasionalism whereby any instance of secondary causality is conceived of as nothing more than the occasion for the exercise of the primary cause's causality. On the model of causality offered here, the hand and stick are not just occasions for the mind to bring about motion, but they themselves have motion from the mind to bring about their respective effects. So when God is in place of the primary cause, we can still say that creatures can exercise their own (secondary) causality, rather than affirming without nuance that it is all down to God. The metaphysics of the per se series does not permit any occasionalism which would remove creaturely causality since it grants a role to secondary causes in exercising their own causality, which they derive from the primary cause.[6]

Not only that, such secondary causality ought not to be interpreted in the emanationist or Lombardian fashion whereby, in the strong sense, the primary cause imparts causality to something secondary, and that to something tertiary, and so on, or, in the weaker sense, whereby creatures act as ministers of God's creative causality. Secondary causes have no causal efficacy except for the primary cause, so the primary cause is primarily the cause of every

---

6. See *Summa Contra Gentiles*, Lib. 3, Cap. 69, and *De Potentia Dei*, qu. 3, art. 7, for lengthy rejections by St Thomas of occasionalism.

effect in the per se causal series. The mind moves the hand, and the stick is moved by the mind's moving the hand, and the stone is moved by the mind's moving the hand to move the stick to move the stone. Hence, none of the effects escapes the causality of the primary cause, in which case such causality is not an emanation to lower effects or a deputizing of secondary agents as ministers of such causality. Nevertheless, secondary causes can co-operate with the primary cause in preserving the causality of the primary cause in the series, as the hand and stick are co-operative causes with the primary cause (the mind) in the example above.

Members of *per accidens* series on the other hand do not participate in the causality of that series through its derivation from some primary cause which possesses that causality essentially; rather members of the *per accidens* series themselves possess the causality of the series in virtue of what they are. Thus, as pointed out above, in the fathers-sons series the members of the series possess the causality of paternity in virtue of being the kinds of things they are; they do not need to participate in some primary cause of paternity for their ability to procreate, and this is precisely because as biologically functioning men they have that ability in themselves. The symbolic representation captures this since in the series we merely have a single cause producing a single effect and with that the causality of the cause is completed. Thus, we link cause and effect in such a series as an accidental causal chain made up of causal units of one cause and one effect. This representation has the benefit of divorcing a previous causal unity, say w's causing x, from a subsequent causal unity, x's causing y, which in turn permits us to envisage the fact that previous members can drop out but the series can continue. In this context we cannot distinguish between primary and secondary causes, since we do not have secondary members of a series participating in the causality of some primary cause. Rather, we can simply enumerate the members of the chain.

Given the metaphysics of the matter, per se causal series are necessarily finite, that is, they cannot be without a primary cause, since to be so would be for the members of that series not to have a cause of their causality, which would be to annihilate the causality of the series. *Per accidens* causal series do not need a primary cause with respect to the causality of the series, e.g. a father of all fathers, precisely because each member of the series possesses causal efficacy in itself and so it is its own primary cause with respect to the causality of the series. This does not mean that there is no cause of the members in *per accidens* series or for the causality involved therein *tout court*; for whilst the members of that series possess the causality of the series themselves, the actuality of members possessing that causality does require a cause, in which case there must be something independent of the series itself which is responsible for the being of the members and hence their intrinsic ability to act as the causes they are. So fathers and sons possess the causal efficacy of paternity in themselves, but that is not to say that they are not caused in some other line of causality, i.e. in their existence. Hence, in order to account for the actuality of the members of the *per accidens* series, that series itself must be embedded in some other causal series whereby the actuality of those members is explained.

Now when it comes to God, Aquinas's typical method for demonstrating God's existence is to find some causal feature of beings, locate that causality within a per se series, and thereby infer a primary cause Who is capable of originating that causality. Insofar as causality is conceived of in terms of actuality, what lies behind all of Aquinas's various demonstrations of God is a recognition of the actuality of things, which actuality things do not possess of themselves but as distinct from their essences; this is to say, Thomas is concerned with the very *esse* of things without which nothing would be. Hence, essence/existence composites require a cause for their existence because they do not possess existence essentially. The causality of *esse* then is involved in such reasoning, and since no essence/existence composite possesses *esse* essentially, such causality is independent of the things in the series that possess it. That then entails that a causal series in which *esse* is the causal property under consideration is a per se series, in which case, given the metaphysics of the matter, there must be a primary cause of *esse* which does not have *esse* as distinct from its essence but is simply *esse* itself—one of Aquinas's favourite designations of God. It is that from which all existence, all actuality flows, in which case anything which in any way exists depends on that primary cause of *esse*.

This argumentation is Thomas's general strategy for demonstrating God's existence, explicit in the proof in the *De Ente et Essentia*, Chapter 4, and implicit in many of his other demonstrations. What is important to bear in mind is that what is being accounted for is the *esse* of things, that without which there would be nothing. All reality, all actuality, comes from *esse*; so by locating such causality in a per se series and discovering a primary cause of such causality in that which is *esse* itself, we find a cause of all things, and without that there would be nothing. All things then participate in this primary cause of *esse* and themselves would have no actuality were it not for this primary source of all actuality.

Now, I noted above that in the *per accidens* series, whilst there is no need for a cause of the causality that the members of the series exercise, because they possess it in themselves, there must indeed be a cause for the actuality of those members. And so *per accidens* series must themselves be embedded in the wider context of some other causal series which does account for their actuality. That series must be a per se series because it is the actuality of the members of the *per accidens* series themselves which is being accounted for (the actuality of the fathers and sons for example) and which such members do not possess of themselves. Thus, the very actuality of the members of the *per accidens* series without which they could not exercise causality is itself caused, and this then is the wider context of a per se series.

An individual per se series may have a primary cause which is primary with respect to the causality of that series, but that primary cause is perhaps secondary with respect to some other kind of causality, e.g. the mind is primary with respect to motion but with respect to some other causality, e.g. its actual existence, it is not primary. So per se series can be embedded in other per se series, and, as I have argued, *per accidens* series are embedded in per se series. We are in danger of getting lost in a complex web of causal interrelations, but the decisive simplicity of Aquinas's reasoning is that he has focussed on that causal property, *esse*, without which there would be no actuality hence no causality whatsoever. So no matter how complex the interweaving of per se and *per accidens* series becomes, all members of those series will be in some way dependent on something for their actuality—they are not identical with the actuality they have, their *esse*, of which they also make use in order to act as causes. Thus, the per se series with greatest causal scope in which all *per accidens* and per se series are embedded is that whose causality is the causality of *esse* and whose primary cause is *esse* itself.

God as creator of all things is the supreme source of *esse*, and as such all actuality and hence causality comes from Him. So God's creating *ex nihilo* is characterized as His being the primary cause of the per se series whose causal property is *esse*. God is the primary cause precisely because He is that without which there would be no actuality, no *esse*, whatsoever. This characterization of primary causality distances Thomas from any account of God's creative causality as a primacy in terms of being first. Rather primacy here is interpreted in terms of dependency, such that what is primary is what is independent with respect to causality, and what is secondary is what is so dependent with respect to the causality in question.[7] When it comes to *esse*, what is primary is

7. The objections of Christopher Williams and Anthony Kenny to Aquinas's reasoning on infinite causal series, to the effect that the notion of secondary cause is unintelligible unless one presuppose a primary cause, are thus groundless; for here a secondary cause is simply one that is dependent for the causality in question whereas a primary cause is a cause not so dependent. Thomas's reasoning has nothing to do with secondary causality being conceived of as what comes after (and hence presupposes) what is primary. For Williams, see C. J. F. Williams, ' "Hic Autem Non Est Procedure in Infinitum . . ." ', *Mind*, 69 (1960), 403–405, and for Kenny see *The Five Ways* (London: Routledge and Kegan Paul, 1969) pp. 26–27, 44. For my response, see 'Aquinas's Argument for the Existence of God in *De Ente et Essentia* Cap. IV: An Interpretation and Defense', *Journal of Philosophical Research*, 37 (2012), 119–121.

what does not depend on anything for its *esse*, i.e. that whose essence is its *esse*, whereas what is secondary is what does so depend. God is primary with regard to *esse*, and this is an absolute primacy since without *esse* there is nothing, in which case there is nothing independent of God on which He could depend for actuality. Accordingly, whatever is primary with regard to *esse*, i.e. whatever is *esse* itself, is absolutely primary, and this is what we understand God to be.

In characterizing the general nature of per se series above, I pointed out that the effects of the series cannot exercise causality without participating in the causality of the primary cause. Effectively, none of the effects would have causality without the influence of the primary cause. Returning to the mind-hand-stick-stone series, the hand, stick, and stone would be inert and immobile unless something granted them the causality of motion; take away this primary cause of motion, and they return to being causally inert. So if you take the mind out of the series, the hand, stick, and stone become motionless, or some other source of motion itself primary in another causal series takes over. What is important here is that unless the effects participate in the causal efficacy of the primary cause, they themselves are causally inefficacious; they are without the causality in question.

This reasoning entails then that in per se series there is no real distinction between the origin of causality and its preservation. It is one and the same act by which the primary cause grants motion to the series and preserves it therein. In acting as the source of motion for the hand, stick, and stone the mind, by that very act, ensures that motion remains in the hand, the stick, and the stone; for if you remove the causal influence of the mind, you remove the causality from the series. Turning to God then, God creates by granting *esse* to things, and such things exist and remain in existence for as long as they participate in the *esse* so granted. Hence, as primary cause of *esse*, God not only originates *esse* in all things but also preserves such things in *esse*, since if God's causal influence were to be removed from the series, the members of the series would be without *esse*, and so would not be.

We can think this through in another way by considering creaturely dependence. A creature cannot exist without *esse*, and such *esse* is caused in the creature by God. Now a creature's existence is not all at once but is stretched out over time, and the creature exists over such a period of time because it has *esse*. But its having of *esse* is a result of God's creative causality, in which case it is not by two different dependencies that a creature exists and remains in existence; there is a single dependency on *esse* which is derived from God, in which case there is a single creative act of God by which the creature exists and remains in existence.

Consequently, God does not grant *esse* to things first of all and then by a different act preserve them in their *esse*; that's not how causality in per se series works. The very granting of causality to things in a per se series involves the preservation of causality therein, since if such things did not participate in the causality of the series, *esse* in this case, they would be causally inefficacious; in this case they would be nothing. Those things participating in *esse* can be causes of the preservation of *esse* for other things, such as the causality of the sun with respect to life on earth. But all such causality that creatures exercise is a participation in the primary causality of God. Hence, such secondary causality, whilst preservative, is so precisely because it participates in the primary causality of God. Hence, creation is a single causal act which both originates and preserves in *esse* anything that in any way exists.[8]

Enough has been established to reject any suggestion of existential inertia, which is a belief that existing things do not need a sustaining cause for their existence but, as in mechanical inertia, go

---

8. See *Summa Contra Gentiles*, Lib. 3, Cap. 65: 'Esse autem cuiuslibet rei est esse participatum: cum non sit res aliqua praeter Deum suum esse, ut supra probatum est. Et sic oportet quod ipse Deus, qui est suum esse, sit primo et per se causa omnis esse. Sic igitur se habet ad esse rerum operatio divina, sicut motio corporis moventis ad fieri et moveri rerum factarum vel motarum. Impossibile autem est quod fieri et moveri alicuius rei maneat, cessante motione moventis. Impossibile ergo est quod esse alicuius rei remaneat nisi per operationem divinam.' See also *Summa Theologiae*, Ia, qu. 104, aa. 1–2, and *De Potentia Dei*, qu. 5, art. 1.

on existing until some other cause brings it about that they cease to exist. Given Aquinas's account of causality (and the metaphysics of *esse*), effects exist insofar as they participate in the primary causality of the efficient cause; otherwise they would not have the causal actuality in question, *esse* in this case. So if such effects did not have *esse* in any other way than through their participation in God's primary causality, they would not be unless for every moment of their being they were caused to be by God. Hence, God's causing things to be and leaving them to be by some sort of inertia is impossible, since if He withdrew His causal influence, things would cease to have *esse*, in which case they would cease to be.[9]

When we think of the mind's causal influence on the hand-stick-stone series and affirm that in causing the motion of the members such causal influence is also responsible for the preservation of causality in the series, we tend to think of that primary cause being present to the members of the series, such that if it were not presently involved with each one of them they would not be able to enjoy the causality that the primary cause imparts. This then carries with it the suggestion that the primary cause is contemporaneous with the effects of the per se series. Thinking of God's primary causality in terms of the per se causal series would thus seem to threaten God's independence of creatures, and in particular His eternity, because in that case God would be contemporaneous with temporal effects, so that for as long as there are any temporal effects which God brings about, God is present to them. This entails that at t_1 through t_2 to t_n God causes x to exist. Hence one might object that locating God's primacy in the fact that He is the primary cause of a per se causal series whose causality is *esse*

---

9. For details of the doctrine of existential inertia see Mortimer Adler, *How to Think about God: A Guide for the 20th Century Pagan* (New York: Collier/Macmillan, 1980), Chapter 13; John Beadouin, 'The World's Continuance: Divine Conservation or Existential Inertia?', *International Journal for Philosophy of Religion*, 61 (2007), 83–98. For discussion and response see Edward Feser, *Five Proofs of the Existence of God*, pp. 232–238, and 'Existential Inertia and the Five Ways', *American Catholic Philosophical Quarterly*, 85 (2011), 237–267.

stands in tension with some key commitments of Aquinas's classical theism.

But what is the mode of presence that the primary cause has to its effects in per se series? The primary cause is primary because it possesses the causality of the series in itself, whereas the effects are effects precisely because they don't possess such causality—they depend on it. In so depending the effects participate in the causality of the primary cause; they draw from its actuality in some way and make it their own. So in order to have the causality that they have, the effects must be present to the primary cause, whereas the primary cause can have that causality, that actuality, irrespective of the being of the effects: the mind still has the causality of motion even if it does not exercise it over the hand, stick, and stone. It follows then that the causality of the per se series is not so much a case of the primary cause's being present to the effects in a way that the primary cause is subject to the being of the effects; rather it is the reverse: the effects are made present to the being of the primary cause as causing their causality. The primary cause is not subject to the conditions of the effects of that series; and so whilst in many cases the primary cause happens to coincide with its effects, there is no strict necessity that it do so. Hence it is only a coincidence that primary cause and effects are contemporaneous in some per se series (i.e. temporal ones); it is not a necessity that they be so.

Given Thomas's account of God, God does not share in the being of creatures, and in particular He does not share in their temporality. As the primary cause of the per se series whose causality is *esse*, God is primary insofar as all things which have *esse* distinct from their essences, i.e. all things other than Him, depend on Him for their *esse*. It is they who in being so dependent are made present to God; God is not made present to them in the sense that He is subject to their temporal conditions. (God does not have a real relationship to them as was seen in the previous chapter when considering creation as a relation.) Hence in granting *esse* to things God causes a being, x, to exist at t_1 through t_2 to t_n, but He Himself does not exist at t_1 through t_2 to t_n. The being that is so caused by

God is subject to temporal conditions and experiences its being (present to God) in a temporal fashion; but God as eternal sees all things that are created from the point of view of eternity, such that in a single act of creation all things are granted being.

3 THE POTENCY OF CREATURES

It is time now to say something about the potency of creatures. I have already emphasized that the actuality involved in the causality of creation is that of *esse* and that its correlative potency is essence. Hence in creating God grants *esse* to essence, so that all creatures are things whose *esse* has been granted to their essences. But Aquinas then leads us to envisage creation as God's adding something (*esse*) to something (essence), and this in turn suggests that God has a set of materials with which to create, thereby undermining creation *ex nihilo*. Added to that is the consideration that nothing would be without *esse*, so that nothing of the creature is actual unless *esse* has been granted to it. But if essence is nothing unless it has *esse*, how could it be that *esse* is added to it prior to its actual being? The very notion of adding *esse* to essence seems absurd in the extreme.[10]

The first and obvious thing to say here is that essence is not a thing, i.e. it is not a substance. Essence is a key component of an individual substance along with *esse*, and it is this composite substance of essence and *esse* which is brought about in creation. Thus,

---

10. Gerald Phelan, 'The Being of Creatures', *Proceedings of the American Catholic Philosophical Association,* 31 (1957), 121: 'However scrupulous one may be to exorcise that essentialism by due distinctions and refinements, the impression still remains, in spite of all protests to the contrary, that something called esse is given by a Being called Creator to a being called creature; something called esse is shared by God and creatures; something else called essence is distinct from esse in creatures, but not in the Creator. In other words, the very words we use, being grammatically nouns or substantives, it is difficult to avoid thinking that what they designate are things or substances with a nature of their own.'

essence is not itself created but is cocreated in the thing along with its *esse*. The *esse* of the thing is united with its essence when the substance is created, and as such both the essence and the *esse* are cocreated by God with the total substance being the creature that is produced. So whilst we can talk about *esse* being composed with/ united to/added to essence etc., this is not to be taken in the sense that essence and *esse* are themselves things that are mixed together to produce the created substance.

Nevertheless, the problem remains that essence has to have some distinct ontological positivity aside from the actuality it gains from *esse*. This is all the more so given Aquinas's commitment to a principle concerning the determination of *esse* that was observed in Chapter 2, to the effect that unreceived act is unlimited, so that when actuality, *esse*, is received by essence as a distinct limiting potency, that actuality is limited to the confines of the potency it actuates. But if nothing can exist without *esse*, so that there is nothing prior to God's creating things, then there is no distinct essence which can receive the *esse* that God grants in creating.

A tempting way out of this impasse is to suggest that there is a realm of possibility independent of both God and creatures from which God selects possible essences and to which essences He grants *esse*. On this view such *possibilia* don't actually exist and so don't actually precede creation. Hence creation is taken to be a kind of determining by God of a set of possibilities, making them more than just possibilities: effectively making them actualities.

A version of this thinking was familiar to Aquinas in the form of the Latin Avicenna, wherein the being of essence (*esse essentiae*) and the being of existence (*esse existentiae*) were distinguished. All essences enjoy *esse essentiae* independently of both God and creatures; but only actually existing things enjoy *esse existentiae*. The essence on this account is topped up as it were with actual existence.[11] A similar view has been advocated in more contemporary

---

11. It is debatable whether or not this view can be attributed to the historical Avicenna; certainly the language of *esse essentiae* and *esse existentiae* is not that of Avicenna but

philosophical discourse by Meinong and his distinction between *Bestand*, which all objects enjoy, real or not, and *Existenz*, which only existing objects enjoy. Moreover, the possible worlds metaphysics of Plantinga, Adams, and Kripke seems to endorse a somewhat similar view to the effect that actuality is derivative of possibility, in which case possibility is more fundamental than actuality. Though the actualists would of course deny that possible worlds are anything other than expressions of how this world might have been, in which case they would deny the independent reality of a realm of possibility, they still make possibility a fundamental component in understanding the actuality of things.[12]

Such views are not available to Aquinas precisely because of his own view on the constitution of objects. Essence/existence composites are not such that they are composed of something enjoying a kind of being, an *esse essentiae*, which is in turn added to and made actual by *esse existentiae*. Rather, if a thing does not have *esse*, then it is nothing, plain and simple. So what exists is exhaustively divided into God and creatures; there is no third realm of possibility. Hence, the potency of creation has to be accounted for in some other manner.

Now, the essence with which *esse* is united need not itself pre-exist other than as an idea in God's intellect. In God's intellect the essence has being, but it is not real being, nor indeed is the essence *a* being; it is simply a possibility of being that God understands He could bring about. All created essences (and many more besides) signify possibilities open to God's power. They are not constituents

---

of Henry of Ghent; see Fabro, *Participation et Causalité*, p. 282–284. Nevertheless, some telling texts from Avicenna do suggest that he was committed to the reality of essence in itself independently of both God and creatures, and that the essence of a creature has something more added to it, see the texts listed in Gyula Klima, ed., *Medieval Philosophy: Essential Readings with Commentary* (Wiley-Blackwell, 2007), pp. 225–226. And it should be noted that Aquinas criticizes Avicenna precisely for holding that *esse* is something that happens to or is added to essence in the manner of an accident, see *In IV Met.*, lect. 2, nn. 556 and 558.

12. For a discussion of these views, see my *Aquinas's Way to God*, Chapter 3, Section 2.

of a possible world to which God has access and selects from in creating; rather they are ways in which God could manifest His power, and they are known to God insofar as He knows Himself perfectly. Hence a certain potency does preexist creation, but this is not a passive potency opposed to act and receiving the action of something else. Rather it is the active power or *potentia* of God to bring about any such possibility that He chooses.[13] Hence, there is no passive potency preexisting creation, only active potency signifying God's power.[14] Hence, God Himself is the formal principle of creation insofar as He has available to His power an understanding of the various things that He could create and does not need to inspect a range of possibilities existing independently of Him and creatures, which possibilities signify some preexisting passive potency necessary for creation.

In creatures there are various passive potencies, e.g. matter in respect of form and essence in respect of *esse*. Such potencies are nothing more than the passive relationship that an ontological principle has to its coprinciple of actuality. So given the example of a statue, its matter stands in passive potency to its form; yet the matter at no point in the sculpting of the statue was without form. It always had a form, and its matter stood in a relationship of passive potency to it. Passive potency then can only be delineated in an already constituted substance such that the passive potency pertains to the relationship that a principle of potency has to its principle of actuality. The same applies to creatures.

Given that a creature exists, we can discern its principle of passive potency (its essence) in relation to its principle of actuality (its existence). But we can only take it that a creature exists if the act of creation has already been accomplished. Thus, passive potency

---

13. *Summa Theologiae*, Ia, qu. 25, art. 1, ad. 1: 'Potentia activa non dividitur contra actum, sed fundatur in eo. . . . Potentia vero passiva dividitur contra actum.' For more details on the distinction of active and passive potency see *In IX Met.*, lect. 1.

14. *Compendium Theologiae* (Turin: Marietti, 1954), Cap. 99: 'Si autem secundum aliquam potentiam dicitur possibile mundum esse, non est necessarium quod dicatur secundum potentiam passivam, sed secundum potentiam activam.'

is only a feature of creatures already existing, it is not one of the ingredients by which God creates. Consequently, passive potency is an effect of creation, not its condition.[15] In creating God wills to bring into existence some possibility open to His power. He has knowledge of this possibility, and given His power He is able to bring it about. There is no passive potency involved here. Having created, i.e. having made something to exist, there exists something in which essence and existence are distinct, and so there is evident in the relationship between the two metaphysical components a passive potency pertaining to the essence and actuality pertaining to the act of existence. So only after creation has been achieved does passive potency emerge, it is not required for creation. Thus the creature is brought about whole and complete, including all of its compositional structures. With that in mind then, the limitation of act by potency in creation is not to be thought of like the pouring of a liquid into a preexisting container; rather the creature is brought into existence by God's power, and having been so brought to be it can be inspected for its compositional structures, and the limitation of *esse* by essence can thereby be affirmed.

4 CONCLUSION AND TRANSITION

I have made a start in articulating Aquinas's causality of creation. To create is to bring the total substance into being; hence a creative cause is something that can do the latter. God is the primary originative principle of *esse* such that nothing would be were it not for God's granting *esse* to it. As such God is the originating source of all things.

In this chapter I have emphasised that Aquinas conceived of God's causality in creation as that of a primary cause in a per se

---

15. *Summa Theologiae*, Ia, qu. 44, art. 2, ad. 2: 'passio est effectus actionis. Unde et rationabile est quod primum principium passivum sit effectus primi principii activi, nam omne imperfectum causatur a perfecto.'

ordered series whose causality is that of *esse*. Hence, whatever is secondary in the series depends on that primary cause for its causality, its *esse*; nothing that is would be unless it depended on God. In characterizing God's causality as that of a primary cause in a per se series Aquinas is able to argue that there is no real distinction between God's originating actuality and the preserving of it in the series, since given the metaphysics of *per se* series the effects participate and thereby depend on the causal efficacy of the primary cause both for the origin of their causality and for its preservation.

Now if we focus on the mind-hand-stick-stone example it can be noted that the preservation of causality in the series is with a view to some end: the primary cause causes the causality of the members of the series in order to pursue some end, e.g. the movement of the stone. The same then can be said for God's primary causality since He originates and preserves causality in the series with a view to some end; and I will consider this in the final chapter when I integrate Aquinas's concept of final causality with his concept of God's primary efficient causality as envisaged in this chapter.

For now I will transition to the next chapter by considering that in the previous section I noted that the metaphysical components of a creature are not primarily created by God; rather, the substance itself is created and its components are cocreated with it. That way it can be said that some potential essence to which God adds *esse* does not preexist, but that in the creature having been produced there is an essence and a distinct act of existence with the former standing to the latter as potency to act. This then draws on Aquinas's metaphysics of substance such that substances are the primary referents of being, they are properly what are, and as such it is they that are created. I must now consider the metaphysics of substance as integral to the metaphysics of creation bearing, in mind the account of God's primary causality offered in this chapter.

5

▼

THE OBJECT OF CREATION

IN THIS CHAPTER I WILL CONSIDER the object of creation, i.e. what God in fact produces when He creates. As is clear from the discussion so far the total substance is the product of creation.[1] Hence God's creative action is terminated in the production of a substance whole and complete. Despite that, if *esse* is the act of all acts and so metaphysically prior to any other component in the creature, then it would seem to be that *esse* (the *esse commune* proper to every individual creature) is what is primary in creation; all else is created subsequent to *esse* and dependent thereon.[2] Indeed, Thomas explicitly states that *esse* is the proper effect of God.[3] Accordingly, *esse* has a greater primacy than that of substance.

So we have a tension; *esse* in a certain sense is primary amongst creatures such that everything depends on it and it depends on nothing but the divine essence itself. Nonetheless, it is clear that Aquinas holds that creation is the production of the total substance

---

1. Aquinas, *In II Sent.*, dist. 1, qu. 1, art. 2: 'Hoc autem creare dicimus, scilicet producere rem in esse secundum totam suam substantiam.'
2. In the *De Causis*, Prop. 4, the anonymous author argues that *esse* is the first of all created things because after the primary cause there is nothing higher than *esse*, so that whilst *esse* is lesser than the primary cause, it is prior to all else, in which case it is the first of all in creation; substance then on this account would be secondary to *esse*. See *De Causis*, Prop. 4: 'Quod est: quia esse est supra sensum et supra Animam et supra Intelligentiam et non est post Causam primam latius neque prius causatum ipso.'
3. *Summa Theologiae*, Ia, qu. 45, art. 5: 'Illud autem quod est proprius effectus Dei creantis, est illud quod praesupponitur omnibus aliis, scilicet esse absolute.'

in being. So what is the object of creation—the total substance or the *esse commune* by which any substance is?

We can resolve this tension if we focus closely on the notion that creation is the production of the total substance *in being*. The 'in being' qualification refers to *esse*, so that creation is the granting of *esse* and thereby production of existing things. The things that exist are substances, yet they exist only insofar as they possess a principle of actuality by means of which they exist. This principle is *esse*, in which the existing thing participates in order to be. It is substances that are produced in being, but the metaphysical structure of substance is an ordered one whose primary principle is *esse*, which in turn actuates form, which, if it is a material creature, in turn actuates matter. As it is the *total* substance that is brought into being, God simultaneously composes essence and *esse* in order that a creature be produced. The ordering of the metaphysical components does not signify a temporal ordering such that the primary component (*esse*) is what is produced first; rather each component has a part to play in the constitution of the total substance which is properly the object of creation. This ties in with what I articulated in the previous chapter to the effect that the component parts of the substance are not first produced and then comingled so that the substance is produced; rather the substance is produced and its parts cocreated with it. Hence whilst *esse* is primary in the substance, *esse* itself is not the substance that is produced. Accordingly, substance is the primary product of creation.

Nevertheless, there is a legitimate sense in which *esse* can be said to be the proper effect of creation precisely because *esse* is that without which there is nothing, in which case *esse* is presupposed for all creation. Given this presupposition, nothing would be without *esse*, in which case the *esse* of creatures is properly and primarily what God brings about when He creates. *Esse* is the most universal, the most common, the most formal, the most intimate of all created acts. It is the aspect of being whereby creatures come to be related to God through participating in His divine *esse* so that they may be something rather than nothing.[4] Yet as the distinction of essence and *esse* in creatures makes clear, the creature is not to be identified with its *esse* but is a composite of essence and *esse*. Hence what is created properly so called is not the *esse* by means of which the creature actually exists but the composite creature itself composed of essence and *esse*. Indeed, Fabro warns that despite the emphasis on the fundamentality of *esse* in Aquinas's metaphysics, one must not be led to think that God simply creates *esse* and leaves it to be as if it were self-subsisting. Only God is self-subsisting *esse*, whereas creatures participate in the created *esse commune* by which they are. It is not just *esse* which comes from God in creation; the other metaphysical components as well are cocreated with *esse* in the creature.[5] Hence it is the composite substance that must be taken as the object of creation.

It is this composite substance, the product of creation, that I propose to consider in this chapter. I will begin with a consideration of substance in general (Section 1), then I will consider the creation of substance (Section 2), and finally I will consider the creation of necessary things which apparently resist causal influence (Section 3).

1 SUBSTANCE

Given that when God creates He produces the total substance in being, whatever else a being is, it is first and foremost a substance; anything else is an accident of substance. Substance then

---

4. Fabro, *Participation et causalité*, pp. 371–372: 'C'est dire que l'*esse* exprime ce point unique incomparable du réel où Dieu rencontre la créature et la créature rejoint Dieu. Par suite l'*esse* est ce qu'on peut appeler la "ratio propria creationis". . . . Le terme proper de la création est donc la participation de l'*esse* par lequel les créatures sont actualisées, tirées hors du néant.'
5. *Participation et causalité*, p. 374.

is the primary referent of being.[6] Beings are substances, and so for Aquinas, substances are primary and exist in themselves.[7]

In characterizing substance, Aquinas takes four significations thereof and reduces them to two. The four significations are: (i) particular bodily things we see around us such as earth, fire, rocks, etc.—these are not said of any other more fundamental subject, but things are said of these, and they correlate with Aristotle's first or primary substance in the *Categories*;[8] (ii) the intrinsic principles of primary substances, for example the substantial forms of sensible things;[9] (iii) the parts of primary substances which limit them and make them divisible, for example surfaces, lines, points, and numbers;[10] (iv) the quiddity or essence of the thing which is signified by the definition.[11]

As noted, Aquinas reduces these four to two, and he begins by isolating the primary substance (sense (i)) as the ultimate subject of which other things are predicated. Primary substance is

---

6. *In VII Met.*, n. 1252: 'alia entia non sunt entia nisi secundum quod referuntur ad substantiam.'

7. *In IV Met.*, n. 539: 'Alia enim dicuntur entia vel esse, quia per se habent esse sicut substantiae, quae principaliter et prius entia dicuntur'; see also *In V Met.*, n. 898, *In VII Met.*, n. 1246, and *De Potentia Dei*, qu. 9, art. 1, for the same. Strictly speaking Aquinas's terminology is to the effect that a substance exists per se—through itself. I choose to translate this as 'in itself' so as to avoid confusion with Thomas's more characteristic metaphysical view that what exists per se is that in which there is no distinction of essence and *esse*, whereas things that are so distinct exist *per aliud* (cf. *De Ente et Essentia*, Cap. 4). By speaking of substance as existing in itself, I here capture the true signification of substance, which is to be so as not to exist in another. See Wippel, *The Metaphysical Thought of Thomas Aquinas*, p. 229, n. 112.

8. *In V Met.*, n. 898: 'Haec enim omnia praedicta dicuntur substantia, quia non dicuntur de alio subjecto, sed alia dicuntur de his. Et haec est descriptio primae substantiae in predicamentis.' See also *In VII Met.*, n. 1273, for correlation of the ultimate subject of predication with primary substance in Aristotle's thought.

9. *In V Met.*, n. 899.

10. Ibid., n. 900; Aquinas attributes this position to the Pythagoreans and the Platonists.

11. Ibid., n. 902: 'Dicit quod etiam quidditas rei, quam significat definitio, dicitur substantia uniuscuiusque.'

properly basic and thus subsists in itself; it is distinct from others and separable, hence it is incommunicable to others.[12]

Turning then to substance as form (sense (ii)), Aquinas justifies the distinction between this and substance as essence (sense (iv)) insofar as he holds that the essence of a thing is not signified by its form alone, but by all the essential principles of the thing, which for material substances includes both matter and form; hence he says that substance as essence is related to substance as form as the soul is to humanity.[13] What I take him to mean here is that the soul is only a formal part of what it is to be human; it is not the only part, since the soul must inform a body as well and does not naturally exist by itself. So essence or quiddity is not totally synonymous with form but, for a material thing at least, includes the thing's matter. There is thus a distinction between a thing's essence and its form, since the essence expresses something more than its form (at least in material things; for immaterial things form and essence are identical). Elsewhere Thomas distinguishes between the *forma partis*, which is the component form of the substance informing prime matter, and the *forma totius*, which is the overall form or essence of the composite substance including both its matter and its *forma partis*. Such a distinction of forms (between part and whole) would seem to be what he has in mind here when he distinguishes substance as form (ii) from substance as essence (iv).[14]

---

12. *In V Met.*, n. 903: 'substantia duobus modis dicitur: quorum unus est secundum quod substantia dicitur id quod ultimo subjicitur in propositionibus, ita quod de alio non praedicetur, sicut substantia prima. Et hoc est, quod est hoc aliquid, quasi per se subsistens, et quod est separabile, quia est ab omnibus distinctum et non communicabile multis.'

13. Ibid., n. 902: 'Haec autem quidditas sive rei essentia, cuius definitio est ratio, differt a forma quam dixit esse substantiam in secundo modo, sicut differt humanitas ab anima. Nam forma est pars essentiae vel quidditas rei. Ipsa autem quidditas vel essentia rei includit omnia essentialia principia.'

14. For instances in which Aquinas distinguishes *forma totius* from *forma partis* in the way that I have explained here, see *In IV Sent.*, dist. 44, qu. 1, art. 1, qc. 2, ad. 2, *Summa Contra Gentiles*, Lib. 4, Cap. 81, *Quodlibet IX*, qu. 2, art. 1, ad. 4, *Quodlibet II*, qu. 2, art. 2, *De Ente*, Cap. 2, *In V Met.*, lect. 5, n. 822, *In VII Met.*, lect. 9, n. 1469. Lack of distinction between the overall essence of the thing, including its matter if

Despite their distinction, both substance-(ii) and substance-(iv) express the thing's formal nature, and so Aquinas sees substance-(ii) as falling within the scope of the wider ranging substance-(iv). Thus, substance-(ii) and substance-(iv) signify the same thing, which is the essence of the primary substance-(i). However, whereas form (*forma partis*) is correlated with the matter that it informs, the essence (*forma totius*) is correlated with the primary substance, or what Aquinas calls the 'supposit', of which it is the essence. Hence the material thing has the form that it has because of its *forma partis* (substance-(ii)), whereas the individual thing is the kind of thing that it is because of its essence or *forma totius* (substance-(iv)). Thus, substance-(ii) and substance-(iv) are indeed distinct from substance considered as the individual supposit (i) and are not simply diverse logical significations of one and the same thing.[15]

Turning then to substance-(iii), that is those parts of a primary substance-(i) which limit it and make it divisible, e.g. surfaces, lines, points, numbers, Aquinas holds that these are actually properties of substance and thus derivable from substance and so should not be confused with substance itself.[16] Thus, Aquinas rejects the third mode of substance as a proper mode at all, because it confuses the

---

it's material, and the form of a thing is a position that Aquinas attributes to Averroës; see Armand Maurer, 'Form and Essence in the Philosophy of St Thomas', *Mediaeval Studies*, 13 (1951), pp. **165–176**, Section 1. One of the motivating reasons for such a distinction in Aquinas's thought is that insofar as essence is subject to *esse*, all essential components of the existing thing must be so subject and included in the essence of the thing, which would entail that the thing's matter be so included as well. I discuss this issue in *Aquinas's Way to God*, pp. 37–45.

15. *In V Met.*, n. 904: 'Essentia enim et forma in hoc convenient quod secundum utrumque dicitur esse illud quo aliquid est. Sed forma refertur ad materiam, quam facit esse in actu; quidditas autem refertur ad suppositum, quod significatur ut habens talem essentiam.'

16. Ibid., n. 901: 'Iste autem modus non est verus. Nam hoc quod communiter invenitur in omnibus, et sine quo res esse non potest, non oportet quod sit substantia rei, sed potest esse aliqua proprietas consequens rei substantiam vel principium substantiae.'

properties of a substance with the substance itself; so substance-(iii) is discharged.

We accordingly arrive at two significations of substance: (i) primary substance or supposit (or particular individual), and (ii) the essence (comprehending the form of the thing). As primary substance the supposit needs no foundation or support other than itself, for it subsists in itself.[17] As such, the supposit is the support and foundation for accidents which do not subsist in themselves but are such that they subsist in another.[18]

In the *Categories* Aristotle clearly defines primary substance as what is said neither of nor in a thing, and this is substance properly so called, whereas secondary substances are the genera and species in which primary substance is realized; for example an individual human being (primary substance) is of the species human (secondary substance) of the genus animal (secondary substance).[19] It has already been shown that Aquinas correlates the supposit with Aristotle's primary substance, but we should not assume that he correlates essence with Aristotle's secondary substance. This is because substance as essence is common to many supposita and does not include the individual matter by which

---

17. Let us bear in mind that we are not dealing with the thing's existence here, but only its reality as a substance, and as such it does not exist in another.

18. *De Potentia Dei*, qu. 9, art. 1: 'Substantia vero quae est subiectum, duo habet propria: quorum primum est quod non indiget extrinseco fundamento in quo sustentetur, sed sustentatur in seipso; et ideo dicitur subsistere, quasi per se et non in alio existens. Aliud vero est quod est fundamentum accidentibus substentans ipsa; et pro tanto dicitur substare.' See also *In VII Met.*, n. 1291.

19. For Aristotle, see *Categories*, Chapter 5, 2a11–19. For Thomas's awareness of such a twofold signification of substance in Aristotle's thinking, see *De Potentia Dei*, qu. 9, art. 1: 'Dicendum quod Philosophus ponit substantiam dupliciter dici: dicitur enim uno modo substantia ipsum subiectum ultimum, quod non praedicatur de alio: et hoc est particulare in genere substantiae; alio modo dicitur substantia forma vel natura subiecti'; see also *In VII Met.*, n. 1275; note in particular the following denial that essence (*quod quid erat esse*) is to be identified with either genus or species: 'Hoc autem quod quid erat esse hic ponitur, sed ibi [i.e. *Categories*] praetermittitur, quia non cadit in praedicamentorum ordine nisi sicut principium. Neque enim est genus neque species neque individuum, sed horum omnium formale principium.'

each supposit is individual. Hence, in material substances at least, we cannot predicate the essence of an individual supposit, e.g. we cannot say that Socrates is humanity. On the other hand Aristotle's second substance—genus and species—can be predicated of the individual supposita, because the latter are realized in these second substances; so we can say that Socrates is a man or that Socrates is an animal. There is nothing contained under second substance that is not already contained under first substance; first substance signifies the same generic (animal) and specific (human) natures subsisting individually.[20] On the other hand with Aquinas's distinction between supposit and essence, the supposit contains something that the essence does not contain, and this is the individuating principles by which the supposit is an individual substance; essence does not contain such individuating principles since it can be predicated of many.[21]

Given all of this, Aquinas sees Aristotle's division of primary and secondary substance as one of reason and not *secundum rem*, since all that is contained in second substance is contained in primary substance, so the distinction between primary and secondary substance is not that of diverse species within the genus of substance but of different ways of signifying one and the same genus, with secondary substance signifying it absolutely and

20. *De Potentia Dei,* qu. 9, art. 2, ad. 6: 'nihil contineatur sub secunda substantia quod non sit in prima.'

21. *De Potentia Dei,* qu. 9, art. 1: 'Quidquid ergo est in re ad naturam communem pertinens, sub significatione essentiae continetur, non autem quidquid est in substantia particulari, est huiusmodi. Si enim quidquid est in substantia particulari ad naturam communem pertineret, non posset esse distinctio inter substantias particulares eiusdem naturae. Hoc autem quod est in substantia particulari praeter naturam communem, est materia individualis quae est singularitatis principium, et per consequens accidentia individualia quae materiam praedictam determinant. Comparatur ergo essentia ad substantiam particularem ut pars formalis ipsius, ut humanitas ad Socratem. Et ideo in rebus, ex materia et forma compositis, essentia non est omnino idem quod subiectum; unde non praedicatur de subiecto: non enim dicitur quod Socrates sit una humanitas.'

primary substance signifying it individually.[22] On the other hand the division between supposit and essence is real and not merely a division of reason, because the supposit contains real principles by which it is individual, principles not included in the essence of the thing, thereby dividing the essence from the supposit. Given the real distinction between supposit and essence we can say that Socrates (primary substance) has but is not identical with humanity (substance as essence), whereas given the lack of real distinction between primary and secondary substance we can say that Socrates (primary substance) is a human animal (secondary substance expressing species and genus).

These general considerations lead us to consider three related issues: (i) the individuation of substance, (ii) the relation of the essence of a thing to the individual thing (the supposit), and (iii) the relation of substance to accidents.

1.1 Matter, Form, and Individuation

In material substances, the supposit is the particular individual, and it is distinct from the essence that it has. The essence is predicable of many, yet it resides in the individual substance. There is something then about the individual supposit not included in the essence which thereby distinguishes it from the essence, and this is the substance's individuating principle. Now Aquinas holds that the individuating principle of material things is matter, so that the substantial form of the thing when composed with matter produces an individual substance; but Aquinas also distinguishes between the form which is in the thing as composed with matter (the *forma partis*) and the total essence of the thing, including its matter (the *forma totius*). If the individual substance is distinct from essence, and is so because of its individuating principle of matter, then the

---

22. *De Potentia Dei*, qu. 9, art. 2, ad. 6: 'Nam secunda substantia significat naturam generis secundum se absolutam; prima vero substantia significat eam ut individualiter subsistentem.'

matter which is the principle of individuation must be different from the matter that is present in the essence as one of the thing's essential components.

The matter which is the principle of individuation is designated matter, say Peter's flesh and bones, whereas the matter which is included as a formal element in the definition of the thing is nondesignated matter, flesh and bones as such. It is the designated matter that the individual has by which it is an individual. This is not the general notion of matter included in the essence, the *forma totius* of the thing, nor is it prime matter that is informed by the substantial form of the thing (the *forma partis*). It is the matter of the composite material individual which comes to exist in three dimensions, the matter to which we can point and that we can touch. Thus, designated matter is the only actual matter in existence; all other matters are either abstractions (nondesignated matter) or available to us under some form (prime matter). Designated matter on the other hand is the matter that is available to us for ostensible observation, and it is this matter by means of which a thing is an individual.[23]

This account of individuation of course raises the issue of how prime matter comes to be designated. Consider that prime matter is itself unformed, and so it is nothing but pure potency until united with substantial form, at which point it is formed and a substance produced. Hence prior to the production of an individual substance, there is no designated matter that can serve to delimit the scope of the form that comes to it. Indeed designated matter with its three-dimensionality, like the lines and surfaces of substance-(iii), would seem to be a consequence of an individual substance and not a principle thereof. So how can Aquinas hold that designated matter is the principle of individuation of material substances?

---

23. Historically, the distinction between designated and nondesignated matter is found principally in Avicenna; see M-D Roland-Gosselin, Le 'De Ente et Essentia' de s. Aquinas d'Aquin (Paris: Librairie Philosophique J. Vrin, 1948), pp. 59–69, for details.

The first thing to note in answer to this issue is that the way in which I have framed it as a problem for Thomas is in a temporal manner, hence the unqualified talk of designated matter's being prior to the substance serving as the principle of individuation. But this is not how we should think about the components of a substance and their coming to be composed therein. As I noted at the beginning of the chapter, a substance is produced in being whole and complete; such a substance is analysable into its metaphysical components, and these metaphysical components have diverse causal roles to play in the being of the substance. Bearing that in mind, we come to consider designated matter as the principle of individuation and how in fact it functions as such a principle in an already constituted substance, but this does not entail that such designated matter has to preexist the substance of which it is the matter in order that it may individuate it.

Whilst it is prime matter with which substantial form is composed, Thomas maintains throughout his career that form is not individuated by prime matter as such. This is because there is no diversity to prime matter taken in itself, for it is wholly un-formed; but without diversity of matter, we cannot distinguish diverse material particulars. Therefore, there must be some addition to prime matter that allows it to diversify the form it receives, thereby constituting diverse individuals of that form. According to Aquinas, what diversifies prime matter is dimensive quantity, and such dimensive quantity follows upon matter's corporeity. Such corporeity comes about through the substantial form's informing the (prime) matter, such that the substantial form makes matter corporeal. It is this dimensive quantity consequent on corporeity that individuates form.[24]

24. Aquinas affirms this in a number of places; see *In I Sent.*, d. 8, qu. 5, art. 2, *In II Sent.*, dist. 3, qu. 1, aa. 1 and 4; dist. 30, qu. 2, art. 1, *In III Sent.*, dist. 1, qu. 2, art. 5, ad. 1, *In IV Sent.*, dist. 12, qu. 1, art. 1, sol. 3, ad. 3; dist. 44, qu. 1, art. 1, ad. 3, *De Ente et Essentia*, Cap. 2, p. 371: 73–77, *De Veritate*, qu. 2, art. 6, ad. 1, *Quodlibet VII*, qu. 4, art. 3, *Summa Contra Gentiles*, Lib. 4, Cap. 65. For a representative argu-ment see, *De Trinitate*, qu. 4, art. 2: 'Forma fit haec per hoc quod recipitur in ma-teria. Sed cum materia in se sit indistincta, non potest esse quod formam receptam individuet, nisi secundum quod est distinguibilis. Non enim forma individuatur per hoc quod recipitur in materia, nisi quatenus recipitur in hac materia distincta et

So it is through being taken under dimensive quantity that matter can be parcelled off as this or that matter, and hence as designated, and hence as individuating. To be sure Thomas does vary his terminology when discussing the dimensions of matter by which it is designated. Some of the texts in note 24 speak of matter taken under indeterminate dimensions (e.g. the texts from the commentary on the *Sentences*, Lib. 2 and 4, and on the *De Trinitate*), and others speak of matter taken under determined or determinate dimensions (e.g. those from the commentary on the *Sentences*, Lib. 3, *De Ente et Essentia*, and *De Veritate*). The difference is that in the former matter is simply taken as dimensioned, but the exact dimensions are not fixed, since, as the *De Trinitate* text makes clear, the determined dimensions of a substance are often changing whilst the individual remains the same, so the determined dimensions cannot be what individuates given their

determinata ad hic et nunc. Materia autem non est divisibilis nisi per quantitatem. Unde philosophus dicit in I physicorum quod subtracta quantitate remanebit substantia indivisibilis. Et ideo materia efficitur haec et signata, secundum quod subest dimensionibus. Dimensiones autem istae possunt dupliciter considerari. Uno modo secundum earum terminationem; et dico eas terminari secundum determinatam mensuram et figuram, et sic ut entia perfecta collocantur in genere quantitatis. Et sic non possunt esse principium individuationis; quia cum talis terminatio dimensionum varietur frequenter circa individuum, sequeretur quod individuum non remaneret semper idem numero. Alio modo possunt considerari sine ista determinatione in natura dimensionis tantum, quamvis numquam sine aliqua determinatione esse possint, sicut nec natura coloris sine determinatione albi et nigri; et sic collocantur in genere quantitatis ut imperfectum. Et ex his dimensionibus indeterminatis materia efficitur haec materia signata, et sic individuat formam, et sic ex materia causatur diversitas secundum numerum in eadem specie.' For discussion of Thomas's position in general see Wippel, *The Metaphysical Thought of Thomas Aquinas*, pp. 351–375, Joseph Bobik, 'Dimensions in the Individuation of Bodily Substances', *Maynooth Philosophical Studies*, 4 (1954), 60–79, Joseph Owens, 'Thomas Aquinas (b. ca. 1225; d. 1274)', in *Individuation in Scholasticism: The Later Middle Ages and the Counter Reformation*, ed. by J. J. E. Gracia (New York: State University of New York Press, 1994), pp. 173–194, and Owens, 'Thomas Aquinas: Dimensive Quantity as Individuating Principle', *Mediaeval Studies*, 50 (1988), 279–310; despite the penetrating lucidity of Owens's treatment of many issues of Thomistic metaphysics, I can't quite follow him in his view that existence is the cause of individuality in Aquinas's thought.

variability over the stability of the individual. On this account then, whilst dimensionality may be essential to any material substance since it follows upon its corporeity, its determined dimensions are not essential but accidental. However, in the texts where Thomas simply speaks of matter under determinate dimensions as what individuates, he takes the actual determined dimensions to do the individuating work, and not simply the dimensioned nature of the substance. (Wippel points out that this is Thomas's final position on the matter).[25]

There is no consistent way of reading Aquinas here. Commentators such as Owens attempt to downplay the shift in terminology, whereas Wippel in particular has difficulty in agreeing with such an interpretation. Be that as it may, for my purposes I need not untangle that web, since I am concerned with the problem that the designation of matter seems to be a consequence of matter/form composition rather than being a principle by which form is individuated. Thus, Aquinas's account of how matter comes by its dimensionality would indicate that individuation is a consequence of the composition of matter and form, since for him the corporeity and hence the dimension-ality of matter is a result of form.[26] So what we need to do is ex-plain how designated matter, i.e. matter as subject to quantitative

---

25. Wippel, *The Metaphysical Thought of Thomas Aquinas*, p. 371.

26. See *In I Sent.*, dist. 8, qu. 5, art. 2: 'Et propterea materia prima, prout consideratur nuda ab omni forma, non habet aliquam diversitatem, nec efficitur diversa per aliqua accidentia ante adventum formae substantialis, cum esse accidentale non praecedat substantiale. Uni autem perfectibili debetur una perfectio. Ergo oportet quod prima forma substantialis perficiat totam materiam. Sed prima forma quae recipitur in materia, est corporeitas, a qua nunquam denudatur. . . . Ergo forma corporeitatis est in tota materia, et ita materia non erit nisi in corporibus.' *In II Sent.*, dist. 3, qu. 1, art. 1: 'cum enim uni perfectibili debeatur una perfectio, et in materia prima non sit ulla diversitas, oportet quod omnis forma antequam possit in ea esse ulla diversitas, nec intelligi, investiat eam totam. Sed ante corporeitatem non potest intelligi aliqua diversitas, quia diversitas praesupponit partes, quae non possunt esse nisi praeintelligatur divisibilitas quae consequitur quantitatem, quae sine corporeitate non est. Unde oportet quod tota materia sit vestita forma corporeitatis.'

dimensions, can function as a principle of individuation when such matter appears to be a consequence of an already formed and thus individual substance.

Substantial form is what is united with prime matter and gives it its corporeity and hence dimensionality. Substantial form then has a causal role to play in its relationship to matter, but this does not mean that matter cannot itself have a causal role to play in relation to form, albeit a role which is not formal but material. Thomas is quite clear that when it comes to the four causes, a cause can be a cause in one respect and an effect in another (something observed in the previous chapter). So for instance in the *De Principiis Naturae*, Cap. 4, Aquinas notes that form is a cause in one respect, i.e. as informing matter, whereas it is an effect in another respect, i.e. as depending on matter as a receptive principle of form.[27] So the substantial form is the principle by which prime matter is formed corporeally and hence having dimensionality, but simultaneously in being a receptive principle of form matter receives such dimensions and in turn limits the form to the realization of the particular determinations of those dimensions. Hence whilst dimensionality is a result of formal causality, the particular dimensions in question are a result of the receptivity of matter in being so informed.

Add to that the fact that with respect to creation, *esse* has overall causal priority so that nothing is actual within the thing unless participating in the thing's *esse* granted to it by God. The composite of matter and form is what exists and so is subject to *esse*, in which case the thing's matter and form are cocreated simultaneously with the thing, so that all at once form gives dimensionality to matter whereas matter (in being so dimensive) makes form individual. It is not the case that we first have dimensionless matter, then afterwards form is composed with it to give it dimensionality,

---

27. *De Principiis Naturae*, Cap. 4: 'Materia enim dicitur causa formae, inquantum forma non est nisi in materia; et similiter forma est causa materiae, inquantum materia non habet esse in actu nisi per formam.'

and only after that form is individuated by such matter. Rather, there are interlocking lines of causal interaction which occur simultaneously, so that for as long as a matter/form composite exists, its form gives it dimensionality but its matter as so dimensioned delimits the universality of the form. So much then for material substances.

Immaterial substances on the other hand are individuated in themselves, in which case they are not individuals of a species but individual species of a genus. Their individuation is not dependent on some principle such as matter; rather the individuation of such substances is an intelligible feature of the form itself, making it that form or species of the genus as opposed to another. Hence for Aquinas, individual angels are individuals of themselves, not requiring a material principle of individuation, as others maintained.[28] All of this then would suggest that an individual immaterial substance is identical with its nature, since it is a species of itself; hence there would seem to be no distinction between essence and supposit in an immaterial substance. So I am led to the second issue connected with the general discussion of substance: that the relation of essence to supposit.

28. The others here to whom I refer are those who held that all creatures are composed with matter in some way and who, in order to avoid the absurdity of suggesting that immaterial creatures are composed of matter, distinguished between corporeal and incorporeal matter, holding that immaterial creatures have incorporeal matter and so are not bodily, whereas creatures typically taken to be material have corporeal matter and so are bodily. This position is known as universal hylemorphism. From the earliest stage of his career until the end Aquinas rejected universal hylemorphism, not only as an explanation of the individuation of immaterial creatures but also as offering an explanation of the potency of such creatures; the real distinction of essence and *esse* was Aquinas's way for accounting for the potency of creatures without holding that all such potency requires matter. For some historical details on the role this doctrine played in the intellectual climate of the thirteenth century see Wippel, *The Metaphysical Thought of Godfrey of Fontaines* (Washington, DC: Catholic University of America Press, 1981), pp. 275–277.

1.2 Essence and Supposit

Aquinas often argues for the distinction between essence and supposit based on the fact that the individual supposit has something that the nature does not have. Hence, the nature is common, but the supposit is individual because it has matter as an individuating principle. In such cases there is a clear distinction between essence and supposit, but this of course only pertains to things that are individuals of a nature, and hence to material things. When Aquinas argues in this mode, he holds that in simple immaterial things, i.e. things without matter, there is no such distinction, and this is because the supposit is the very nature itself. So this mode of argumentation makes explicit appeal to some feature of the supposit that is not included in the essence of the thing thereby entailing that supposit and essence are distinct; and this is a form of argumentation that does not apply to immaterial creatures.[29]

Such argumentation is often employed by Thomas in order to safeguard God's simplicity, but in doing so it is clear that he does not distinguish between God and immaterial substances, so that in this regard God and immaterial substances are alike in their

---

29. Aquinas employs this mode of argumentation in *In III Sent.*, dist. 5, qu. 1, art. 3, *De Potentia Dei*, qu. 9, art. 1, and *Summa Theologiae*, Ia, qu. 3, art. 3. See the following representative argument from the *Summa Theologiae* text: 'essentia vel natura comprehendit in se illa tantum quae cadunt in definitione speciei, sicut humanitas comprehendit in se ea quae cadunt in definitione hominis, his enim homo est homo, et hoc significat humanitas, hoc scilicet quo homo est homo. Sed materia individualis, cum accidentibus omnibus individuantibus ipsam, non cadit in definitione speciei, non enim cadunt in definitione hominis hae carnes et haec ossa, aut albedo vel nigredo, vel aliquid huiusmodi. Unde hae carnes et haec ossa, et accidentia designantia hanc materiam, non concluduntur in humanitate. Et tamen in eo quod est homo, includuntur, unde id quod est homo, habet in se aliquid quod non habet humanitas. Et propter hoc non est totaliter idem homo et humanitas, sed humanitas significatur ut pars formalis hominis; quia principia definientia habent se formaliter, respectu materiae individuantis. In his igitur quae non sunt composita ex materia et forma, in quibus individuatio non est per materiam individualem, idest per hanc materiam, sed ipsae formae per se individuantur, oportet quod ipsae formae sint supposita subsistentia.'

simplicity. But we know that the simplicity of God cannot be like that of immaterial creatures, because the latter are subject to essence/*esse* distinction and composition whereas God is not. In another text wherein Aquinas again considers the distinction between supposit and essence but this time with the thing's *esse* in mind, he denies the identity of essence and supposit in all things other than God, even immaterial creatures; that text is *Quodlibet II*, qu. 2, art. 2.

In this text, Aquinas goes over once again his metaphysics of substance, essence, and supposit. Interestingly for my purposes he includes in the first objection the argumentation for distinction of essence and supposit that I have just been considering, namely that if the supposit has something such as individuating matter not included in the essence then essence and supposit differ. Accordingly, the objection goes on to conclude that such does not apply to immaterial creatures (angels), in which case supposit and essence are identical therein.[30] It is interesting that a mode of argumentation endorsed by Aquinas elsewhere appears here as an objection, since it is a position with which he intends to disagree.

In the body of the article Aquinas argues that distinction and composition of matter and form is not sufficient to distinguish between essence and supposit. This is because such reasoning takes for granted that essence is signified by form, and when form is united with matter in the supposit essence is therefore distinct from the supposit. But making use of his distinction of the *forma partis* from the *forma totius* Thomas reasons that the essence (*forma totius*) of a material thing must include its matter in some way, because the essence is signified by the definition of the thing. Thus, a thing's essence already involves its matter, and so the possession of matter is not enough for a *de*

---

30. *Quodlibet II*, qu. 2, art. 2, obj. 1: 'In his enim quae sunt composita ex materia et forma differt suppositum et natura: quia suppositum addit supra naturam speciei materiam individualem; quod non potest esse in Angelo, si Angelus non sit compositus ex materia et forma. Ergo in Angelo non differt suppositum et natura.'

jure (as opposed to de facto) distinction of essence and supposit, in which case we cannot move easily to the identity of the two in immaterial creatures.

Considering the question anew, Aquinas develops the working principle that if something can happen (*accidere*) to the supposit, which something is not within the thing's nature, there is distinction of essence and supposit; for if something can happen to the thing which is distinct from the essence of the thing, the thing itself, i.e. the supposit, will have that which can happen to it *and* its essence, so that the thing which supposits for both will differ from each.[31]

Now, immaterial creatures are not identical to the *esse* that they have, in which case the supposit of the creature can have something (*esse*) which, as is well known, is not identical to its essence. On this basis it follows that in immaterial creatures nature and supposit are not identical, whereas in God there is such identity since in Him there is no distinction of essence and *esse*.[32] Evidently here Aquinas is taking supposit in an all-inclusive fashion, including both its essence and its *esse*, so that essence is regarded as a formal part of the whole, which is the supposit, the individually existing thing; and this observation is key to cohering the argumentation in *Quodlibet II* with what Aquinas argues elsewhere.

31. Ibid.: 'Secundum hoc ergo, cuicumque potest aliquid accidere quod non sit de ratione suae naturae, in eo differt res et quod quid est, sive suppositum et natura. Nam in significatione naturae includitur solum id quod est de ratione speciei; suppositum autem non solum habet haec quae ad rationem speciei pertinent, sed etiam alia quae ei accidunt.' See also *Summa Theologiae*, IIIa, qu. 2, art. 2: 'Si qua vero res est in qua omnino nihil est aliud praeter rationem speciei vel naturae suae, sicut est in Deo, ibi non est aliud secundum rem suppositum et natura, sed solum secundum rationem intelligendi, quia natura dicitur secundum quod est essentia quaedam.'

32. *Quodlibet II*, qu. 2, art. 2: 'In solo autem Deo non invenitur aliquod accidens praeter eius essentiam, quia suum esse est sua essentia, ut dictum est; et ideo in Deo est omnino idem suppositum et natura. In Angelo autem non est omnino idem: quia aliquid accidit ei praeter id quod est de ratione suae speciei: quia et ipsum esse Angeli est praeter eius essentiam seu naturam.'

If we think of the individual simply in terms of what it is, i.e. in a quidditative sense, and not as the whole that it is, then essence and supposit will differ only in material things, because in such things the essence is multiplied in individuals through being the formal component of a thing. However, if we take the individual thing as the whole that it is and think of it not just in terms of what it is but also in terms of its being, its *esse*, something which *is*, then the thing is an individual that not only has an essence but also an act of existence, so that unless the individual is God, it is distinct from both its essence and its *esse*, in which case essence and supposit will differ in anything that is not identical with its *esse*, which is the case for all creatures.[33]

Thinking of creatures in an existential sense, i.e. as beings, as opposed to thinking of them in an essential sense, i.e. merely as having an essence, is central to thinking of creatures precisely as creatures; for as I have outlined creation is the granting of *esse* to a thing, in which case thinking of a creature from the point of view of its existence is thinking of it precisely as something created. So with regard to the metaphysics of creation, we can say that in all creatures there is distinction and composition of essence and supposit. I will now turn to a consideration of accidents.

1.3 Substance and Accident

Substance is one way in which being is divided, so that one way of being is being a substance; indeed, this is the primary way of being because it is substances that are the primary referents of being. Nevertheless, there are certain modes of being that are not that of substance but ways in which substance is modified, and that is via accidents. So the being of accident signifies another mode of being. If a substance is what exists in itself, an accident is what exists in

---

33. For discussion of this issue see Wippel, *The Metaphysical Thought of Thomas Aquinas*, pp. 243–253. This resolution of the tension tracks a similar strategy adopted by Wippel.

another; the very term 'accident' betrays such a signification since an accident happens (*accidit*) to some substance.

There are three classes or ways of being an accident for Aquinas, which are divided through a consideration of how the kind of accident in question relates to the subject. First, there are accidents which are caused by the principles of a thing's essence, and these are proper accidents; they are found wherever any being of that kind is found, for example, the ability to laugh in man is an accident that is caused by the principles of man's essence, i.e. his rational animality. Second, there are accidents that are caused by the principles of the individual substance in question (as opposed to the species) and are permanent: these are inseparable accidents; examples of them would be masculine and feminine, which are not themselves caused by the principle of the species, i.e. rational animality, but are caused by the principles of the individual substance of that species. Third, there are accidents that are caused by the principles of the individual substance and are separable from that substance; for example walking or sitting are accidents which are caused by an individual man, but a man can be perfectly well without them.[34] Regardless of which class of accident is under consideration, all of them depend on the subject, i.e. the substance in which they inhere, for their being. This is not to say that they are drawn from the subject, since separable accidents clearly are not so. Nevertheless even for separable accidents, they would not be were it not for some subject to which they happen.[35] Hence, as

34. *Quaestiones Disputatae De Anima*, art. 12, ad. 7: 'tria sunt genera accidentium: quaedam enim causantur ex principiis speciei, et dicuntur propria sicut risibile homini; quaedam vero causantur ex principiis individui. Et hoc dicitur quia, vel habent causam permanentem in subiecto, et haec sunt accidentia inseparabilia, sicut masculinum et femininum et alia huiusmodi; quaedam vero habent causam non permanentem in subiecto, et haec sunt accidentia separabilia, ut sedere et ambulare.'

35. *In I Sent.*, dist. 17, qu. 1, art. 2, ad. 2: 'Tamen sciendum, quod omnibus accidentibus, communiter loquendo, subjectum est causa quodammodo, inquantum scilicet accidentia in esse subjecti sustentantur; non tamen ita quod ex principiis subjecti omnia accidentia educantur.'

I will show below in more detail when I come to consider the creation of substance, the being of accidents is that of the substance of which they are accidents.

Substance and accident express the modes of being for creatures (the *predicamenta* or categories), and taken together there are ten such modes. Whilst this may coincide with Aristotle's thinking, and doubtless it was unlikely that Thomas would have derived any categories other than those outlined by Aristotle, it is nevertheless the case that Aquinas offers some justification for there being these ten categories and not others; this is something that Aristotle does not do (at least not in the *Categories*).

Aquinas derives the categories on the basis of predication, so that there is a distinct category for a distinct mode of predication. In proceeding, it should be kept in mind that for Thomas there is a correlation between our predicating something of some subject and the mode of existence of that subject, since every mode of predication for him signifies a mode of being for some existing thing.[36] Given that we deduce the categories on the basis of predication, he outlines a threefold way in which something can be said of something else: (i) when the predicate signifies the very subject itself; (ii) when what is predicated is taken according as it belongs to a subject; and (iii) when what is predicated is taken from what is extrinsic to the subject.[37]

In the first case, the predicate expresses the very subject itself (i), so when I say Socrates is an animal, it is Socrates himself who is the animal. So this manner of predicating signifies the concrete

---

36. *In V Met.*, n. 890: 'ens contrahatur ad diversa genera secundum diversum modum praedicandi, qui consequitur diversum modum essendi; quia 'quoties ens dicitur' idest quot modis aliquid praedicatur, 'toties esse significatur', idest tot modis significatur aliquid esse. Et propter hoc ea in quae dividitur ens primo, dicuntur esse praedicamenta, quia distinguuntur secundum diversum modum praedicandi.'

37. Ibid., nn. 891–892: '[i] Uno modo cum est id quod est subiectum. . . . [ii] Secundo modo ut praedicatum sumatur secundum quod inest subiecto. . . . [iii] Tertio modo ut praedicatum sumatur ab eo quod est extra subiectum.'

substance, Socrates; hence we have the category of substance (primary substance).[38]

In the second case, when what is predicated is taken according as it belongs to the subject, what is predicated belongs to the subject either (ii.i) per se and absolutely, or (ii.ii) nonabsolutely but in respect of something else. If absolutely (ii.i), what is predicated belongs to the subject either (ii.i.i) as a consequence of its matter, in which case we have the accident of 'quantity', or (ii.i.ii) as a consequence of its form, in which case we have 'quality'. If what is predicated belongs to the subject nonabsolutely but in respect of something else (ii.ii), we have the accident of 'relation'.

In the third case what is predicated is taken from what is extrinsic to the subject, and this can occur in a twofold manner: first, (iii.i) what is predicated is wholly other (*extra*) than the subject, and second, (iii.ii) what is predicated is other than the subject but predicated because of something in the subject. Concerning the first (iii.i), if what is predicated is wholly other than the subject but not its measure (iii.i.i), we have the category of 'habit' (*habitus*), for example when we say Socrates is clothed, we are signifying by clothing that Socrates is habited in some sort of way—he has some feature which does not measure him but nevertheless is a feature of him. On the other hand if what is predicated is wholly other than the subject but is its extrinsic measure (iii.i.ii), that measure concerns either time (iii.i.ii.a), in which case we have the category of 'when', or place, but not the order of the thing distributed in place (iii.i.ii.b), in which case we have the category of 'where', and if the measure does consider the order of parts of the thing distributed in place (iii.i.ii.c), we have 'position'. Concerning the second (iii.ii), if what is predicated is other than the subject but predicated because of something in the subject, and if it is predicated so because of a principle in the subject (iii.ii.i), we have the category of

38. Ibid., n. 891.

THE OBJECT OF CREATION | 145

'action' (*agere*), but if it is so predicated because the subject is the terminus of an action of another (iii.ii.ii), we have the category of 'passion'.[39]

We can schematize the foregoing as follows.

(i) Predicate expresses the subject itself: *substance*
(ii) Predicate belongs to the subject
  (i) Per se and absolutely
    (i) as a consequence of matter: *quantity*
    (ii) as a consequence of form: *quality*
  (ii) Nonabsolutely but in respect of something else: *relation*
(iii) Predicate is extrinsic to the subject
  (i) Is wholly other than the subject
    (i) is not the measure of the subject: *habit*
    (ii) is the measure of the subject
      (a) pertaining to time: *when*
      (b) pertaining to place but not to the order of parts: *where*
      (c) pertaining to place and the order of parts: *position*
  (ii) is other than the subject but because of something in the subject:
    (i) because of a principle in the subject: *action*
    (ii) because the subject is the terminus of an action: *passion*

---

39. For Aquinas's deduction of the categories in this manner see ibid., nn. 891–892; a slightly different deduction but delivering the same set of categories can be found in *In III Phy.*, lect. 5, n. 322. The differences between these two deductions occur in the third division where Thomas divides how predicates are applied to a thing on the basis of certain extrinsic features. I do not intend to go into this issue because my focus here is on the fact that being is so richly divided for Thomas and how that can be so in light of his metaphysics of creation, but for a discussion of both these deductions see Wippel, *The Metaphysical Thought of Thomas Aquinas*, pp. 208–228.

What this deduction seeks to map are the various modes of being that pertain to substance. So whilst substance is primary, it can be modified in various ways. Such modifications are captured by the different predications which seek to signify how the substance is in reality, and so these categories all signify being in some way.

Given all of what I have outlined about substance and accident, one would naturally assume that substance is defined as a being that is not in a subject, or a being that exists in itself, in which case the corresponding definition of accident would be what does exist in a subject. But Aquinas, following Avicenna, denies that this is the definition of substance; in fact he denies that substance can be defined. Why is this so?[40]

The answer revolves around the mode of defining. We define something by first stipulating something general (the genus) and then specifying what is being defined by including a difference. So to take a classic example, we define man as an animal that is rational. Man is a member of something more general than him, i.e. something that includes more species than that of man, and so man stands out from this genus by having some differentiating feature outside of the genus that picks him out from other animals, and that is his rationality. Thus, we define man as an animal that is rational.

Now, to define substance as 'a being that is not in a subject' (or what amounts to the same: 'a being that is in itself') will not do, for two reasons.

First, the genus out of which the species 'substance' stands would be being, but being cannot be a genus because any difference that could be used to specify it in some way would be a being and so included in it.[41]

---

40. For further details of Aquinas's reasoning that I shall proceed to unfold as well as the Avicennian influence on Aquinas, see Étienne Gilson, 'Quasi Definitio Substantiae', in *St Thomas Aquinas 1274–1974: Commemorative Studies* (Toronto: Pontifical Institute of Medieval Studies, 1974), I, pp. 111–131; for discussion see Wippel, *The Metaphysical Thought of Thomas Aquinas*, pp. 228–238.

41. *De Potentia Dei*, qu. 7, art. 3, ad. 4: 'Ens enim non potest esse alicuius genus, ut probat philosophus, cum nihil possit addi ad ens quod non participet ipsum; differentia vero non debet participare genus.'

Second, the differentiating feature, 'not in a subject', is inappropriate because it involves a negation and not a positive feature, such as rationality, that can differentiate a species.

Hence, 'a being that is not in a subject' is not the definition of substance. More generally, the genus in which a species falls signifies its quiddity, i.e. it tells us something about what the thing is; but being is not the quiddity of anything; it rather signifies the act of existing of the thing, in which case positing being as the genus out of which substance stands tells us nothing about the quiddity of substance.[42]

All of this tells us that the definition of substance as a being that is not in a subject or a being in itself is lacking in some respect; but what about Aquinas's contention that substance cannot in principle be defined—why does he think that?

That contention follows immediately from Aquinas's denial that being can be a genus. If the most fundamental kind of existents are substances, then substance is the primary referent of being. But if that is the case, then there is no more general strata of being as a genus from which substance emerges and is specified. Consequently, substance does not admit of a formal definition per genus and difference. However, we can offer a quasi-definition of substance to the effect that it is that which has a quiddity to which

---

42. Aquinas, *In I Sent.*, dist. 8, qu. 4, art. 2, ad. 2: 'Ista definitio, secundum Avicennam, non potest esse substantiae: substantia est quae non est in subjecto. Ens enim non est genus. Haec autem negatio non in subjecto nihil ponit; unde hoc quod dico, ens non est in subjecto, non dicit aliquod genus: quia in quolibet genere oportet significare quidditatem aliquam, ut dictum est, de cujus intellectu non est esse. Ens autem non dicit quidditatem, sed solum actum essendi, cum sit principium ipsum; et ideo non sequitur: est non in subjecto: ergo est in genere substantiae'; *Summa Contra Gentiles*, Lib. 1, Cap. 25: 'In definitione substantiae non est ens per se. Ex hoc enim quod dicitur ens, non posset esse genus, quia iam probatum est quod ens non habet rationem generis. Similiter nec ex hoc quod dicitur per se, quia non videtur importare nisi negationem tantum; dicitur enim ens per se, ex hoc quod non est in alio, quod est negatio pura, quae non potest naturam vel rationem generis constituere, quia sic genus non diceret quid est res, sed quid non est.'

it belongs to be not in a subject.[43] Similarly for accidents, an accident is 'a thing to which it belongs to be in another', and this being-in-another belongs to accident by its very nature and cannot be separated from it.[44]

Substance and accident are thus taken as expressing the modes of being of things so that the schematism of categories above is not some logical construction imposed on being; rather it is derived from a consideration of the nature of things themselves. Hence, these modes of being are built into the very being of creatures, and so they accompany creation in some manner. My account of Aquinas's metaphysics will have to explain how such a rich division and composition of being can be accounted for in light of the fact that creation is the production of the total substance in being.

2 THE CREATION OF SUBSTANCE

Whatever exists depends on God for its existence, and it so exists because God grants to it an act of existence (*esse*). To create then is to produce the total substance in being, so there is nothing that pertains to the substance that is not created by God. All actuality then, all existence, is rooted in God, Who is pure *esse* itself. God does not stand at the beginning of a chain of causes in some linear fashion but is the primary cause on which all things depend. When Aquinas says that creation is the production of the total substance in being, he must be interpreted in this context, i.e. that there is

---

43. *In IV Sent.*, dist. 12, qu. 1, art. 1, qc. 1, ad. 2: 'definitio, vel quasi definitio, substantiae est res habens quidditatem, cui acquiritur esse, vel debetur, ut non in alio'; *De Potentia Dei*, qu. 7, art. 3, ad. 4: 'si substantia possit habere definitionem, non obstante quod est genus generalissimum, erit eius definitio: quod substantia est res cuius quidditati debetur esse non in aliquo.'

44. *In IV Sent.*, dist. 12, qu. 1, art. 1, qc. 1, ad. 2: 'similiter esse in subjecto non est definitio accidentis, sed e contrario res cui debetur esse in alio; et hoc nunquam separatur ab aliquo accidente, nec separari potest: quia illi rei quae est accidens, secundum rationem suae quidditatis semper debetur esse in alio.'

nothing actual in the substance that does not come within the scope of God's causality.

Now, it has been seen that there are a number of compositional structures pertaining to substance, i.e. supposit and essence, matter and form, substance and accident. What is important is that insofar as it is the total substance which is produced, the substance is created with these structures. Substances involve metaphysical components, but those components are not what are created; the substance is created, and the components are created with the substance; they come to be with the coming to be of the substance. The components of the substance are then cocreated with the substance but not created themselves; hence it is the substance which has an act of existence, not its matter, form, or accidents, which only participate in the act of existence of the substance itself.[45] Given that the components of a creature are only cocreated with the substance, it is not the case that God first takes some essence, then takes some *esse*, and then unites the two of them in the supposit. Creation is a single act of bringing creatures into being, in which case the substance is brought into being with all of its metaphysical components.

The components of creatures have their origin in God, and this can clearly be seen from an advertence to the divine ideas. In God's divine mind there are ideas of every possible essence, and included in these are the essences of the material and immaterial things He actually creates. It is not the case that God has ideas of the individual components of these essences (matter, form, etc.); rather He has ideas of the essences, and He knows the components as components of the essences of which He has ideas. Thus, God knows matter and form as constitutive components of material

---

45. *De Potentia Dei*, qu. 3, art. 1, ad. 12: 'Neque materia neque forma neque accidens proprie dicuntur fieri; sed id quod fit est res subsistens. Cum enim fieri terminetur ad esse, proprie ei convenit fieri cui convenit per se esse, scilicet rei subsistenti; unde neque materia neque forma neque accidens proprie dicuntur creari, sed concreari.'

essences, but He does not have individual ideas of the matter and of the form of the material essence.[46] In creating, God grants *esse* to these essences so that individually existing things are brought about which have these essences and all of the components entailed therein.

Despite all of this, the creation of material things is often thought to pose a special challenge to the idea of creation *ex nihilo*. One can readily conceive how immaterial creatures can come from God, and this because of the appeal of an emanationist kind of thinking. This kind of thinking envisages God, in a somewhat Neoplatonic fashion, as like the sun, the source and origin of visible light, whose rays are limited manifestations of the light of the source. Immaterial creatures are then thought to be like such imitations, and with that backdrop in mind there is not the radical discontinuity between God and immaterial creatures that there appears to be between God and material creatures; for the latter have an added extra (matter) which the former do not. Given that setup there seems to be an ontological chasm between God and material creatures, which chasm requires more effort on God's part to bridge than there is required for creating immaterial things.

Needless to say, Aquinas rejects such emanationist thinking, since God creates voluntarily and not by necessity of nature. Given that God chooses to create there is a radical discontinuity between God and *all* creatures, not just material ones, since had God chosen not to create, there would have been no creatures, material or immaterial. Hence the discontinuity between God and creatures is not on the basis that creatures are a lesser emanation out of the being of God with immaterial creatures being slightly less and material creatures being lesser still; rather creatures are nothing

---

46. *De Potentia Dei*, qu. 3, art. 1, ad. 13: 'Nam proprie loquendo, materia non habet ideam, sed compositum, cum idea sit forma factiva.' It should be said that to deny that God has ideas of form and matter alone is to deny in Him ideas of form alone as the constitutive principle of a material essence. In the case of an immaterial essence, God has an idea of form alone, but this is because that is what the essence is, not because God has an idea of an individual component of a composite substance.

without God. Hence, it is not the case that immaterial creatures simply flow from God but material creatures need some extra effort on God's part. The creation of an immaterial being requires no less an act of omnipotence than the creation of a material one, since neither naturally exists, and both require God to bring them into being by granting them *esse*.

The exercise of omnipotence is necessary for the creation of anything at all, since creation is the origination of being, which can only come from the power of that which is pure *esse* itself. So both material and immaterial creatures require an exercise of God's omnipotent power in order to be. Consequently, on the Thomist account, God knows all the possibilities to which His power extends, He wills to create some of them, and through His power He does so. It is by the same act of power that God creates both material and immaterial things, and whilst some of the metaphysical principles of these may differ, it is by the same act by which both are brought into being. Creating matter out of nothing is no more a challenge for God than is creating anything at all out of nothing. If we grant that God can create out of nothing (and we do since He is omnipotent), then there is no special problem concerning God's creation of matter out of nothing.

Having said all that, material things are metaphysically more complex than immaterial things; for material things are subject to a kind of composition (matter and form) to which immaterial things are not subject. But once again, this metaphysical complexity is no challenge for God. God produces all creatures by His power, and some of these are metaphysically more complex than others because they have more metaphysical components. Nevertheless, the act of granting *esse* to some potentially existing essence in order to produce a concrete substance is the same for immaterial creatures as it is for material creatures. It is the creatures themselves that are analysed differently, not the act by which they are produced.

I will now turn to accidents, and as should be clear, the creation of any accident as a metaphysical component of a creature is like that of the creation of other metaphysical components, such that unless the component depends on *esse* in some way, it simply will not be. The *esse* of accidents is that of the substance such that accidents signify a modification of the being of the substance, in which case they share in its being. That is not to say that accidental *esse* is a distinct kind of *esse* differing from substantial *esse* as if individual accidents had their own distinct act of existence as a substance does; rather, whatever *esse* an accident has derives from that of the substance of which it is an accident. The justification then for distinction of accidental *esse* from substantial *esse* is not that accidental *esse* is a distinct act of existence united with its accident but that it signifies a modification of the being of the substance and not the very substance itself.[47]

The whole plethora of accidents outlined in the previous section signifies the various modes by which substance can be; they are all modifications of substance, and so they all signify what can happen (*accidit*) to substance. It is true to say that such accidents would not be unless substance were such that it could be affected in some way, whether through material potency or intellectual potency, but it is even more true to say that such accidents would not *be* (emphasis on the being of accidents) if they did not participate in the actuality of the substance; for the being of accidents is not a distinct *esse* they have of their own but is that of their substance. So accidents will only be in a substance if they participate in the substance's being; otherwise they have no principle of actuality and so are not. Whatever then the temporal coming and going of accidents, none escapes the actuality of the *esse* of a given

---

47. *De Veritate*, qu. 27, art. 1, ad. 8: 'Similiter accidentia, quia non subsistunt, non est eorum proprie esse; sed subiectum est aliquale secundum ea; unde proprie dicuntur magis entis quam entia. Et ideo, ad hoc quod aliquid sit in praedicamento aliquo accidentis, non requiritur quod sit compositum compositione reali, sed solummodo compositione rationis ex genere et differentia.' My interpretation here is in contrast to that of Barry Brown, who holds that accidents have their own *esse* by which they are actuated, an *esse* distinct from that of their substance and distinct from their essence. See Barry Brown, *Accidental Being: A Study in the Metaphysics of St Thomas Aquinas* (Lanham: University Press of America, 1985). For further discussion see Wippel, *The Metaphysical Thought of Thomas Aquinas*, pp. 253–266.

substance. To participate in the being of substance is to participate in its *esse*, and this is a participation in God's divine *esse*, which participation is to be understood as the relation of creation. So we can say then that accidents are cocreated with the thing insofar as to be actual at all they have to depend on the *esse* of the thing which is created.

3 WHAT IS UNCREATABLE

Throughout this chapter my goal has been to articulate Aquinas's metaphysics of creation with special emphasis on the object of creation. The object of creation is the concretely existing substance, and it has several components to it all of which depend on *esse* for their actuality. Hence, whatever is of act in the substance is so because of the *esse* granted to it by God. But what about things independent of God that are arguably uncreated? I mean such so-called entities as mathematical truths, numbers, universal properties, etc. which in their necessity resist any kind of causal influence?

This problem is the traditional challenge of Platonism; unless we grant the existence of abstract universals which are what they are in themselves, we cannot account for the intelligibility of reality as exhibiting properties of those universals. But if we grant the existence of universals, we must grant that they depend on nothing but themselves for their existence. Unless one is a voluntarist when it comes to universals (and Aquinas is not) God does not make these universals what they are; He makes it that there are things that exhibit such universal properties. So the universals themselves are uncreated whereas things are created after them. It is considerations such as these that have led Alvina Plantinga and Nicholas Wolterstorff, amongst others, to affirm that there are some things that exist uncreated by God precisely because they are uncreatable.[48]

---

48. See Plantinga, 'Which Worlds Could God Have Created?', *Journal of Philosophy*, 70:17 (1973), 539–552; note in particular p. 541: 'Properties are not creatable: to

It will not be enough to respond that Aquinas is working with a different conception of God and creation from those of Plantinga, Wolterstorff, and others. For even accepting a full-blooded Thomist view, one has to accept the existence of universals that could not be otherwise, hence are necessary, yet are not created substances like men and angels. How then do such realities fit into Aquinas's philosophy of creation wherein all that in any way exists depends on God for its existence?

The resolution to this problem will not be to deny the existence of universals or our ability to grasp and affirm universal properties of concrete substances. Rather, it will be to modify what the existence of such universals consists in so as not to go to the extreme of affirming real existent universals independent of the substances which manifest them whilst at the same time granting the fact that such universals are what they are irrespective of divine influence.

Aquinas is in agreement with Aristotle in rejecting Platonic universals. He believes that the Platonists confused the mode of existence of forms in the intellect, i.e. as separate and universal, with their mode of existence in reality, and so they concluded

suppose that they have been created is to suppose that, although they exist now, there was a time at which they did not; and this seems clearly false. Again, since God did not create numbers, propositions, pure sets, and the like, he did not actualize the states of affairs consisting in the existence of these things.' For Wolterstorff see *On Universals: An Essay in Ontology* (Chicago: University of Chicago Press, 1970), pp. 290–297. Wolterstorff concedes that his view diverges from those of important authorities in Christian theology both Protestant and Catholic, but he nevertheless argues that his view is in accord with scripture. See also Thomas V. Morris and Christopher Menzel, 'Absolute Creation', *American Philosophical Quarterly*, 23 (1986), 353–361, for what I take to be a non-Thomist way to resolve this issue (non-Thomist because a key argumentative move for Morris and Menzel is to affirm that God creates His own nature); note in particular their statement of the issue on p. 353: 'The question then is whether any divine creative activity can consistently, and even plausibly, be held by theists to be the source of necessary existence and necessary truth, or to put it another way, whether such existence and truth can in any defensible way be held to be dependent on God.'

that the mode of existence in reality mirrors that of the intellect.[49] Aquinas argues that it need not be the case that what we think about abstractly actually exists in such an abstract fashion. For him what exists are individual substances, and these exist as formed. Whilst universal in themselves, forms exist individually in things; nevertheless such forms can be thought of in themselves through abstraction by means of the agent intellect. In so abstracting form, the intellect can understand the universal form of things, but that does not mean that the form exists universally. Hence for Aquinas there are real universals, but they do not exist universally in things, only in the intellect in thinking about such things. Consequently, one need not affirm the separate existence of forms in order to affirm that the human intellect can grasp them.

Now, as I articulated in Chapter 2, God creates by means of His intellect (and will and power) such that He sees every possibility of being and chooses to grant existence to some of these possibilities. In knowing these possibilities God does not cause the possibilities to be the possibilities that they are, i.e. He does not decide that they be so. Nevertheless, such possibilities are possibilities *of* being and so are dependent on their being the possibilities that they are because of the being of which they are possibilities. But that being is God's being—such possibilities exhibit to God's intellect the range of His power. Hence, whilst it is not the case that God could make what is genuinely a square to be genuinely a circle, it is the case that the natures of each signify distinct ways in which things could be, and so distinct possibilities that are open to God's power. In such a manner, squares, circles, and all other universals are dependent

---

49. *Summa Theologiae*, Ia, qu. 84, art. 1: 'Videtur autem in hoc Plato deviasse a veritate, quia, cum aestimaret omnem cognitionem per modum alicuius similitudinis esse, credidit quod forma cogniti ex necessitate sit in cognoscente eo modo quo est in cognito. Consideravit autem quod forma rei intellectae est in intellectu universaliter et immaterialiter et immobiliter, quod ex ipsa operatione intellectus apparet, qui intelligit universaliter et per modum necessitatis cuiusdam; modus enim actionis est secundum modum formae agentis. Et ideo existimavit quod oporteret res intellectas hoc modo in seipsis subsistere, scilicet immaterialiter et immobiliter.' See also *In I Met.*, lect. 10, n. 158, for the same.

on God for being the possibilities that they are. Whilst they are causally independent in their intelligibility, they do not exist independently of God unless things have been created which manifest such universal properties.

Given that such universals are causally independent of God in their essences but do not exist independently of Him, Aquinas can deny on the one hand universals existing separately from God and creatures, whilst on the other hand he can affirm that such universals come within the scope of God's causal power in bringing creatures into being. And back of that Aquinas can deny that there exists anything other than God which has not been created, whilst still granting the central insight of the Platonist position, namely that universals are not caused to be the way they are; they are that way in themselves, i.e. because they manifest some way in which being could be.

The same reasoning goes *mutatis mutandis* for mathematical objects, necessary truths, propositions, and all other such things that motivate this kind of Platonism in metaphysics. Such things manifest intelligible features of being and as such signify ways in which being could be. As ways in which being could be, such necessities signify some distinct manifestation of the divine essence, i.e. something to which God's power could extend. God does not make it be by the fiat of His will that such intelligible necessities have the intelligibility that they have, but their intelligibility is nevertheless not independent of God's being, since it is a manifestation thereof—the intelligible necessity of such things is conditional upon God's being.[50] And, of course, in choosing to create God forms creation on the basis of such intelligibilities. Hence, there is no need to affirm the necessary and independent existence of things other than God.

To bring this chapter to a close then and look forward to the next: I have built on my previous considerations of Aquinas's metaphysics of creation. I have considered the things to which

50. *Summa Theologiae*, Ia, qu. 44, art. 1, ad. 2.

esse is granted, i.e. concrete substances and their metaphysical components, affirming that whatever is actual in the substance is so because of the *esse* that the substance has received from God. Accordingly, I have shown that Aquinas has remained closely committed to his definition of creation, namely the production of the total substance in being, and not only that but managed to avoid the shortcomings of those philosophers who failed to arrive at a universal consideration of the being of things. Whatever is actual in the substance is so because of its dependence on *esse,* which is from God; there is nothing actual in creatures that is not caused to be by God. God's creation then embraces all that is without remainder.

In considering Aquinas's definition of creation in Chapter 3, I noted that for Aquinas the philosopher can affirm (i) that in creation nothing is presupposed of the thing created, and (ii) that non-being precedes the being of the creature. Hence when God creates He makes use of nothing but His own resources, and creatures in themselves would not exist were it not for the being that they receive from God. But also to be noted is a third feature of creation, one to which Aquinas is committed but one which he believes is incapable of demonstration in philosophy: the beginning of creation in time. Aquinas maintains that the latter can only be affirmed by faith and so is a truth that is divinely revealed.[51] It is now time to consider how Aquinas's metaphysics of creation integrates with what he takes to be divinely revealed about creation. In the next chapter I will consider the history of creation, and this history will cover both the temporal beginning of things and their development.

---

51. *In II Sent.,* dist. 1, qu. 1, art. 2: 'Si autem accipiamus tertium oportere ad rationem creationis, ut scilicet etiam duratione res creata prius non esse quam esse habeat, ut dicatur esse ex nihilo, quia est tempore post nihil, sic creatio demonstrari non potest, nec a philosophis conceditur; sed per fidem supponitur.'

6

THE HISTORY OF CREATION

SO FAR I HAVE OBSERVED THAT Aquinas views creation as a dependency relation whereby all creatures that in any way exist stand as effects to God as their cause; there is nothing that is that has not been caused to be by God. I have shown that this notion of creation is articulated in Aquinas's metaphysics in terms of *esse*, and that it is such that all creatures participate in the *esse* they receive from God in order to be. Given what I have considered on both the causality of creation and the object of creation, it is not the case that in causing things God simply gets the ball rolling and then steps back to let it roll. As is now clear, if God's causal activity were not present to every creature, then nothing would be. So if God simply got the ball rolling and then stepped back, things would cease to be as soon as they were originated. Creation has a history it would not have were it not for God's creative act originating and thus sustaining the existence of all things. In this chapter I will consider that history.

First, I will consider the beginning of creation. Thomas is clear that creatures have an origin in God, and this origin lies precisely in their *esse* being caused. But this is not to say that creatures have a beginning, since it can be the case that things which don't have a beginning are dependent in some respect (here, in respect of *esse*) and so require a cause for the respect in which they are dependent (a cause of *esse*). Aquinas is notorious for his neutrality on the demonstrability of the beginning or otherwise of creation, and in Section 1 of this chapter I will consider his thinking thereon.

Second, if to be created is to have one's *esse* caused, then the act of creation extends to all things whose *esse* is caused, i.e. all things other than God. That then means that all things in whatever way they exist, and whenever they exist, exist precisely because they participate in the act of creation of God. Creation then is simultaneous and all at once, though it can be differentiated through its ontological hierarchy and temporal succession; so there is a single act of creation with diverse effects. But for many this view stands in tension with the revealed doctrine of scripture, which presents creation as an event with successive stages, a number of days, within which it occurs. I will thus consider Aquinas's thinking on the work of the six days in Section 2.

1 ETERNAL CREATION

In the ancient world, nearly all thinkers held that the universe was without a beginning. What this entailed was varied, but fundamentally such thinkers held that whereas the current arrangement and order of the cosmos had a beginning, i.e. a temporal reference point at which it came to be that way, the matter of the cosmos they took to be without a beginning. Hence different arrangements of matter could come and go, thereby signifying a beginning of this or that particular arrangement, but the matter itself was thought to be without a beginning.[1]

The lack of a beginning to the matter of creation fits nicely with the views of creation that Aquinas considered erroneous outlined in Chapter 1; for they held matter to be uncreated, in which case one may infer that such matter did not begin to be. Nevertheless, it should be pointed out that whilst the operative principle of this view, namely that whatever is uncaused has no beginning, is indeed

---

1. For a presentation of some of these views see Aristotle, *On the Heavens,* Bk. 1, Chapter 10.

a sound one, its converse—that whatever does not have a beginning does not have a cause—is not, since as I will show, a thing can be dependent for its *esse* but lack any sort of temporal beginning.

The notion that there is a beginning to creation, and hence of the matter of creatures, is one that appears to have been developed almost exclusively in Judeo-Christian circles wherein the notion of creation *ex nihilo* most especially belongs.[2] Furthermore, the doctrine of the beginning of creation was defined by the Fourth Lateran council as *de fide* for all Catholics; this is to say that no Catholic can believe that the universe did not have a beginning.[3] Nevertheless, the question of whether or not creation could be eternal, i.e. without beginning, was heavily debated in the Middle Ages by Thomas and his contemporaries.[4] The crux of this debate was whether or not the very notion of creation *ex nihilo* involves a commitment to the beginning of creation in time.

There were three general positions that medieval authors took. There was the position of St Bonaventure to the effect that one could establish philosophically that creation had a beginning. On the other hand there was the view of Siger of Brabant, following the philosophical view of the ancient authors that whilst one may hold

2. Richard Sorabji, *Time, Creation, and the Continuum* (London: Duckworth, 1982), p. 193.

3. The Fourth Lateran Council (1215) decreed that God created all things, both spiritual and material, at the beginning of time *ex nihilo*: 'creator omnium invisibilium et visibilium spiritualium et corporalium qui sua omnipotenti virtute simul ab initio temporis utramque de nihilo condidit creaturam spiritualem et corporalem angelicam videlicet et mundanam ac deinde humanam quasi communem ex spiritu et corpore constitutam.'

4. The debate over the eternity of the world was conducted in terms of the world's being eternal—*de aeternitate mundi*. However, the debate was concerned neither with the world exclusively nor with eternity; what was at issue was the finitude or otherwise of the duration of creatures. If the duration of creatures is infinite, then creation is without a beginning; if finite, then a case can be made for its having a beginning. Following the medieval precedent, I shall freely interchange all designations of 'eternity of the world' with all designations of 'beginninglessness of creation.' The awkwardness of the terminology is a hangover from the medieval debate; for discussion see Kretzmann, *The Metaphysics of Creation*, pp. 142–143.

by faith that there is a beginning of creation, reason nevertheless leads us to affirm its beginninglessness; what is interesting about Siger's position is that he did not deny the Catholic view of creation; he simply held that on the basis of philosophy we have to affirm that it is beginningless. Third, there was the intermediate view of Aquinas, following Moses Maimonides (*Guide for the Perplexed*, Pt. 2, Chapter 16), who held that neither the arguments for nor the arguments against a beginning were decisive, and that it is a position that could only be held *firmiter* on the basis of revelation.[5] In agreement with Siger and against Bonaventure, Aquinas holds that a beginningless creation is possible;[6] yet, in agreement with Bonaventure and against Siger, Aquinas holds that the philosophical argumentation for a beginningless creation is not decisive.[7]

Thomas was well aware of the doctrine of the Fourth Lateran Council; indeed he states that among the various errors excluded in its creed is that of Aristotle, who on Aquinas's view held that all things were from God but did not have a beginning.[8] This is

5. For details see Fernand Van Steenberghen, 'La controverse sur l'éternité du monde au XIIIe siècle', in *Introduction à l'étude de la philosophie médiévale* (Louvain: Publications Universitaires, 1974), pp. 512–530. For texts see *St Thomas Aquinas, Siger of Brabant, St Bonaventure, On the Eternity of the World*, ed. and trans. by Cyril Vollert et al. (Milwaukee: Marquette University Press, 1964).

6. Wippel has argued that Aquinas did not defend this possibility until quite late in his career, with the *De Aeternitate Mundi*. Nevertheless, the possibility of an eternal creation is consistent with the metaphysics of creation that he articulated throughout his career. See Wippel, 'Thomas Aquinas on the Possibility of Eternal Creation', in *Metaphysical Themes in Thomas Aquinas*, pp. 191–215.

7. Siger's position is somewhat nuanced because whilst it would seem that he defends an eternal creation, after the condemnations of 1270 he seems to have modified his view somewhat and, drawing himself closer to the Thomist position, Siger held that neither set of arguments are decisive and that it is a truth held by faith; it would seem that Boethius of Dacia also held a similar view. For details see Van Steenberghen, 'La controverse sur l'éternité du monde au XIIIe siècle', p. 520, n. 17 (for Siger) and p. 525 (for Boethius of Dacia).

8. Aquinas, *Super Decretales*, E35: 'Alius error fuit Aristotelis ponentis quidem omnia a Deo esse producta, sed ab aeterno, et nullum fuisse principium temporis, cum tamen scriptum sit Gen. I, 1: *in principio creavit Deus caelum et terram*. Et ad hoc excludendum addit, *ab initio temporis*.'

an interesting observation because Aquinas indeed attributes a doctrine of creation to Aristotle, since he interprets Aristotle as holding that all things are from God. Nevertheless, Aquinas doesn't interpret Aristotle as holding *the* doctrine of creation, i.e. the one defined by the council, since Aristotle also held that creation is without a beginning.

Setting aside the historical accuracy of Aquinas's interpretation of Aristotle, what this indicates is that in Thomas's mind to be created is not incompatible with not having a beginning. So here we have an indication that for Aquinas a beginningless creation is possible; God could bring about all things without their having had a beginning; such is not beyond His power to do.[9] Contrast this with the view of St Bonaventure, who argued that it is essential to the very notion of creation that it have a beginning; the two cannot be divorced. Hence, the one who affirms creation affirms a beginning of creation.[10]

In dealing with the arguments offered by a number of philosophers for there being a beginning of creation, Aquinas rejects all of them for being problematic in some way. He expresses from the outset a need for a higher standard of demonstrability than what is needed in other matters; and this is because the beginning of creation is an article of faith binding on all Catholics. So if any argument is offered for this view and can be subject to doubt, it will bring about derision from non-Catholics.[11] Ultimately Aquinas

---

9. *De Potentia Dei*, qu. 3, art. 14: 'Si ergo consideretur hoc enuntiabile, aliquid diversum in substantia existens a Deo fuisse semper, non potest dici impossibile secundum se, quasi sibi ipsi repugnans: hoc enim quod est esse ab alio, non repugnat ei quod est esse semper.'

10. See for instance Bonaventure, *In I Sent.*, dist. 44, art. 1, qu. 4. For a general discussion of Bonaventure's view see Bernardino Bonansea, 'The Impossibility of Creation from Eternity According to St Bonaventure', *Proceedings of the American Catholic Philosophical Association,* 48 (1974), 121–135.

11. *Summa Theologiae*, Ia, qu. 46, art. 2: 'Et hoc utile est ut consideretur, ne forte aliquis, quod fidei est demonstrare praesumens, rationes non necessarias inducat, quae praebeant materiam irridendi infidelibus, existimantibus nos propter huiusmodi rationes credere quae fidei sunt'; *Summa Contra Gentiles*, Lib. 2, Cap. 38, n. 8: 'Hae autem rationes quia non usquequaque de necessitate concludunt, licet

holds that whilst philosophy can demonstrate some things about creation, such as its being *ex nihilo* and the priority of nonbeing over being in the creature, the beginning of creation is held as a matter of faith.[12]

Even though he rejects the arguments in favour of a beginning, Aquinas cannot be swayed by the opposing arguments in favour of a lack of beginning; for this would entail that a truth established by reason is contrary to faith (something that Siger of Brabant at one point seems to have affirmed). Hence in considering the arguments for the eternity of the world, Aquinas maintains that none of them are demonstrable. Nevertheless, given the divorce between being created and having a beginning, Aquinas certainly maintains that it is possible for there to be a beginningless creation, but he also maintains that with revelation we know that creation does indeed have a beginning.

I do not propose to go painstakingly through the arguments for and against the beginning of creation; Thomas has already done that in various places, e.g. the commentary on the *Sentences*, Lib. 2, dist. 1, qu. 1, art. 5, *De Potentia Dei*, qu. 3, aa. 14 and 17, *Summa Contra Gentiles*, Lib. 2, Cap. 31–38, and *Summa Theologiae*, Ia, qu. 46. Not only that, such an argumentative tennis match is liable to obscure the metaphysics that really informs Thomas's views. What

probabilitatem habeant, sufficit tangere solum, ne videatur fides Catholica in vanis rationibus constituta, et non potius in solidissima Dei doctrina. Et ideo conveniens videtur ponere qualiter obvietur eis per eos qui aeternitatem mundi posuerunt.'

12. Note the statement in *In II Sent.*, dist. 1, qu. 1, art. 2, that I have had cause to consider before: 'Respondeo quod creationem esse, non tantum fides tenet, sed etiam ratio demonstrat. . . . Sciendum est autem, quod ad rationem creationis pertinent duo. Primum est ut nihil praesupponat in re quae creari dicitur. . . . Secundum est, ut in re quae creari dicitur, prius sit non esse quam esse: non quidem prioritate temporis vel durationis, ut prius non fuerit et postmodum sit; sed prioritate naturae, ita quod res creata si sibi relinquatur, consequatur non esse, cum esse non habeat nisi ex influentia causae superioris. . . . Et secundum ista duo creatio dupliciter dicitur esse ex nihilo. Si autem accipiamus tertium oportere ad rationem creationis, ut scilicet etiam duratione res creata prius non esse quam esse habeat, ut dicatur esse ex nihilo, quia est tempore post nihil, sic creatio demonstrari non potest, nec a philosophis conceditur; sed per fidem supponitur.'

sort of metaphysical picture of things does Thomas have in place which permits him to believe that there was a beginning of creation but that it is possible for there to be creation without a beginning? The answer to this question is the more interesting one for elucidating Aquinas's metaphysics of creation.[13]

The metaphysics of creation involves the metaphysics of *esse* such that creation is the granting of *esse* to things. What is created is such that it is not the source of its own *esse* but has its *esse* from another, ultimately from God, Who is the source of all *esse*. All creatures then are dependent on God for their *esse*. So long then as we preserve dependency on *esse* in the thing under consideration we can say that that thing is created; effectively, if a thing is a composite of essence and *esse* then it is a creature. Within this metaphysics, the temporal geography of creatures is incidental to their being dependent for their *esse*, and thus being creatures. Hence, whatever the temporality of creatures, whether they have a beginning or not, that is independent of their being essence/*esse* composites and hence created. So creation does not essentially involve having a beginning, and to see this more clearly we can consider Aquinas's metaphysics of time.

Following Aristotle, Aquinas holds that time whilst not identical to motion nonetheless pertains to motion.[14] One who perceives motion perceives time, and the particular perception of motion by which one perceives time is the before and after involved in the succession of motion. Hence time is the before and after in a process of change (motion). It follows then that whatever

---

13. For a list of the various arguments offered for and against the eternity of the world considered by Aquinas and his contemporaries see Cyrille Michon et al., *Thomas d'Aquin et la controverse sur L'Éternité du monde* (Paris: Flammarion, 2004), pp. 385–394. For presentation and commentary of Aquinas's consideration of the various arguments for and against a beginningless creation see Kretzmann, *The Metaphysics of Creation*, Chapter 5. For a treatment of the pre-Thomist authors who advanced many of these arguments, see Sorabji, *Time, Creation, and the Continuum*, Chapters 14–15.

14. *In IV Phy.*, lect. 17, n. 572.

is not subject to change is not temporal and so cannot be subject to temporality. Only God is immutable, so only God is atemporal. Time then is applied to things insofar as they are changing, and this is the case even for the angels since they are subject to some succession in their intellectual potencies, and so they are subject to temporality. The temporality of angels of course is not the same as that to which material things are subject, but it is a temporality nonetheless; it is called aveiternity or sempiternity insofar as it is a kind of mean between eternity, given their immateriality, and time, given their mutability.[15]

Now, the act of creation is not a process of change; this is because change requires some underlying components presupposed for the change, whereas creation as the granting of *esse* presupposes nothing. However, when changeable things are brought into existence, we have the necessary components for temporality since we have all the components brought into existence by which change can occur. Fundamentally change will involve some kind of potency, whether the potency of matter or the intellectual potency of the angelic essence. And so, given that changeable things are brought into being without any change being involved in creating them, time, as pertaining to the process of change, is created along with the things that can change. The finitude or otherwise of the duration of such temporal things is not determined by their being originated; since an infinite number of such changeable things can be originated, i.e. there can be an infinite number of essence/*esse* composites, all of which are dependent for their *esse* on God. Given such an infinity, there would be no beginning to things subject to time, yet both the things so subject and the time itself would be originated. Hence, there being a beginning of creatures is not essentially involved in the origination of creatures.

Nevertheless, one might argue that such reasoning leads to some unacceptable conclusions with regard to the actual infinite.

15. *Summa Theologiae*, Ia, qu. 10, aa. 5–6, and qu. 61, art. 2, ad. 2.

It is generally accepted on Aristotelian grounds that an actual infinite is impossible, and indeed Aquinas himself, though he wavered on the issue of an actual *per accidens* infinite, held that the actual infinite is impossible.[16] Now, if creation were without a beginning, there would be an infinite number of created changeable things, and the latter would entail one of the following: (i) an actual infinity of things, or (ii) an actual infinite causal series pertaining to those things, or (iii) (an objection Aquinas found particularly pressing) an actual infinity of human souls that have persisted beyond the deaths of their bodies.[17] So granting the possibility of a beginningless universe would be the first step towards affirming any of conclusions (i)–(iii) and hence an actual infinite, in which case Aquinas cannot consistently reject the actual infinite but affirm the possibility of an eternal creation.

On the contrary, Aquinas maintains that conclusions (i) and (ii) do not follow from creation's being without a beginning, and that in the case of (iii) the actual infinity of immortal souls is not a problem. Concerning (i) and (ii), Aquinas holds that if there were an infinity of changeable things, such an infinity would not be an actual infinity, because as time progresses things in the past would perish and new things come to take their place. So given such succession we do not have an actual infinity of things (or causal processes pertaining to those things) but only a potential one, whereby a new thing (or component of the causal series) succeeds a previous one. In that case, what we have at any one time is actually finite but potentially infinite. It is different for (iii), the actual infinity of immortal souls, since new souls given their immortality do not succeed the old ones that have perished; rather the old continue to exist alongside the new. So if there were an infinity of such souls, we would have an actual infinity. Hence if one were to grant

---

16. See *Aquinas's Way to God*, pp. 129–135, for details.
17. These objections or variations thereof are made in *In II Sent.*, dist. 1, qu. 1, art. 5, s.c. 3, 5–6, *Summa Contra Gentiles*, Lib. 2, Cap. 38, *Summa Theologiae*, Ia, qu. 46, art. 2, arg. 6–8.

the beginninglessness of the universe, i.e. its infinity, one would have to grant an actual infinity of immortal souls.

Aquinas grants that this is a pressing problem, but he argues that it does not undermine the possibility of an eternally created universe. God need not have created the universe with human souls, or the human souls that were created could have been created at a certain (later) moment and so are not coextensive with the infinity of created things; or even if there were an actual infinity of souls, this need not be problematic because the souls are only related *per accidens* and not per se. (This latter concession would suggest that Aquinas did not see the actual infinite itself as problematic, only an actual infinite in which the multitude are related per se and not *per accidens*.)[18]

One may not feel altogether satisfied with Aquinas's reasoning here, since he seems not to tackle head on the objection inspired by the actual infinity of souls but to navigate his way around it. Indeed, Kretzmann accuses St Thomas of an *ad hominem* since in the various places where he responds to this argument he points out that the one proposing it will have to sacrifice some other

---

18. There is also confirmation outside the context of the eternity of the world that Aquinas did not see an actual infinite as impossible in itself, just that it would be against the wisdom of God to bring such about; *Quodlibet XII*, qu. 2, art. 2: 'Cum ergo quaeritur utrum sit possibile Deo facere aliquid infinitum in actu, dicendum quod non. Potentiae enim agenti per intellectum aliquid repugnat dupliciter: uno modo quia repugnat potentiae eius; alio modo quia repugnat modo quo agit. *Primo modo non repugnat potentiae Dei absolutae, quia non implicat contradictionem* [my emphasis]. Sed si consideretur modus quo Deus agit, non est possibile. Deus enim agit per intellectum et per verbum, quod est formativum omnium; unde oportet quod omnia quae agit sint formata. Infinitum autem accipitur sicut materia sine forma; nam infinitum se tenet ex parte materiae. Si ergo Deus hoc ageret, sequeretur quod opus Dei esset aliquid informe; et hoc repugnat ei per quod agit, et modo agendi; quia per verbum suum omnia agit, quo omnia formantur.' Following Torrell's dating in *St Thomas Aquinas: The Person and His Work*, trans. by Robert Royal, (Washington, DC: Catholic University of America Press, 2005), p. 211, the majority of scholars date *Quodlibet XII* as coming after 1270, so it is contemporaneous with the *De Aeternitate Mundi*, c. 1271, wherein he also holds the possibility of an actual infinite. It is likely then that the treatment in *Quodlibet XII* signifies Aquinas's final thoughts on the matter.

principle that he (Aquinas's opponent) holds good. So really, according to Kretzmann, Thomas charges his interlocutor with inconsistency in even making this objection and does not resolve it.[19]

But I think Kretzmann misses the point. Of course, it may be the case that those who push the actual infinity of souls might have to sacrifice other principles to which they are committed; and it is right and just that Thomas point that out. Nevertheless, the real thrust of his retort is that the infinity of immortal souls objection does not succeed in running together being created with having a beginning, in which case it fails to establish that the former necessitates the latter; for an infinity of immortal souls can still be dependent for their *esse*, i.e. their *esse* is not identical with them, in which case they are caused to be. Thus, there is still a divorce between being created, i.e. being an essence/*esse* composite, and having a beginning. And that's all Aquinas needs to do to show that the argument in question does not satisfactorily establish that creation must have had a beginning.

Aquinas's position then is that the granting of *esse* to things is not inconsistent with there being an infinity of things, in which case it is not inconsistent that such things lack a beginning. Despite such beginninglessness, creatures themselves in their metaphysical constitution are such that their essences are not identical with the *esse* they have; they possess *esse* as a distinct principle of actuality by which they exist.[20] In so possessing *esse* their nonbeing naturally precedes their being—they are naturally nothing—and in granting them *esse* God presupposes nothing, so on both counts they are created *ex nihilo*, yet there is no beginning to creation. In contrast to Bonventure, Aquinas holds that being *ex nihilo* does not entail that things come to be *post nihilum*, but as clarified in Chapter 3, being *ex nihilo* signifies the fact that God presupposes nothing in creating things and that the nonbeing of a creature is naturally prior to its being, i.e. it is naturally nothing without *esse*.

---

19. Kretzmann, *The Metaphysics of Creation*, p. 181.
20. See the *De Potentia Dei* text in note 9 above.

So, *pace* Bonaventure, on the metaphysics of *esse* it is possible to have a beginningless creation *ex nihilo*.

What all this entails is that God's causality in granting *esse* cannot be a kind of motion; for all motion is successive and permits us to plot a temporal geography such that the cause will be temporally prior to its effect. If God were such a cause, then all time would come after Him, and the origin of creation would be the beginning of creation. But by conceiving of God as a cause of *esse* not acting as a motive cause on some underlying material, Thomas divorces God's creative causality from motion, in which case creation does not happen successively but is instantaneous.[21]

The lack of succession in God's creative causality draws on reasoning I presented in Chapter 4 with regard to God's being the primary cause. God is the primary cause of things such that He is primary in a per se ordered series whose causality is *esse*. Nothing would be in that series if not for God's causal influence. Hence anything in the causal series, i.e. anything that is, exists precisely because it is caused to be by God. If God simply began the series by giving it its first push, then there would be a beginning to the series, but subsequent members would not depend on God for their being; they would depend on their immediately preceding causes. On the contrary, given the metaphysics of per se ordered series, the primary cause (God) does not give the first push to the series; He is

---

21. *Summa Theologiae*, Ia, qu. 46, art. 2, ad. 1: 'Considerandum est quod causa efficiens quae agit per motum, de necessitate praecedit tempore suum effectum, quia effectus non est nisi in termino actionis, agens autem omne oportet esse principium actionis. Sed si actio sit instantanea, et non successiva, non est necessarium faciens esse prius facto duratione; sicut patet in illuminatione. Unde dicunt quod non sequitur ex necessitate, si Deus est causa activa mundi, quod sit prior mundo duratione, quia creatio, qua mundum produxit, non est mutatio successiva, ut supra dictum est.' *Summa Contra Gentiles*, Lib. 2, Cap. 38, n. 9: 'Quod enim primo dicitur, agens de necessitate praecedere effectum qui per suam operationem fit, verum est in his quae agunt aliquid per motum: quia effectus non est nisi in termino motus; agens autem necesse est esse etiam cum motus incipit. In his autem quae in instanti agunt, hoc non est necesse: sicut simul dum sol est in puncto orientis, illuminat nostrum hemisphaerium.'

that on which the very causality of the series depends, so no matter at what point in the series a being is found, it is dependent on God for its being. Hence, God's causality is omnipresent throughout the series at whatever temporal juncture. This does not mean that God is subject to the temporality to which the things He causes are subject, but that temporal things, i.e. things that are mutable, are subject to God for their being. (He does not become mutable, and hence temporal, in causing them.) From eternity God can will that temporal things come to be and have a beginning without Himself being subject to the time at which they come to be.[22] Hence, as I have already had occasion to note, their being created and their being conserved are by one and the same act in God, whereas the temporal being of creatures allows us to experience our conservation as distinct from our creation and extended through time.

Despite the real possibility that creation is without a beginning, Thomas is at pains to argue that none of the arguments for a beginningless creation are demonstrable, that is to say, whilst it may be possible for creation to be without a beginning, there is no (good) reason to think that such is the case. He even goes so far as to argue that Aristotle's arguments for the beginninglessness of creation were not intended as demonstrations at all but signify only probable reasonings.[23] In any case, as with the arguments in

---

22. *Summa Contra Gentiles*, Lib. 2, Cap. 35.
23. Aquinas, *In II Sent.*, dist. 1, au. 1, art. 5: 'Dico ergo, quod ad neutram partem quaestionis sunt demonstrationes, sed probabiles vel sophisticae rationes ad utrumque. Et hoc significant verba philosophi dicentis quod sunt quaedam problemata de quibus rationem non habemus, ut utrum mundus sit aeternus; unde hoc ipse demonstrare nunquam intendit: quod patet ex suo modo procedendi; quia ubicumque hanc quaestionem pertractat, semper adjungit aliquam persuasionem vel ex opinione plurium, vel approbatione rationum, quod nullo modo ad demonstratorem pertinet.' For some of Aristotle's arguments for creation's being beginningless see *Physics*, Bk. 1, Chapter 9, 192a25–34, Bk. 8, Chapter 1, 251a9–b28, *Metaphysics*, Bk. 12, Chapter 6, 1071b3–11, Chapter 7, 1072a21–26; for commentary see Sorabji, *Time, Creation, and the Continuum*, Chapter 17. By the time Aquinas comes to write his commentary on the *Physics*, he no longer holds the view that Aristotle did not really mean to demonstrate the eternity of the world; see *In VIII Phy.*, lect. 2, n. 986.

favour of there being a beginning of creation, Aquinas painstakingly goes through the arguments for creation's being without a beginning, arguing that none of them are decisive.

Now an interesting feature of creation emerges in Thomas's response to some of these arguments, and it is a feature which gives us an insight into his personal approach to the matter. Some philosophers, as I have noted, entertained an emanationist interpretation of creation such that all creatures naturally emanate by blind necessity from the creator so that there must be creatures for as long as there is a creator. Creatures then are coeternal with the creator.[24]

On the contrary, Thomas holds that creatures would only be coeternal with God in that way if God did not create voluntarily but by necessity of nature. So if God cannot help but create, He cannot determine creatures as with or without a beginning. Thomas then emphasizes the voluntary aspect of creation as a way of avoiding the eternity of creation, so that creation on Aquinas's account is a free creation, one that has been willed to be by God.[25]

---

24. See for instance *Summa Theologiae*, Ia, qu. 46, art. 1, arg. 9: 'posita causa sufficienti, ponitur effectus, causa enim ad quam non sequitur effectus, est causa imperfecta, indigens alio ad hoc quod effectus sequatur. Sed Deus est sufficiens causa mundi; et finalis, ratione suae bonitatis; et exemplaris, ratione suae sapientiae; et effectiva, ratione suae potentiae; ut ex superioribus patet. Cum ergo Deus sit ab aeterno, et mundus fuit ab aeterno'; and arg. 10: 'cuius actio est aeterna, et effectus aeternus. Sed actio Dei est eius substantia, quae est aeterna. Ergo et mundus est aeternus.'

25. *Summa Theologiae*, Ia, qu. 46, art. 1, ad 9: 'Ad nonum dicendum quod, sicut effectus sequitur a causa agente naturaliter secundum modum suae formae, ita sequitur ab agente per voluntatem secundum formam ab eo praeconceptam et definitam, ut ex superioribus patet. Licet igitur Deus ab aeterno fuerit sufficiens causa mundi, non tamen oportet quod ponatur mundus ab eo productus, nisi secundum quod est in praedefinitione suae voluntatis; ut scilicet habeat esse post non esse, ut manifestius declaret suum auctorem'; and ad. 10: 'Ad decimum dicendum quod, posita actione, sequitur effectus secundum exigentiam formae quae est principium actionis. In agentibus autem per voluntatem, quod conceptum est et praedefinitum, accipitur ut forma quae est principium actionis. Ex actione igitur Dei aeterna non sequitur effectus aeternus, sed qualem Deus voluit, ut scilicet haberet esse post non esse.' See also *De Potentia Dei*, qu. 3, art. 15.

Insofar as creation is voluntary and not the result of blind necessity, the nature of creation is a result of God's will and so is as He wills it. Hence, given that a beginningless creation is possible and thereby perfectly open to God's omnipotence to bring about, the beginning or otherwise of creation is something that God chooses, and so is something that can only be firmly established by appeal to God's choices, which is to say how He decides to manifest His goodness.[26] Aside from what we can know about God's will from considering the things He has willed, we cannot know His will unless we turn to revelation, in which case in order to establish firmly that God has created things from the beginning of time we need revelation.[27] Thus it is only through appealing to what has been revealed and is accepted by faith that we can firmly establish the beginning of creation or otherwise. All else is open to challenge. And this seems to be Thomas's own personal approach to the matter, that to establish firmly the beginning of creation one needs access

26. *De Potentia Dei*, qu. 3, art. 17: 'Cum autem de toto universo loquimur educendo in esse, non possumus ulterius aliquod creatum invenire ex quo possit sumi ratio quare sit tale vel tale; unde, cum nec etiam *ex parte* divinae potentiae quae est infinita, nec divinae bonitatis, quae rebus non indiget, ratio determinatae dispositionis universi sumi possit, oportet quod eius ratio sumatur ex simplici voluntate producentis'; later in this same article Aquinas roots the quantity of time for the universe in the will of God: 'Unde patet quod ex simplici Dei voluntate dependet quod praefigatur universo determinata quantitas durationis, sicut et determinata quantitas dimensionis. Unde non potest necessario concludi aliquid de universi duratione, ut per hoc ostendi possit demonstrative mundum semper fuisse'; *Summa Contra Gentiles*, Lib. 2, Cap. 38: 'Potest autem efficacius procedi ad hoc ostendendum ex fine divinae voluntatis. . . . Finis enim divinae voluntatis in rerum productione est eius bonitas inquantum per causata manifestatur. Potissime autem manifestatur divina virtus et bonitas per hoc quod res aliae praeter ipsum non semper fuerunt. Ex hoc enim ostenditur manifeste quod res aliae praeter ipsum ab ipso esse habent, quia non semper fuerunt. Ostenditur etiam quod non agit per necessitatem naturae; et quod virtus sua est infinita in agendo. Hoc igitur convenientissimum fuit divinae bonitati, ut rebus creatis principium durationis daret.'
27. *Summa Theologiae*, Ia, qu. 46, art. 2: 'Voluntas enim Dei ratione investigari non potest, nisi circa ea quae absolute necesse est Deum velle, talia autem non sunt quae circa creaturas vult, ut dictum est. Potest autem voluntas divina homini manifestari per revelationem, cui fides innititur. Unde mundum incoepisse est credibile, non autem demonstrabile vel scibile.'

to the mind of God, which access in this respect is only provided by revelation and so is safeguarded by faith, not natural reasoning.

2 THE WORK OF THE SIX DAYS

The second theme to be dealt with in the history of creation is the actual history of the created universe. Granted that it is a truth of faith not demonstrated by reason that creation had a beginning, there is a story (a history) of things developing from that beginning. This is of interest in consideration of the metaphysics of creation because as is clear from contemporary discoveries in science and as was clear to St Thomas from his reading of Genesis, the created universe has undergone development from its initial starting point to the stage at which it is now. Thus far, Aquinas's metaphysics of creation has stressed that so long as anything exists it is present to God for its existence and so is continually in a state of being created. Nevertheless, whilst there is no change in the creator, there are continual changes in creatures which are present to the creator. Thomas was convinced of this, given the Genesis account of creation, and we are convinced of it today given big bang cosmology and the evolution of the species. So now I will take up these issues.

Thomas of course was not aware of the scientific confirmation that the universe has undergone development over the course of its existence. Ernan McMullin points out that it wasn't until as late as the eighteenth century that philosophers began to take seriously the prospect of a longer time scale than that envisaged by the Bible for the history of the universe.[28] Nevertheless, whilst unaware of the lengthy time scale involved, Aquinas was convinced of the development of creation given what is narrated in Genesis

---

28. See Ernan McMullin, *Evolution and Creation* (Notre Dame, IN: Notre Dame University Press, 1986), Introduction, Section 8.

concerning it. St Thomas deals with these issues in his discussion of the work of the six days, what has come to be known in the history of such commentary as the Hexaemeron.

When it comes to the work of the six days Aquinas had at his disposal the writings of the Church Fathers, which divide into those who interpret the days as signifying temporal periods (he mentions Basil, Ambrose, Chrysostom in this regard), and those, represented primarily by Augustine, who see the days as an ordering of nature amongst things and not a literal temporal expanse.[29] On the Augustinian view, the developing creation described in scripture is interpreted in terms of the ordering of the natures of things and is not literally a temporal ordering; whereas Basil and the others view the development of things as occurring over a period of time. Aquinas himself shows favour for the Augustinian option but adopts an interpretation of the six days that can suitably be applied to both interpretations, holding that in this matter there can be legitimate disagreement amongst Christians.[30]

29. Speaking of the diverse opinions about the formation of material things, Aquinas writes, *Summa Theologiae*, Ia, qu. 66, art. 1: 'Augustinus enim vult quod informitas materiae corporalis non praecesserit tempore formationem ipsius, sed solum origine vel ordine naturae. Alii vero, ut Basilius, Ambrosius et Chrysostomus, volunt quod informitas materiae tempore praecesserit formationem.' See also qu. 68, art. 1, and qu. 74, art. 2. For a short but informative introduction to the Patristic literature on the work of the six days see Frank Egleston Robbins, *The Hexaemeral Literature: A Study of the Greek and Latin Commentaries on Genesis* (Chicago: University of Chicago Press, 1912). See also McMullin, 'Darwin and the Other Christian Tradition', *Zygon*, 46:2 (2011), 291–316, for an account of the atemporal interpretation of Genesis with particular focus on its compatibility with Darwinian evolution by natural selection.

30. See *In II Sent.*, dist. 12, qu. 1, art. 2: 'circa mundi principium aliquid est quod ad substantiam fidei pertinet, scilicet mundum incepisse creatum, et hoc omnes sancti concorditer dicunt. Quo autem modo et ordine factus sit, non pertinet ad fidem nisi per accidens, inquantum in Scriptura traditur, cujus veritatem diversa expositione sancti salvantes, diversa tradiderunt. Augustinus enim vult, in ipso creationis principio quasdam res per species suas distinctas fuisse in natura propria, ut elementa, corpora caelestia, et substantias spirituales; alia vero in rationibus seminalibus tantum, ut animalia, plantas, et homines, quae omnia postmodum in naturis propriis producta sunt in illo opere quo post senarium illorum dierum Deus naturam prius conditam administrat. . . . Ambrosius vero, et alii sancti ponunt

The hexaemeral literature typically divided the work of the six days into three: (i) the work of creation (*opus creationis*), (ii) the work of distinction (*opus distinctionis*), and (iii) the work of adornment (*opus ornatus*), and Aquinas does the same.[31] This discussion will follow this division.

2.1 Opus Creationis

Aquinas interprets Genesis as beginning with an announcement of creation: in the beginning God created the heaven and the earth. This creation is the act of God's conferring *esse* on things both spiritual and corporeal.[32] So the actual work of creation is the exercise of God's power in creating things. This work is in the beginning, and for Aquinas it is a truth of faith that part of the signification of this beginning is that there is a beginning of time. But Aquinas also sees the beginning as having several other senses serving the need to exclude various errors. Thus, the beginning can also signify that creatures have their beginning in God, in the Son, the Word through Whom all things are made, serving the need to remove the error of those who might think that along with

ordinem temporis in distinctione rerum servatum: et haec quidem positio est communior, et magis consona videtur litterae quantum ad superficiem; sed prior [the Augustinian view] est rationabilior, et magis ab irrisione infidelium sacram Scripturam defendens: quod valde observandum docet Augustinus super Genes. ad Litt., libro 1, cap. 19, ut sic Scripturae exponantur, quod ab infidelibus non irrideantur; et haec opinio plus mihi placet; tamen utramque sustinendo, ad omnia argumenta respondendum est.' For details of Aquinas's relation to Patristic and medieval thought in this respect see the commentary of William Wallace on qq. 65–74 of the *Summa Theologiae*, Prima Pars, in the Blackfriars edition of the *Summa*, Vol. 10, Appendices 7–8.

31. *Summa Theologiae*, Ia, qu. 65, Proem.: 'Post considerationem spiritualis creaturae, considerandum est de creatura corporali. In cuius productione tria opera Scriptura commemorat, scilicet opus creationis, cum dicitur, *in principio creavit Deus caelum et terram*, etc.; opus distinctionis, cum dicitur, *divisit lucem a tenebris, et aquas quae sunt supra firmamentum, ab aquis quae sunt sub firmamento*; et opus ornatus, cum dicitur, *fiant luminaria in firmamento* et cetera.'

32. *Summa Theologiae*, Ia, qu. 66, art. 4.

God there is a principle of evil that is also responsible for creation. The beginning can also signify that heaven and earth were created before all else, i.e. before any other causal agent, so that God's creation is of *all things* and not through the mediation of any spiritual creatures.[33]

Whilst the 'work' or the activity of creation is eternal and all creatures at whatever point in time they exist participate in that action, God nevertheless does make some things exist at the beginning of time (though of course He is not subject to such time), and these are those things which come to be not through generation from matter but through a direct act of creation. They are (i) the angelic nature, (ii) the empyrean heaven, (iii) unformed corporeal matter, and (iv) time itself.[34]

First, angels are immaterial and so must be directly created by God, since they cannot be generated from any preexisting matter. Hence, they are created in the beginning.

33. Ibid., art. 3: 'illud verbum Genes. I, *in principio creavit Deus caelum et terram*, tripliciter exponitur, ad excludendum tres errores. Quidam enim posuerunt mundum semper fuisse, et tempus non habere principium. Et ad hoc excludendum, exponitur, in principio, scilicet temporis. Quidam vero posuerunt duo esse creationis principia, unum bonorum, aliud malorum. Et ad hoc excludendum, exponitur, in principio, idest in filio. Sicut enim principium effectivum appropriatur patri, propter potentiam, ita principium exemplare appropriatur filio, propter sapientiam, ut sicut dicitur, omnia in sapientia fecisti, ita intelligatur Deum omnia fecisse in principio, idest in filio; secundum illud apostoli ad Coloss. I, in ipso, scilicet filio, condita sunt universa. Alii vero dixerunt corporalia esse creata a Deo mediantibus creaturis spiritualibus. Et ad hoc excludendum, exponitur, in principio creavit Deus caelum et terram, idest ante omnia.'

34. Ibid., art. 4: 'communiter dicitur quatuor esse primo creata, scilicet naturam angelicam, caelum Empyreum, materiam corporalem informem, et tempus.' See also qu. 46, art. 3. Aquinas notes that Augustine only lists the angelic nature and corporeal matter as being in the beginning. He harmonises this Augustinian view with the 'other saints' who add the empyrean heaven and time insofar as Augustine typically thinks of creation in terms of the division of an ordered hierarchy rather than ordered points of time. Hence for Augustine the angelic nature and corporeal matter are in the beginning, whilst time only proceeds from that, and presumably so does the empyrean heaven which ultimately contains all corporeal things. See also *Summa Theologiae*, Ia, qu. 66, art. 1.

Second, the empyrean heaven is the highest heaven, the farthest and most luminous reaches of material space, and so contains all that is within material space. It is created in the beginning as an anticipation of man's bodily glory that he will attain through the resurrection.[35] As creation develops more heavens are distinguished, but in the beginning at least there is the empyrean heaven.[36]

Third, unformed corporeal matter has a multiple signification. On the Augustinian view, whereby scripture is interpreted as signifying an ordering of nature, the unformed matter in the beginning is prime matter standing in potency to form. This is said to be prior to form not in time but insofar as it is the receptacle of form.[37] On the other hand for those saints who adopt a temporal interpretation of scripture, the unformed matter in the beginning signifies both the elements of the world (earth, air, fire, and water) and the matter of the heavenly bodies.[38] Whilst technically the elements (and the matter of the heavenly bodies) are formed in the beginning, their being unformed pertains to a certain lack of distinction and decoration which will come in later works.[39]

---

35. *Summa Theologiae*, Ia, qu. 66, art. 3.
36. In accord with the astronomical thought of his time, there are three heavens according to Aquinas: (i) the empyrean, which is wholly luminous, (ii) the aqueous or crystalline, which is wholly diaphaneous, and (iii) the heaven of the stars, which contains the eight spheres, the sphere of the fixed stars, and the seven planetary spheres. See *Summa Theologiae*, Ia, qu. 68, art. 4.
37. *Summa Theologiae*, Ia, qu. 66, art. 1: 'Augustinus enim accipit informitatem materiae pro carentia omnis formae. Et sic impossibile est dicere quod informitas materiae tempore praecesserit vel formationem ipsius, vel distinctionem. . . . [S]i informitas materiae referatur ad conditionem primae materiae, quae secundum se non habet aliquam formam, informitas materiae non praecessit formationem seu distinctionem ipsius tempore, ut Augustinus dicit, sed origine seu natura tantum, eo modo quo potentia est prior actu, et pars toto.'
38. Ibid., qu. 74, art. 2: 'Alii vero Sancti per terram et aquam primo creatas, intelligunt ipsa elementa mundi sub propriis formis existentia; per sequentia autem opera, aliquam distinctionem in corporibus prius existentibus.'
39. Ibid., qu. 66, art. 1: 'Alii vero sancti accipiunt informitatem, non secundum quod excludit omnem formam, sed secundum quod excludit istam formositatem et decorem qui nunc apparet in corporea creatura. Et secundum hoc dicunt quod informitas materiae corporalis duratione praecessit formationem eiusdem.'

It is prudent at this point to dwell on the matter of the elements and the heavenly bodies for a moment. The matter of each is quite distinct for Aquinas, since whilst both *qua* matter signify some potency, the matter of the heavenly bodies is fully actualized by the form of the body in question. Hence, such matter is in potency only to the substantial form of that heavenly body and exhibits no other potency except with respect to position in space. The elements on the other hand are the most basic kind of substances. As elemental substances, the elements are composed out of prime matter and substantial form, but there is nothing more basic than them. Once more complex mixed bodies come to be from the elements, the elements lose their form and integrate with the form of the new substance generated from them. Nevertheless, for Aquinas the elemental powers are not lost (mixed bodies are hot, cold, dry, wet, given the elemental powers which remain after their generation), and the elements themselves are retrievable with the decomposition of the substance. As opposed to heavenly bodies then, the elements are corruptible when composed to form a more complex substance, in which case the matter of such is not like that of the heavenly bodies, since it is in potency to more than one form.[40]

Now insofar as the heavenly bodies are not subject to any substantial form other than the one they have, they cannot be composed out of the elements; hence they cannot come to develop over time, in which case they cannot come at a later point of development in creation. The heavenly bodies then are ungenerated and so must be in the beginning. But scripture does not tell us that the heavenly bodies were created in the beginning; in fact they do not appear until the fourth day. So we have a problem: how is it that

---

40. See ibid., art. 2, for details on the difference in matter between that of the elements and that of the heavenly bodies. For Aquinas's thought on the elements as the most basic kinds of substance see *De Mixtione Elementorum* (Rome: Editori di San Tommasso, 1976), and for commentary see Joseph Bobik, *Aquinas on Matter and Form and the Elements: A Translation and Interpretation of the 'De Principiis Naturae' and the 'De Mixtione Elementorum' of St Thomas Aquinas* (Notre Dame, IN: University of Notre Dame Press, 1998), pp. 103–129.

the heavenly bodies, whilst ungenerated, appear only on the fourth day and not in the beginning with the elements?

Aquinas deals with this very objection from the outset of his consideration of the coming to be of the heavenly bodies. It is worth considering that objection in full: 'It would seem that the lights ought not to have been produced on the fourth day. For the heavenly luminaries are by nature incorruptible bodies: wherefore their matter cannot exist without their form. But as their matter was produced in the work of creation, before there was any day, so therefore were their forms. It follows, then, that the lights were not produced on the fourth day.'[41]

Aquinas responds in a threefold manner. First, on the Augustinian view there is no issue here, for Augustine envisages the work of the six days not as progressing over a period of time but as signifying a hierarchical ordering. Thus, unformed matter does not precede the formation of the heavenly bodies in time, in which case it did not exist by itself unformed (or under another form) only for the heavenly bodies to be formed from it on the fourth day. Second, for those who hold that the heavenly bodies are composed out of the nature of the four elements, such as followers of the Presocratics and Plato (cf. *Summa Theologiae*, Ia, qu. 68, art. 1), there is still no problem, since the heavenly bodies then would be formed out of some pre-existing formed matter. Third, for those who hold, like Aquinas, that the heavenly bodies are of a nature different from the elements but who, unlike Aquinas, do not favour the atemporal Augustinian view, it must be that the heavenly bodies are substantially created in the beginning (with the elements), but their power is determined on the fourth day. Aquinas notes some spiritual value in this in that it serves to preserve people from the worship of the heavenly bodies.[42]

Assuming that the second way is unavailable to Thomas since he rejected the idea that the heavenly bodies are of the same

41. *Summa Theologiae*, Ia, qu. 70, art. 1, obj. 1.
42. *Summa Theologiae*, Ia, qu. 70, art. 1, ad. 1.

nature as the elements, Aquinas can either hold with Augustine that there is no temporal preexistence of unformed matter to the heavenly bodies, the elements, or anything else, or he can go with the other saints holding that whilst there is temporal preexistence and whilst the elements are there from the beginning, the heavenly bodies are there too, at least substantially, but not with a determination of their power, which determination comes on the fourth day; either way the heavenly bodies are brought about by a direct act of creation. Hence it can be coherently held (i) that unformed matter is distinct from both the elements and the heavenly bodies, and (ii) that the heavenly bodies do not appear until the fourth day.

Fourth, then, time is also created in the beginning, and time is the measurement of the succession of changeable things, in which case it comes to be through the creation of such things. This applies both to the aveiternity of the angels and to the time proper of material things; hence time comes to be with God's creation in the beginning when changeable things are first created.

So these four are created in the beginning. Whilst they are there in the beginning, we should bear in mind that the act of creation covers all of time, beginning, middle, and end, insofar as anything that in any way exists participates in God's act of creation in order to exist. The Augustinian view of Genesis sits naturally with such an outlook, since it envisages the priority and posteriority in scripture as signifying a priority and posteriority of metaphysical components all of which simultaneously participate in the act of creation. Nevertheless, the temporal view of Basil and others can also sit with the Thomistic metaphysics of creation insofar as the four things which are created in the beginning and which play a role in the development of the universe over time also participate in God's act of creation. As I emphasized at the beginning, the history of creation falls under the aegis of the act of creation, so that whilst that act is eternal, creatures themselves are successive yet would not be unless present to the eternal act of creation from God.

Despite these four being created in the beginning, the created universe is not simply made up of these four. There are various developments that have occurred in the history of creation, and these pertain to the distinction and ornamentation of things. To these works I now turn.

2.2 *Opus Distinctionis*

Concerning the work of distinction, we can consider distinction in general and then distinction more particularly as it refers to the work of the six days. Generally speaking the distinction of things in the universe pertains to one thing's not being another thing, and in Aquinas's time there were various competing accounts of how this came to be, some of which I will allude to below.[43] Aquinas firmly holds that God is responsible for the distinctions that pertain to creatures, and this is because whatever exists exists because it has *esse* and so could not be unless caused to be by God.

To begin with, God creates voluntarily, that is to say that when God creates He does so by envisaging the various things He could create and freely undertaking to bring some of those into being. Creation is not a necessary emanation from God's being but is intelligently and voluntarily brought forth. This then entails that the distinctions that pertain to creatures are not a result of chance or blind necessity, but that God wills them.[44]

For Thomas the latter conclusion eliminates the views of the Presocratic philosophers, some of whom held there to be a single material principle diversified by condensation and rarefaction, or many material principles which are spontaneously formed in

---

43. In *Summa Contra Gentiles*, Lib. 2, Cap. 40–44, Thomas denies: (i) that matter is the principle of distinction, (ii) that there are many principles of distinction, (iii) that distinction follows the order of secondary agents that emanate from the first cause, (iv) that distinction is the result of secondary agents giving form to things, and (v) that distinction is the result of a hierarchical ordering of things based on merit and demerit. Cap. 45 provides a summary of these views.
44. Ibid., Cap. 39.

different ways; these views undermine any role for God's intelligent and free creation of things. Not only that, the conception of God as a voluntary agent bringing forth all creatures entails that matter cannot be the principle of the distinction of things, as if all distinct things were somehow primordially contained in matter and had to be drawn out into distinction by God. Rather, Thomas reasons that the divisions amongst the matters of things are for the sake of the distinct forms that God chooses to bring into existence and not somehow contained confusedly in matter itself. This outlook in turn ties in with Aquinas's general metaphysical view that the determined dimensions of matter are a result of its substantial form and they in turn individuate the form, a position I dealt with in the previous chapter. Thus is eliminated the view of Anaxagoras, who postulated an infinite multitude of material principles which were initially mixed and confused but separated by intellect.[45]

If God is responsible for the distinction of things, then things are distinguished not by chance but intelligently. This is so because as I outlined in Chapter 2, God does not act unless by will, and His will is informed by His intellect. Hence, when God brings about things in their distinctions He does so by means of His intelligence. Now, God's intelligence is His self-understanding, and in so understanding Himself God understands everything that could be understood—all the forms that being could take. Hence, in bringing about distinctions in things, God distinguishes things according to such forms. In other words, God's distinguishing of things is His granting of substantial forms to things. So there are humans, dogs, cats, and the like because God chose to create these things.

In spite of all this, when considering chance, Aquinas holds that what is by chance is what could have been otherwise and so involves possibility. Now, matter, not form, is the principle of possibility, because matter can be otherwise; it can take on another

45. Ibid., Cap. 40.

form. But if matter plays an essential role in individuation, then surely in accord with this reasoning, individuals must be by chance, since individuals are so on account of their matter. This would then imply that whilst the kinds (the forms) of things are not by chance but willed by God, the individuals of those kinds are by chance given that matter is the principle of individuation.[46]

Kretzmann seems to accept this conclusion. He holds that whilst nothing comes to be apart from God's intending it, understood in the sense that nothing comes to be which is contrary to or falls short of God's intention, it can be the case that things can come to be having been neither intended by God nor disappointing or contrary to His intention.[47] Thus, individuals can come to be by chance and apart from God's intention in the sense of not being contrary to His intention, but not in the sense of being against His intention. So presumably then individual things can come about in their material differentiation by chance without God's intending them.

I have a problem with Kretzmann's reading here, and my problem is as follows. On Aquinas's metaphysics of creation, God creates by granting *esse* to things. It is the concrete substance that God creates and that is the object of creation; all metaphysical components of the creature are cocreated with it. Thus, the individual creature is created in its entirety and participates in that act of creation for as long as it is. If Kretzmann is correct and individual things can come to be by chance not contrary to God's intention, then we have the case that such things are created but not intended by God, i.e. not directly willed by Him; rather they merely come

---

46. Ibid., Cap. 39: 'Cum casus sit tantum in possibilibus aliter se habere; principium autem huiusmodi possibilitatis est materia, non autem forma, quae magis determinat possibilitatem materiae ad unum; ea quorum distinctio est a forma, non distinguuntur casu: sed forte ea quorum distinctio est a materia. Specierum autem distinctio est a forma: singularium autem eiusdem speciei a materia. Distinctio igitur rerum secundum speciem non potest esse a casu: sed forte aliquorum individuorum casus potest esse distinctivus.'

47. Kretzmann, *The Metaphysics of Creation*, p. 209.

about by means of secondary causal processes occurring amongst material things. But if that is the case, where do they get their *esse*? No creature can be the cause of *esse* for another creature; only God can cause *esse*. Certainly, as secondary causes creatures can co-operate with God's causality in bringing forth other individuals, but they do not originate the *esse* of that individual; that is reserved for God alone. But on Kretzmann's reading individuals can come to be by chance and independent of God's intention, so it must be that individual creatures can get their *esse* from a source other than God, and this plainly contradicts Aquinas's view that only God can create. Thus, an alternative reading of the distinguishing of individuals is required.

It cannot be denied that God has knowledge of individuals or that God brings into existence all the individuals that do exist; for in dealing with God's knowledge it was shown that He has knowledge of individuals because they come within His power.[48] God's power extends over both what kinds of things there are and the individuals that there are, and this because God brings into being both the forms of things and their matter, by which things are individuals. So every individual that exists is brought into existence and determined in its being the individual that it is by God. From God's point of view, there is no chance involved, and everything that is so because God intends it to be.

Nevertheless we must grasp the nettle of the affirmation that chance pertains to matter, and Thomas's explicit affirmation that material things can come to be by chance.[49] This can be done if we delve deeper into Aquinas's account of chance.

---

48. *Summa Theologiae*, Ia, qu. 14, art. 11: 'cum Deus sit causa rerum per suam scientiam, ut dictum est, intantum se extendit scientia Dei, inquantum se extendit eius causalitas. Unde, cum virtus activa Dei se extendat non solum ad formas, a quibus accipitur ratio universalis, sed etiam usque ad materiam, ut infra ostendetur; necesse est quod scientia Dei usque ad singularia se extendat, quae per materiam individuantur.'
49. Cf. *Summa Contra Gentiles*, Lib. 2, Cap. 39.

In commenting on Aristotle, Aquinas points out that just as certain earlier philosophers wanted to reduce all fortuitous events to some ordaining cause called fortune, so too is it the case that all things are ordered by providence.[50] Aquinas sees fortuitous events as being reducible to some ordering cause, which is God in the exercise of His providence.

Fortune is a kind of cause, but it is not a per se cause; rather it is a *per accidens* cause. A per se cause is one that is such as to bring about its effect, e.g. the cause of the house is the house builder who has the art of building; whereas a *per accidens* cause is one accidentally related to the effect, e.g. if the builder were musical one could say the musician is the cause of the house, but the musician is only the cause of the house insofar as the same person who is a musician is also a builder. Thomas then adds the further refinement that sometimes a per se cause produces something and in doing so brings about some further effect outside the intention of the cause; in this case what is brought about is accidentally united to the effect and is brought about by the agent (though outside the agent's intention). For example, a gravedigger whilst digging a grave may discover treasure. The agent's intention was the digging of the grave, and it is of that of which he is the per se cause, whereas he is the *per accidens* hence fortuitous cause of the discovery of the treasure, which is outside his intention. It is in this sense that fortune is a *per accidens* cause.[51]

Chance is something more extended than fortune. Fortune happens in those things in which something is said to happen well,

---

50. *In II Phy.,* lect. 7, n. 206: 'Volebant enim quod omnes fortuiti eventus reducerentur in aliquam divinam causam ordinantem, sicut nos ponimus omnia ordinari per divinam providentiam.'

51. Ibid., lect. 8, n. 214: 'Et hoc modo dicitur fortuna esse causa per accidens, ex eo quod effectui aliquid coniungitur per accidens; utpote si fossurae sepulcri adiungatur per accidens inventio thesauri. Sicut enim effectus per se causae naturalis est quod consequitur secundum exigentiam suae formae, ita effectus causae agentis a proposito est illud quod accidit ex intentione agentis: unde quidquid provenit in effectu praeter intentionem, est per accidens.'

and so pertains to practical action. Thus, fortune pertains only to those who act voluntarily. On the other hand chance occurs in things which do not act voluntarily, e.g. brute animals, or do not act of themselves at all, e.g. inanimate things. So chance occurrences come to be, and of the things which come by chance those which pertain to voluntary agents are said to be fortuitous.[52]

What is clear is that both fortune and chance occur in situations where there is action for an end, and they happen to occur when something comes about that was not intended by that action. Thus, fortune and chance are embedded in causal contexts whereby there is a per se cause acting to bring about some effect, and they follow *per accidens* from that per se cause.[53] Fortune and chance are therefore derivative of per se causes and so cannot be unless from some already established causal order.[54]

When it comes to material things then, the coming to be of this or that individual may appear to be the result of chance; and this is because an individual's coming to be is the result of a number of variables that happen to be there at the right time so that individual may come to be. However, all of those variables by which the individual comes to be and which from a creaturely point of view are haphazard and seemingly occur by chance would not be unless caused to be so by God. Thus, the causality of chance causes, and hence of the coming to be of things by chance, is subject to God's primary causality in granting *esse* to things. If the distinction of individuals as a result of matter is taken to be by chance, this does not put such distinction beyond the causal power of God.[55] Rather, that very chance itself is ordered by God and so in relation

52. Ibid., lect. 10, n. 232.
53. Ibid., lect. 8, n. 215.
54. Ibid., lect. 10, n. 237: 'quia casus et fortuna sunt causae per accidens eorum quorum intellectus et natura sunt causae per se; causa autem per accidens non est prior ea quae est per se, sicut nihil per accidens est prius eo quod est per se; sequitur quod casus et fortuna sint causae posteriores quam intellectus et natura.'
55. *Summa Theologiae*, Ia, qu. 47, art. 1: 'ipsa materia a Deo creata est. Unde oportet et distinctionem, si qua est *ex parte* materiae, in altiorem causam reducere.'

to God it is not chance, and certainly not outside His intention.[56] All distinctions in creation then are the result of God's causality, both at the level of species and at the level of individuals.

None of what I have said here should bring about any fear of occasionalism. Secondary causes retain their actuality in this framework and hence their causality. Such things can exercise their actuality in the world in their own determinate ways, and different causal paths can cross and bring about effects that appear to be by chance. But such secondary causes would have no actuality unless they participated in the actuality of the primary cause. And they do so precisely insofar as secondary causes depend on God for their *esse* such that they can exercise no causal efficacy unless they have *esse*. Hence all secondary causality is dependent on primary causality, in which case an explanation of the causality of secondary causality would be incomplete without an appeal to the primary cause. This is why we cannot leave the distinction of individuals to chance, since such would be to exclude the influence of the primary cause. Nevertheless, the activity of secondary causes isn't *nothing but* the activity of the primary cause; since secondary causes have their own individual actuality derived from but not identified with that of the primary cause; the case is just that no secondary cause can be the cause of *esse* for anything.

What is clear is that for Thomas, given the primacy of God as creator of all things, the distinction, whether formal or material, of things does not escape His causal influence. That then means that nothing occurs by chance but all is within the power of God. The latter then is the context in which we must read the distinction of things in scripture.

In dealing with the work of distinction, Aquinas follows the tradition and divides the six days in half, with the first three

---

56. *In II Phy.*, lect. 10, n. 238: 'si ea quae fortuito vel casualiter accidunt, idest praeter intentionem causarum inferiorum, reducantur in aliquam causam superiorem ordinantem ipsa; in comparatione ad illam causam non possunt dici fortuita vel casualia: unde illa causa superior non potest dici fortuna.'

signifying the work of distinction and the next three signifying the work of adornment, which I will consider in the next section. Traditionally a correlation of these two halves is envisaged between the days, so that what is distinguished on the first day is adorned on the fourth (first day of adornment), what is distinguished on the second day is adorned on the fifth (second day of adornment), and what is distinguished on the third day is adorned on the sixth (third day of adornment). So on the first three days these are distinguished: (i) the heaven (day 1); (ii) the firmament (day 2), which separates the waters above (the clouds) and below (the seas); and (iii) the earth (day 3). On the next three days each of these is adorned with (i) stars (day 4), (ii) birds and fish (day 5), and (iii) animals on the earth (day 6).

Day	Distinction	Adornment
1	Heaven	Stars
2	Firmament	Birds and fish
3	Earth	Animals on the earth

This is a brief overview of Aquinas's framework for reading the work of the six days. He sees the six days as a self-contained whole expressing all of creation, both distinguished and adorned. Not only that, Thomas is fully aware of the divisions amongst the Church Fathers pertaining to the fine details of what is distinguished and when. When one reads Thomas's own commentary on the six days, it becomes apparent that his attitude is quite synthetic. Where there is division amongst the saints, he seeks to show that they have good reason for holding the positions that they do; he does not show any real urgency in establishing who has *the* correct interpretation. This is because, as I have noted, Aquinas holds that faithful Christians can adopt competing interpretations of scripture, so long as such interpretations are not out of line with its truth. The deeper lesson for the metaphysics of creation is as follows.

One can grant full well that the corporeal universe comes into existence as formed and thereby distinct in some way, and as time goes on this universe develops and brings forth more sophisticated degrees of formation, thereby furnishing the universe that was so created in the beginning. All this occurs through various secondary causes, but no such causes can act unless they receive their *esse* from God. Thus, nothing that occurs in the universe escapes the causal primacy of God's causing it to be, yet given the legitimacy of secondary causality, things within the universe can engage in their own causal processes. It would not be alien to this metaphysical picture then to hold that the cosmos has evolved from a certain initial state, nor, as I will show, that living things have evolved in some way. Aquinas's metaphysics of creation, principally as it pertains to the sort of causality involved in creating, allows for creatures to progress in their own ways without direct miraculous interference by God; yet precisely because such creatures have *to be* in order so to progress the component parts of such a process must participate in God's act of creation for their being. Thus, as science develops it can fill in more of the details of what goes on in the development of the cosmos and the evolution of species, but none of this speaks to the metaphysical picture of creation in which God is seen as creator because He grants *esse* to things. Indeed, all such scientific developments must presuppose God's creative activity; otherwise there would be nothing for the scientist to explain.

With that in mind, what Aquinas takes scripture to be telling us is that (on the temporal reading) in the beginning God created the corporeal universe and historically over time certain distinctions came to be therein: the (corporeal) heaven, the waters, the earth. As so created these parts of creation were not yet adorned; the heavenly bodies did not inhabit the heavens, birds and fish did not occupy the waters, and animals did not occupy the land. Thus, the corporeal universe brings forth these things, but such could not be brought forth were it not for God's granting actuality to the secondary causes which allow them to bring them forth. We are thus led to the work of adornment, but before proceeding, I will briefly consider the fact that scripture tells us that on the third day, the final day of distinction, plants were produced. Yet we typically think of plants as adorning the earth and hence a work of adornment rather than of distinction. Aquinas's response is interesting.

On the temporal reading this is quite straightforward since, as the reader may recall, on the temporal reading, matter's original lack of form does not signify that it was wholly without form but that it stood to be distinguished and provided with its proper decoration. Hence on the third day according to scripture the waters were distinguished from the earth, and its proper décor, i.e. plants, was produced. However, the Augustinian account is slightly different. Recall that Augustine holds an atemporal account, so that distinctions in creation pertain to an ordered hierarchy. Whereas the temporal authors envisaged the plants as being actually produced on the third day, i.e. as signifying some temporal period in the history of the earth, Augustine interprets it in an atemporal sense insofar as the earth is such that it has in itself the ability to bring forth plants. Hence the plants were produced only virtually, i.e. as latent within the causal powers of the earth itself, and not actually.[57] This is the Augustinian doctrine of seminal reasons: that various active potencies lie within things, the earth in this case, which with the appropriate secondary causal factors can bring forth something that is new yet precontained in the old. This view will be especially relevant for my purposes when I come to consider the appearance of new species on the earth. But in relation to the question at hand, whilst they appear to be part of the work of adornment plants are announced on the third day of distinction only virtually, i.e. as pertaining to the power of the earth, itself distinguished on the third day, which can bring them forth. And so it is not unfitting that scripture describes plants as appearing on the third day. Let us now consider the work of adornment.

---

57. *Summa Theologiae*, Ia, qu. 79, art. 2.

2.3 *Opus Ornatus*

Aquinas distinguishes adornment from distinction as follows. There is the work of creation proper, i.e. the bringing into being of the first four things, and scripturally speaking this pertains to the creation of heaven and earth. The heaven and earth that is brought into being must be completed in some way, whether through substantial form being composed with unformed matter (the Augustinian view) or through order being brought to what was not ordered (the more literal view of Ambrose, Basil, et al.). The work of distinguishing therefore pertains to the intrinsic distinctions of heaven and earth. The work of adornment pertains to what is extrinsic to heaven and earth yet moves within those parts which have been distinguished, hence (i) the heavenly bodies, (ii) the birds and fish, and (iii) the animals of the land.[58] When creation is so adorned it is brought to completion; and as is well known, with creation completed, God takes a rest on the seventh day.

As I have shown throughout, in creating, in distinguishing, and now in adorning, God plays a direct and active role. All things exist insofar as they participate in the *esse* given to them by God. All distinction comes about because of the free decisions of the creator to distinguish creatures in the way He chooses. But when it comes to adornment, it is possible for creation to bring forth its own furnishings. Scripture speaks of the various distinguished parts of creation bringing forth that with which it is furnished, and especially so with regard to living things. Hence, creation can bring forth the birds and the fish (fifth day) and the animals of the land (sixth day). The heavenly bodies however that appear on the fourth day are not brought forth by creation but as I have shown either are directly created by God, on the atemporal reading, or are created substantially in the beginning and their power determined on the fourth day, on the temporal reading.

---

58. Ibid., qu. 70, art. 1.

Aquinas holds that creation itself can give birth to living things because of the seminal reasons present in creation, that is, various active potencies within material reality itself by which new substances can come to be which are not actually present in the beginning.[59] Thus, material creation can bring forth various creatures. This bringing forth pertains to the interplay of secondary causality bringing to actuality the latent potentialities of creatures; but as I have shown in Chapter 4 all such secondary causality is inefficacious were it not for that of the primary cause. No secondary cause could act, could be, unless granted its causal efficacy, its *esse*, by God. Hence, whilst creation can bring forth its own furnishings, this does not banish God from any causal involvement in granting such things their *esse*.

Creation thus contains potentially all the things that come to furnish it, and so they were created in the beginning with creation. Despite all things being created in the beginning, they were not created in the beginning as they actually are now; rather all things preexist in the beginning in a number of ways, whether (i) materially, as Eve was made from the rib of Adam; (ii) causally, as things of the same species are generated from their descendants, or new species may arise from the old (something I will consider below); or (iii) by a certain likeness.[60] Hence creation can grow

---

59. Ibid., qu. 69, art. 2, qu. 71, qu. 73, art. 1, ad. 3, qu. 115, art. 2.
60. Ibid., qu. 73, art. 1, ad. 3: 'nihil postmodum a Deo factum est totaliter novum, quin aliqualiter in operibus sex dierum praecesserit. Quaedam enim praeextiterunt materialiter, sicut quod Deus de costa Adae formavit mulierem. Quaedam vero praeextiterunt in operibus sex dierum, non solum materialiter, sed etiam causaliter, sicut individua quae nunc generantur, praecesserunt in primis individuis suarum specierum. Species etiam novae, si quae apparent, praeextiterunt in quibusdam activis virtutibus, sicut et animalia ex putrefactione generata producuntur ex virtutibus stellarum et elementorum quas a principio acceperunt, etiam si novae species talium animalium producantur. Animalia etiam quaedam secundum novam speciem aliquando oriuntur ex commixtione animalium diversorum secundum speciem, sicut cum ex asino et equa generatur mulus, et haec etiam praecesserunt causaliter in operibus sex dierum. Quaedam vero praecesserunt secundum similitudinem; sicut animae quae nunc creantur.'

and develop, furnishing itself with new individuals and even new species which are not actually but only potentially contained in creation in the beginning.

So what we have is a difference between the initial state of the universe and its developed state at whatever particular point in time. The universe's developed state may not actually resemble how the universe was in the beginning, but that state is not anything added on to creation in the beginning; it is rather the unfurling of potentialities lying primordially within matter and duly brought to actuality by secondary causes. Thus, God's direct intervention is not required for creation to evolve and grow and for new features to occur. Nevertheless, without God's primary causality in granting existence to things, such new creatures would not come to be out of the latent potentialities of matter.

All of this then can provide the Thomist with a rather nuanced view when it comes to the evolution of the species. Thomas of course was not aware of Darwin's work or of evolution by natural selection. Thomas was however aware that creation as it is now does not look the way it did in the beginning, if for no other reason than that this is what scripture presents as the history of creation; and as I have shown he builds into his metaphysics, indeed into his reading of scripture, the possibility of new species arising from the old. So he is not committed to a crude fixity of species whereby all species were created once and for all.

For Aquinas a thing is a member of a species owing to its possession of a substantial form uniting it with other members of the species possessing the same form. Form gives structure to prime matter and determines the substance as a substance of that kind. Hence whilst form is a principle of act, it is not a separately existing Platonic form but is something united with the material thing in question. Individuals exist as formed, and individuals can undergo change; in the most extreme circumstances one individual can change substantially into another, and this because the thing's matter can come to take on a new substantial form. Hence, matter is not resistant to some other substantial form.

Given the potentiality of matter, individuals can display various accidents that their generators did not display, and on the basis of various powers that they have they can integrate with and adapt to an environment into which their ancestors did not have to integrate or adapt. For example, parental gametes may exhibit some mutation which is in turn passed on to offspring, which in turn equips offspring to survive in an environment such that over time only offspring that have that mutation come to dominate the environment. Hence, over time and with environmental pressures characteristics that were previously only accidents of the parents become reinforced so that offspring cannot survive in the environment without them, in which case the being of such substances is characterized by such properties. That something can survive in a particular environment where previously its ancestors could not because of certain properties that it has points to the fact that such a thing is of a different kind from its ancestors, a kind which gives rise to those new properties that its ancestors did not possess. Hence, it can be said that such a thing has a substantial form different from that of its ancestors, even though the thing in question is derived from those substantially different ancestors.

I should however stress that such new properties displayed by the thing are not identical with a new substantial form; for something of one form could display such properties merely as separable accidents brought about by mutation, whereas things of a new form display them as proper accidents emerging from their essence, formally constituted by a new substantial form. The detective work of discerning which thing displays such properties merely as separable accidents because of some mutation and which thing possesses them as proper accidents derived from a new form is tricky and often vague; but such vagueness does not undermine the ontological fact that things of one form which wouldn't display various accidental characteristics without some mutation are formally distinct from other things which display such characteristics because they are essentially distinct from their ancestors. In any case, whilst substantial forms cannot themselves change, for example what it is to be human can be nothing other than rational animality, individuals of that form can change (and indeed in the case of extinct species die out), so that over time new substantial forms emerge from species.[61]

Whilst Darwin himself may have had reservations about species kinds (preferring instead to focus on populations and common descent), and whilst many scientists and philosophers today reject biological essentialism,[62] the Thomist view of the metaphysical constitution of substances as being (partially) out of matter and form does not exclude evolution by natural selection, because in that view the potentiality of matter allows for change in accidents which over time can become so embedded that new species begin to emerge.[63] Many of the scientific objections to species are opposed not so much to their explanatory power as to their messiness. When working in the field of biology it is difficult to distinguish one species from another, but this is more of an epistemic than a metaphysical difficulty. Unless a biologist is antecedently convinced that substances are not formed, the biologist must recognize that in certain cases, despite our inability to distinguish in any nonarbitrary way between one species and another, there is a fact of the matter that one is formed in one way and another in another; there are no vague forms, only vague knowledge of form.

61. David Oderberg, *Real Essentialism* (New York: Routledge, 2008), p. 205: 'The essentialist does not need to be a Platonist to hold that species do not turn into distinct species in any sense beyond the causation of individuals of one species to come into existence by individuals belonging to a different species. Any other sense attached to the notion of species change is barely intelligible, as much as when applied to the idea that triangularity could somehow change into sphericity. Neither the essentialist nor the evolutionist has such an idea of species change as part of his picture of what happens in biology or anywhere else.'
62. See ibid., p. 201.
63. For a more general account of the feasibility of an Aristotelian outlook in the context of Darwinian evolution see Étienne Gilson, *D'Aristote à Darwin et retour: Essai sur quelques constantes de la bio-philosophie* (Paris: Librairie Philosophique Vrin, 1971), and Fran O'Rourke, 'Aristotle and the Metaphysics of Evolution', *Review of Metaphysics*, 58:1 (2004), 3–59.

Metaphysical species and hence form can thus be retained whilst granting a certain amount of intellectual parsimony with regard to the recognition of species and a certain pragmatism in their classification.

So understood, Aquinas's metaphysics of matter and form can accommodate the theory of evolution by natural selection. Moreover, and fundamentally, insofar as the metaphysical components of matter and form only exist through participation in the *esse* of the substance whose components they are, which *esse* is granted to them by God, whatever process of gradual development and change occurs in things ultimately depends on the causal activity of the primary cause, which is God's creating of things. This creation is the granting of *esse* to all things from eternity; but the things so created can have their own temporal geography and experience a distinction between their coming to be and their remaining in being. Hence whilst there is a flow and development of beings, whether individually or at the level of species, all such occurs under the causality of the primary cause.[64]

If the Thomist reading of creation can sit nicely with an account of the universe by which it can bring forth its own life and allow

---

64. Other Christian philosophical approaches to evolution are indeed forthcoming, for instance Alvin Plantinga grants the compatibility of evolution with scriptural claims; however, he recommends caution in accepting evolution *tout court* as if it were scientific fact; rather, he suggests that we only accept that for which we have sufficient warrant to accept, and he claims that unless one presupposes naturalism we do not have any greater warrant to accept certain aspects of the theory of evolution than we do for accepting a more literal scriptural position; see 'When Faith and Reason Clash: Evolution and the Bible', in *Intelligent Design Creationism and Its Critics: Philosophical, Theological, and Scientific*, ed. by Robert T. Pennock (Cambridge, MA: MIT Press, 2001), pp. 113–145. Given Aquinas's endeavours to do justice both to the Augustinian atemporal reading of Genesis and to the more literal temporal reading of Basil et al., I do not believe that the Thomist approach is to take direct contradictions between scripture and science and weigh them so as to see which has the greater warrant and side with one accordingly; rather it is to subsume the truth present in both contexts within a philosophy of being which itself is then subsumed within a theology that tells us about God's purposes in creating the universe. I thus submit that Plantinga's approach is not one which would appeal to a convinced Thomist.

life to evolve, it does not sit so easily with the view that human life evolved. This is because of the special nature of the human being amongst living things.

A living material thing for Aquinas is an ensouled thing, such that without a soul no physical thing could be alive. The soul then is the primary principle of life for those things that are alive, that by which a living thing is alive.[65] Now, the soul, the principle of life, does not belong to any bodily thing *qua* bodily, since all bodily things can be without life, in which case life is not essential to such things. A bodily thing is alive not because it is a body but because of the type of body that it is, and that is determined by its form. Given then that (i) the soul is the primary principle of life of a living thing, and (ii) a body is living because of its form, the soul is the form of the body and is united to it as its form and is thereby present throughout the body.[66]

With regard to man then, the human soul is the form of the human body, i.e. that by which the human body enjoys life. But the type of life that is essentially human is the rational or intellectual life, in which case the type of soul possessed by the human is a rational or intellectual soul.[67] The soul then is the principle of the intellectual operation in man. This operation is nonbodily and does not depend on any bodily organ; for man can know the natures of all bodily things through the use of his intellect, but what can know everything in a given range cannot itself be one of the things in that range, since if it were it would not stand in potency to knowing all such things. Thus, man's intellectual operation is not one of the

---

65. *Summa Theologiae*, Ia, qu. 75, art. 1: 'Anima dicitur esse primum principium vitae in his quae apud nos vivunt'; *Sentencia libri De Anima* (Rome: Commissio Leonina, 1984), Lib. 2, lect. 1, p. 70: 207–208: 'Per animam enim intelligimus id quo habens uitam uiuit.'

66. For a general introduction to Aquinas's account of ensoulment see Brian Davies, *The Thought of Thomas Aquinas* (Oxford: Clarendon Press, 1992), Chapter 11.

67. *Summa Theologiae*, Ia, qu. 76, art. 1: 'Hoc ergo principium quo primo intelligimus, sive dicatur intellectus, sive anima intellectiva, est forma corporis'; see also *In II De Anima*, lect. 1, p. 70: 216–223, *Quaestione Disputata De Anima*, art. 1.

bodily things to which it stands in potency to know.[68] Not only that; Thomas argues that it is not even through a bodily organ that man's intellectual operation is exercised since the determinate matter of that organ would impede the intellectual operation, just as if the eye's ability to see were exercised through some coloured medium, the eye would not be able to see all colours. So, given that man's intellectual operation does not have a bodily nature nor does it depend on a bodily organ, it follows that the principle of such an operation, the soul, has an operation of its own independent of the body. This then entails that man's soul is subsistent; for whatever has an operation of its own independent of other things subsists. Man's soul then is a subsistent form not dependent on the body.[69] This account of the soul then has implications for its creation.

Aquinas denies that human life (the human soul) originates in matter; for as a subsistent form of the human body, the human soul is not a result of some organization (or reorganization in the case of evolution) of matter but is an immaterial principle itself responsible for the organization of the human substance. Accordingly, given its immaterial nature the rational soul cannot be educed from principles innate to matter but requires a direct act of creation by God.[70]

68. *Summa Theologiae*, qu. 75, art. 2; see also *In III De Anima*, lect. 1, p. 203: 131–142: 'Omne autem quod est in potencia ad aliquid et receptiuum eius caret eo ad quod est in potencia et cuius est receptiuus . . . ; set intellectus noster sic intelligit intelligibilia quod est in potencia ad ea et susceptiuus eorum sicut sensus sensibilium; ergo caret omnibus illis rebus que natus est intelligere; cum igitur intellectus noster sit natus intelligere omnes res sensibiles et corporeas, oportet quod careat omni natura corporali.'

69. *Summa Theologiae*, Ia, qu. 75, art. 2.

70. *Summa Theologiae*, Ia, qu. 90, art. 2. It is indeed the case that in embryogenesis Aquinas advocates a successiveness of souls from the vegetative to the sensitive and finally to the rational, which latter requires a direct act of creation by God. This is because of Aquinas's understanding of embryology and his belief that biologically speaking the human substance was formed successively rather than from the moment of conception. Nevertheless, when it comes to the rational soul, this calls for direct infusion by God, at whatever point one takes there to be a rational soul (and hence a rational substance) present. For details of this in Aquinas's thought and that of his predecessors, see J. M. Da Cruz Pontes, 'Le problème de l'origine de l'âme de

Having said that, it should not be envisaged that God has at His disposal a set of human souls which He infuses into the individuals that come to be. The human soul is united to the body as its form, and in creating a human being the matter and form of the creature are cocreated. Thus, every creature as participating in its own act of existence is created whole, and its principles (its matter and form) are cocreated with it. Hence, the coming to be of the human body coincides with the direct creation of the rational soul so that at once the human creature is created; human souls do not actually preexist the creation of the human being.[71]

What then does this entail for the consistency of Aquinas's creationism with later evolutionary biology? Aquinas is clear that man's body comes from the earth and is made up of material principles just like any other body.[72] But Aquinas denies that the form of that body is earthly and derived from the reorganization of matter. This denial runs up against evolutionary accounts of human life since on those accounts the form of the human body is something evolved. Human life is not something inexplicable in the context of a biological explanation of life on the evolutionary account.

Nevertheless, we must be careful in suggesting that there is an inconsistency here. Aquinas is not making a biological claim, nor are strict evolutionary biologists (we hope) making metaphysical claims. He is not giving an account of how life has come to be (and they are not telling us the metaphysical principles without which a thing would not be); rather, he is explaining the metaphysical principles that need to be in place for that life to come to be (and they

---

la patristique à la solution Thomiste', *Recherches de Théologie ancienne et médiévale*, 31 (1964), 175–229. For details of Aquinas's thought on the successive biological formation of human life and in particular its application to contemporary debates on abortion, see John Haldane and Patrick Lee, 'Aquinas on Human Ensoulment, Abortion, and the Value of Life', *Philosophy*, 78:304 (2003), 255–278; note in particular the extensive secondary literature on this subject detailed on p. 259, n. 5; see also Haldane and Lee, 'Rational Souls and the Beginning of Life (A Reply to Robert Pasnau)', *Philosophy*, 78:306 (2003), 532–540.

71. *Summa Theologiae*, Ia, qu. 90, art. 4.
72. *Summa Theologiae*, Ia, qu. 91, art. 1.

are telling us how that life came to be through descent). The biologist can tell us all about the history of life, and this may provide an inkling as to what life is; but it is the metaphysician who gives an explanation as to what life is and what there needs to be in order for there to be life, i.e. ensoulment. The biologist works with the metaphysics already in place, presupposed, and thence proceeds to work accordingly.

On the Thomist account, in order to have living things, those things need a special form which distinguishes them as the kind of things they are from nonliving things; thus the need for a soul. The biologist has no need for explanations in terms of soul because ensoulment, hence life, is presupposed before the work of offering a history of life is undertaken; anything further takes the biologist out of biology and into philosophy. Thus the biologist, often unconsciously, presupposes what the metaphysician articulates. The determination of whether or not the soul is directly infused in the creature from its moment of conception or whether the soul evolved from matter is not something that the biologist can establish, because from the viewpoint of biology the materials remain the same in any case. But at the level of metaphysical explanation things are different, requiring recourse to what it is to be alive and the principles by which a living thing is such. The Thomist account is not inconsistent with the evolutionary account precisely because they are not offering competing explanations of the same thing. The biology still looks the same when the human soul is directly created by God as it would look if the human soul had evolved from matter. Given that the biologist qua biologist cannot detect differences that pertain to metaphysical explanation, the biological explanation cannot be taken to be normative for the metaphysics in this case.

Now given that according to Thomas God exercises primary causality over all creation whilst not excluding secondary causality, creation can bring forth its own furnishings. However, in the case of human life, such cannot simply be brought forth by powers latent within creation; rather God must actively intervene and produce that life through the infusion of the human soul in the body. This then entails that the creation of human beings is not a creative run-of-the-mill affair following the order of other creatures but a special undertaking by God. And this entails that humans are created specially by God. Given that they are and that all creative activity by God is an expression of His goodness, the creation of humans is a particularly special expression of the divine goodness. It follows from all this then that humans have a special end for which God has created them. And so it is now time to draw this study to a close with a final chapter on the end of creation and the end of man in particular.

7

THE END OF CREATION

IN THIS FINAL CHAPTER I WILL deal with the end of creation. Throughout this study I have emphasised that according to Aquinas God is creator insofar as all things participate in the existence He bestows on them. This creative causality is often parsed in terms of God's being the primary efficient cause of things, and indeed this is how God was envisaged in Chapter 4. Yet, having explored God's primary causality in respect of the object of creation (Chapter 5) and the history of creation (Chapter 6), I have articulated how such causality not only originates but also preserves creatures in existence. Now, to preserve something in the causality that one grants to it is to exercise one's causality with respect to some end, and so it is the case with God's primary causality in creation—He originates and preserves creatures in their being with respect to some end. Hence, there is finality to God's causality, and I now come to consider such finality.

Accordingly, in this chapter I will explain how the ordered efficient causality which accounts for the origination of *esse* outlined in Chapter 4 can be integrated with final causality, which will allow for God's not only originating but also guiding creation to its end. The picture of God then which emerges is that of both primary and final cause. As primary cause God is that without which nothing would be, i.e. the origin and source of all existence; as final cause God is the good for the sake of which all things are. The goal or purpose of creation is thus to manifest the divine goodness, and this ties in with what I outlined in Chapter 2 to the effect that God cannot but exercise His will for the good, and so His choice to create is a manifestation of His goodness.

This chapter focuses on the end or goal of creation as an expression of God's goodness, and in particular man's final end. Accordingly, the chapter is divided as follows. First (Section 1), I will consider the integration of God's primary causality with His final causality in the creative act; this will require enlarging on my discussion of ordered series in Chapter 4 so as to include final causality. Second, and following on from that (Section 2), I will consider the end of creation as a whole. Third (Section 3), I will consider the end of man as the apex of creation and ultimately his beatitude as the completion of creation. And with that I will conclude this study of Aquinas's metaphysics of creation.

1 PER SE FINAL CAUSAL SERIES

When I considered ordered causality in Chapter 4 I did so primarily with respect to efficient causality, taking as my example for analysis the mind's moving the hand to move the stick to move the stone.[1] Having analysed that example and offered an account of the metaphysics involved therein, I considered God's causality as being the primary cause in a per se ordered series whose causal property is *esse*. Now I shall integrate all of that in the context of the end or purpose of creation, so that the objects which are created and which have a history will be interpreted in the context of God's purposes in creating them.

Now, causality is preserved in per se series insofar as the primary cause (the mind) undertakes to bring about some end (moving the stone) and in doing so makes use of instruments (the hand and the stick) for the attainment of that end. Hence the mind moves the hand *in order* to move the stick *in order* to move the stone. The primary cause engages in causality so as to produce

---

1. The material here and in subsequent sections on per se final causal series originally appeared in my article 'Essentially Ordered Series Reconsidered Once Again', *American Catholic Philosophical Quarterly*, 91:2 (2017), 155–174.

the end, in which case causality is present in the series right up until the production of the end. The latter then entails that the unity and preservation of causality in a per se series requires some appeal to finality, i.e. that for the sake of which a cause acts. So I now consider per se causal series with respect to final causality and whether or not, as in the case efficient causal series, there is a primary cause, which in this case would be an ultimate final cause of the series.

1.1 Final Causal Series

Thomas's notion of final causality is derived from advertence to the goal-directed activity or finality (or teleology) of things. This goal-directed activity is parsed in terms of the 'in order to' or 'that for the sake of which' (*cuius causa fit*), where that for the sake of which something acts is its end.[2] Given that the end is that for the sake of which a thing acts, Aquinas thinks of the end in causal terms; for without the end the thing would not act. So, in the case of finality, given that the end is that for the sake of which the thing acts, it is the end that actualizes the causality of the thing acting towards that end, in which case the end is a final cause of the thing acting.

Now the thing acting for the end is the efficient cause, the principle of motion. But the very motion of the efficient cause, its causality, is for some end such that the end is the terminus of the motion induced by the efficient cause. In other words, the end is that for which the efficient cause induces motion; hence the causality of the efficient cause is for the sake of that end. There is thus a correspondence between the efficient cause and its end,

---

2. *In II Phy.*, lect. 4, n. 173: 'De ratione finis est quod sit cuius causa fit'; *In I Met.*, lect. 4, n. 70: 'Nam motus incipit a causa efficiente, et terminatur ad causam finalem. Et hoc est etiam cuius causa fit aliquid, et quae est bonum uniuscuiusque naturae'; *In III Met.*, lect. 4, n. 374: 'Finis autem, et cuius causa fit aliquid, videtur esse terminus alicuius actus'; *In V Met.*, lect. 18, n. 1039: 'Sed finis non solum habet quod sit ultimum, sed etiam quod sit cuius causa fit aliquid.'

such that the one is the principle of motion and the other its termination.[3]

Given that for Thomas causality is analysed in terms of act and potency, and that the final cause slots in here as that which exercises the causality of the efficient cause such that the efficient cause would be causally inefficacious without it, it follows that whilst the end towards which the efficient cause acts may be independent of it, the causality of that end, i.e. its final causality, is not extrinsic to the efficient cause but is present to it, thus actualizing its efficiency. Final causality is thus immanent in things, whilst the end to which those things aim on the basis of that causality may be extrinsic to things. We can appreciate this further when we consider final causality in respect of its conscious and unconscious manifestations.

Consciously I may decide to devote the rest of my life to, among other things, making a daily attempt to come to an understanding of the thought of St Thomas Aquinas by reading his works, the works of his commentators, and the authoritative journals, by engaging in debate in Thomism discussion groups, etc. My goal here is to understand the thought of St Thomas because for some reason I think that would be a good thing to achieve; I thus take steps to attain that goal, and those steps are themselves many smaller goals which will hopefully (someday, if ever) bring me to the overall goal of understanding St Thomas. What occurs here is that some end or goal is grasped by me as good and is presented to my will as desirable. I thereby will that goal and hence undertake measures to achieve it. In doing so I act as the efficient cause, the first source of motion that will get me to that goal, but I cannot do so unless I have grasped the goal and formed the intention to achieve it. The end is independent of me, but the causality that the end exercises is not; the final causality of the end operates by motivating me, in the form of desire for the end, to take measures to achieve it.[4]

---

3. *In V Met.*, lect. 2, n. 775: 'Efficiens et finis sibi correspondent invicem, quia efficiens est princpum motus, finis autem terminus.'

4. For Aquinas's thought on intentional action, see *Summa Theologiae*, IaIIae, qu. 12; for a summary see Eleonore Stump, *Aquinas* (London: Routledge, 2003), pp. 277–284.

On the other hand a flame is such that it generates heat, so that the end of the flame is the generation of heat. The flame as an efficient cause is the principle by which heat is generated, but the flame would not be a cause unless it caused something—heat. The end (heat) and the efficient cause (the flame) are not independent in this case; nevertheless, the causing of heat is the goal of the flame, and the flame exists in order to cause it; for that is what a flame does. In this case, the final causality which motivates the efficient cause is not some conscious intention formed to attain an end—the flame is unconscious— nevertheless, the flame has a natural inclination to produce the end which is in accord with its nature as a flame. Hence in unconscious things incapable of forming intentions, finality is operative in the form of natural dispositions that a thing has in virtue of what it is.[5]

In both cases, conscious and unconscious, the end is the cause of the causality of the efficient cause.[6] Now I will probe this a little deeper.

In the conscious example, I ascertain some ultimate goal, and in order to achieve it I take various steps that will get me to it. These intermediate steps are themselves ends, but they are ends for the sake of some further end; they are not intended for their own sake but for the sake of the ultimate goal I desire. Thus, I do

---

5. *Summa Theologiae*, IaIIae, qu. 1, art. 1: 'Agens autem non movet nisi ex intentione finis: si enim agens non esset determinatum ad aliquem effectum, non magis ageret hoc quam illud. Ad hoc ergo quod determinatum effectum producat, necesse est quod determinetur ad aliquid certum, quod habet rationem finis. Haec autem determinatio sicut in rationali natura per rationalem fit appetitum, qui dicitur voluntas; ita in aliis fit per inclinationem naturalem, quae dicitur appetitus naturalis'; *Summa Contra Gentiles*, Lib. 4, Cap. 19: 'Res naturalis per formam qua perficitur in sua specie, habet inclinationem in proprias operationes et proprium finem, quem per operationes consequitur; quale est enim unumquodque, talia operatur et in sibi convenientia tendit.'

6. *In V Met.*, lect. 2, n. 775: 'Efficiens est causa finis quantum ad esse quidem, quia movendo perducit efficiens ad hoc, quod sit finis. Finis autem est causa efficientis non quantum ad esse, sed quantum ad rationem causalitatis. Nam efficiens est causa inquantum agit: non agit nisi causa finis. Unde ex fine habet suam causalitatem efficiens'; *De Principiis Naturae*, Cap. 4, p. 43: 16–19: 'Efficiens enim dicitur causa respectu finis, cum finis non sit in actu nisi per operationem agentis: sed finis dicitur causa efficientis, cum non operetur nisi per intentionem finis.'

not read the works of Aquinas just for the sake of reading but for the sake of coming to understand his thought. One can distinguish then between ultimate ends and intermediate or subordinate ends, insofar as the former are willed for their own sake and the latter for the sake of something else.[7]

Of course, it is an open question at this point as to whether or not there is a single ultimate end for all things. Given that Aquinas analyses causality in terms of act and potency, the end can be the principle of the activity of the efficient cause in one respect, but it itself can be subject (and hence in potency) to the activity of some other end in another respect. Hence, the end of mastering the thought of Aquinas, willed by me for its own sake above, can be for the sake of a further end, say that of confuting heretics. On the other hand what was the subordinate end of reading the works of Aquinas, willed so as to understand his thought, can also be willed for no further end than simply the joy of reading the words of the Angelic Doctor. In conscious situations, it is that for the sake of which the agent intends the act which is the act's ultimate end, yet that does not rule out the agent's also intending the various steps as genuine, albeit intermediate, ends by which that end is achieved; in other situations one of those intermediate ends may be willed as the ultimate end of some action.

Turning to unconscious situations, we can observe too that there are ultimate ends and subordinate ends. Take the example of the flame, whose end is the production of heat. In this situation, in order to produce heat, various physical processes must occur, and these are necessary for the production of heat. Should these processes not occur, heat would not be produced. Thus, as with conscious situations, various stages must be passed through

---

7. *Summa Theologiae*, IaIIae, qu. 12, art. 2: 'In motu autem potest accipi terminus dupliciter. Uno modo ipse terminus ultimus, in quo quiescitur, qui est terminus totius motus. Alio modo aliquod medium, quod est principium unius partis motus, et finis vel terminus alterius; sicut in motu quo itur de A in C per B, C est terminus ultimus, B autem terminus, sed non ultimus: et utriusque potest esse intentio.'

in order for a thing to reach its natural end. The difference is that ultimate ends and subordinate ends are much stricter in unconscious than in conscious situations. This is because in conscious situations the ultimate end is that for which the agent intends the action, and that entails that what was merely a subordinate end in one case could be willed as an ultimate end in another. But in the unconscious situation, this cannot be the case, for those stages which were necessary for the attainment of the thing's end, say the production of heat, can hardly obtain as ends in themselves without the production of that end, i.e. heat.

The reason for the necessity in the unconscious situation but not in the conscious one lies in the fact that in the unconscious situation things act for their ends owing to the natural dispositions that they have; these dispositions will only change when the thing itself changes, thereby acquiring new dispositions and hence a different end. On the other hand in conscious situations ends are not determined by natural dispositions but by the will of the agent and can thus change without the agent himself essentially changing.

Given these considerations of the metaphysics of final causality, consider now how such causality can fit into my framework of per se causal series.

1.2 Per Se Final Causal Series

There is a necessary connection between an efficient cause and its end, since the end of an efficient cause is what it produces, so if the efficient cause were not so connected to its end, i.e. if it did not bring about the end, it would fail precisely as an efficient cause. Efficient causes are thus necessarily ordered to their ends; the final cause cannot be divorced from the efficient cause without removing its causality. In that case, the causality of the efficient cause is necessarily caused by the final cause, since without the final cause the efficient cause would not act for the production of some effect and hence would be without its causality.

Now in considering causal series, we distinguish between per se and *per accidens* series insofar as in per se series the effects do not have the causal efficacy of the series in themselves but depend on another for such efficacy. Thus, in the mind-hand-stick-stone example, the hand, stick, and stone do not possess motion of themselves but depend on something other than themselves for their causality—the mind in this case. This distinguishes per se series from *per accidens* series insofar as in *per accidens* series each causal member can possess the appropriate causal efficacy of itself. So in the fathers-sons series, each member of the series is capable of being a father given what it is, i.e. a man, and this is in stark contrast to the mind-hand-stick-stone series, since in the latter only the mind has in itself causal efficacy, whereas in the rest causal efficacy is derived and participated in through the primary cause.

I have pointed out that there is a necessary connection between efficient and final causes such that the final cause is the cause of the causality of the efficient cause; the efficient cause is without its causality were it not for the final cause bringing it into operation. It follows then that efficient causes are per se ordered to final causes; for efficient causes are without their causality were it not for the final cause. Any causal series then wherein final causality is operative is a per se causal series with respect to the finality that is operative therein. The finality of that series is not possessed intrinsically by any member of the series but is ordered to the end of the series, which end motivates the causality of the primary cause. In other words, no causal series in which finality is operative is a *per accidens* series. Hence in the fathers-sons series, finality is not operative in the causal relationship between fathers and sons. This is not to say that finality does not operate per se in reproductive acts but that the *per accidens* series, considered precisely as a chain of fathers producing sons, does not exhibit finality; in order for it to do so it would have to be integrated into a per se series wherein the production of a son (or the biological finality that obtains amongst the sexual organs involved in reproduction) is for the sake of some further end, such as to have a family in order to contribute to society for the greater glory of God etc.; and the latter causal series is quite distinct from that of a chain of fathers producing sons.

Given all of this, I will return to the paradigm example of the per se series and assess the finality thereof: the mind moves the hand to move the stick to move the stone. Finality is evidently operative in this series such that the minded agent moves the hand *in order to* move the stick *in order to* move the stone. It is for some goal that the agent moves the hand/stick/stone. If finality is operative in the series, there has to be some final cause which motivates the finality of the series. But in the above discussion of finality and final causality, it was the action of conscious agents or unconscious substances that exhibited finality and acted towards an end. Here the discussion is about the finality of a per se causal series, something made up of distinct yet connected causal relata; has the discussion switched from the finality of a single entity, conscious or unconscious, to that of a number of entities, and if so is that switch acceptable?

To address these questions, we must consider where in fact the finality in the series lies. The mind moves the hand to move the stick to move the stone. The mind induces causality to the series, and the posterior causal relata would not have their causality unless they participated in that of the mind; their causality is secondary to the mind's. Now it is the mind (or the mindful agent) that is motivated to move the hand to move the stick to move the stone, that is to say, the agent grasps some end he wishes to attain and acts accordingly. (The same series can be erected for an unconscious cause which acts towards an end out of natural disposition.) Hence it is the mind's efficient causality that is brought into operation by the final cause. Just as the mind's efficient causality is participated in by the posterior or secondary causes in the series, so too is the finality with which the primary cause (the mind) acts towards the end. But just as the mind's efficient causality is not possessed essentially by any of the posterior causes, neither is the finality ordered towards the end possessed essentially by any of the members.

So here I am saying not that the series has a final cause but that the primary cause of the series has a final cause, and just as the posterior causes of per se series participate in the causality of the primary cause, so too do they participate in the finality of the primary cause's acting towards its end. Hence, the discussion has not shifted away from single substances acting for an end, in which case the legitimacy of such a shift is not an issue.

To modify the causal series to the case of Dr Smith at the golf course:[8] Dr Smith can go to the golf course to knock balls about, and the knocking of balls about can fit the model of the mind-hand-stick-stone series. So Dr Smith (w) moves his hands (x) to move the club (y) to move the ball (z), hence:

$$w \rightarrow (x \rightarrow (y \rightarrow z)).$$

Now consider that Dr Smith works in a department whose dean is an avid golfer, the opportunity for promotion is coming up, and Dr Smith wants to impress the dean in some way. So he decides to go to the golf course to practice his swing. Thus, Dr Smith moves his hands to move the club to move the ball *in order to* practice his swing *in order to* impress the dean with his golfing skill.

Viewed from the production of the ultimate effect, i.e. the movement of the ball, the Dr Smith series can be explained as a per se series in which there is some primary cause (Dr Smith) who is responsible for the causality of the series and hence of the ultimate effect. However, viewing the situation from the point of view of the overall goal, one must appeal to Dr Smith's motivating desire to impress the dean; otherwise Dr Smith hits the ball for no reason. I now need to modify the model of per se series articulated in Chapter 4 so as to take account of Dr Smith's reasons (the '*in order to*') for hitting the ball.

---

8. Dr Smith first appeared in 'Essentially Ordered Series Reconsidered'.

There are two new causes of which I must take account in modifying the series, and these are both final causes. They are: (i) Dr Smith's desire to improve his swing in order (ii) to impress the dean. Thus, Dr Smith (*w*) moves his hands (*x*) to swing the club (*y*) to move the ball (*z*) *in order to* improve his swing (*B*) *in order to* impress the dean (*A*). Impressing the dean is Dr Smith's overall goal and hence the final cause of the series. But in order to do so, Dr Smith has to improve his swing. Improving the swing is an instrumental end to the goal of impressing the dean, and it is such because whilst undoubtedly an end it is not in this case an end in itself but is subordinate to some further end. So improving the swing, whilst it exercises final causality, is itself subsidiary to the final causality of impressing the dean.[9]

In accordance with my model for representing per se series, I represent the Dr Smith series with the final cause of improving his swing as follows:

$$[w \rightarrow (x \rightarrow (y \rightarrow z))] \leftarrow B.$$

As before, *x*, *y*, and *z* come within the causal scope of *w*, but now that final causality has been taken into consideration, I have to represent *w* and everything that comes within its causal scope (*x, y, z*) as falling within the causal scope of the final cause *B*. Thus, I introduce square brackets to signify final causality with its scope

---

9. It should also be pointed out that insofar as Dr Smith is the mindful agent in this case, it is he who grasps the end of impressing the dean as desirable and institutes a course of action so as to attain that end. To that end he practises his swing to impress the dean, and the actions in which he engages as primary efficient cause in order to practise his swing to impress the dean, i.e. moving his limbs to swing the club to hit the ball, all participate in the finality of his action geared towards improving his swing to impress the dean. In another context wherein impressing the dean is not Dr Smith's desire, but there is some other desire for hitting the ball, e.g. relaxation, the same actions wherein Smith is the primary efficient cause are undertaken, i.e. moving his limbs to swing the climb to hit the ball, but their finality is different, they are no longer geared towards improving his swing to impress the dean, but to relaxation.

ranging over everything between them. Hence, the scope of w, and everything which falls under it (x, y, z), falls under the final causal scope of B. But as noted above, B is only a subsidiary final cause which itself comes under the final causality of A—impressing the dean. Hence, I must introduce the causality of A under which the scope of B and hence w, x, y, and z fall; I represent it thus:

$$[[w \to (x \to (y \to z))] \leftarrow B] \leftarrow A.$$

As is clear from the symbolism, the causal series of w, x, y, and z along with the final causality of B now falls within the scope of A. The primary efficient cause, w, induces causality to the series in order to achieve B, which itself is in order to achieve A. As the bracketing indicates, the initial causal series falls within the scope of B as proximate end, which itself falls within the scope of A as ultimate end. So the greatest causal scope is attributed to A. Thus, the final cause, A in this case, is the cause of the causality of everything in the series such that without A there would be no causality in the series.

What is the order of causality here? The primary final cause is A, and the primary efficient cause is w; w would not act as primary efficient cause without the causality of A as primary final cause. But whilst A is the primary final cause, B is necessary for arriving at A, in which case B also exercises final causality over w. The causality of B in this case is not a causality separate from A; for in this case it is A which is the ultimate (hence primary) final cause, and B is an end necessary for getting there. So the final causality of B is a participation in that of A (just as in the efficient series the causality of x is a participation in that of w). In other contexts, especially conscious ones, B may be the primary final cause and so not secondary to A, but in this case it happens to be secondary to A.[10] Hence the primary effect of A is the movement of w towards it, but

---

10. There is a plausible scenario wherein Dr Smith is new to golf and realizes how bad his swing is so he hits balls about simply to improve his swing. Here the primary end is improving his swing, not impressing the dean.

w cannot move towards *A* unless it moves through *B*, in which case *B* participates in the final causality of *A*'s causing *w* to institute an efficient causal process to reach the end, which is *A*.

In considering the metaphysics of final per se series I have been alluding to quite straightforward series such as Dr Smith on the golf course. Such series exhibit finality insofar as there is a clear goal to which the actions of the series are ordered. But I have not considered final causal series which perfectly overlap, that is to say, final causal series whose ends are distinct yet whose means are identical.[11] The goal of such series is not entirely clear, and that could threaten my account of final per se series.

Consider that in the Smith case I can say that Smith improves his swing in order to impress the dean; but it would sound somewhat odd to subordinate impressing the dean to improving one's swing: Smith moves his arms to swing the club to hit the ball *in order to* impress the dean *in order to* improve his swing. To my mind there is nothing impossible about the latter scenario, just something odd. But now consider the following example. I ride my bike to work, and in doing so I get healthy. Do I ride my bike *in order to* get to work or do I ride my bike *in order to* get healthy? In some cases, I could say I am riding my bike in order to get to work and the getting healthy is a foreseen but unintended outcome of such action; but in other cases I can say that I ride my bike in order both to get to work and to get healthy (a 'two birds with one stone' scenario). The causal series are identical, yet the ends are distinct. So how do I deal with this situation?

Rather than state that two distinct causal series overlap here, what I want to suggest is that this is a single series with a single yet multiply analysable end. As I have shown above, the unity of the final causal series lies in the primary efficient cause, such that the finality of that series originates in the final cause, which motivates the primary efficient cause; the secondary efficient causes participate

11. These considerations were motivated by an anonymous reviewer of my 2017 article 'Essentially Ordered Series Reconsidered Once Again'.

in the primary cause not only for their efficiency but also for their finality. Now as I will argue, final causes are always goods, that is to say, they represent choiceworthy ends for conscious agents (or the perfection/completion of the natural dispositions of unconscious objects). The end then of any final causal series will always be something that is good. Now the good for the particular agent which is the primary efficient cause is unitary for that agent, i.e. it is his good; yet the good of some single agent is multiply analysable. So in the case of my bicycling to work, both getting to work and getting healthy are for my own good; employment and health contribute to my flourishing. In other circumstances employment and health can be attained by different causal series, e.g. I can take the car to work, and I can go to the gym. In the case of riding my bike to work, I am attaining what appear to be two different ends, getting to work and getting healthy, by one and the same means; but these two ends are in fact united in the one end which is my good—my flourishing. This does not harm the analysis offered here of per se final causal series, since the metaphysics of that series remains the same; the difference lies on the descriptive level. Sometimes I may wish to say that I am riding my bike in order to get to work, sometimes I may wish to say that I am riding it to get fit; in reality I am doing both, and both are unified in the fact that they are for my own good.

The same can be said *mutatis mutandis* for causal series in pursuit of some end, e.g. pleasure, which end is not for the sake of some further end. The end that is pursued is always pursued for the good of the primary efficient cause, so that whilst some end pursued can be divorced from any larger teleological context, that context is always there in the form of the good of the agent. And as I will argue, in the order of goods there is one ultimate end which is the end of all ends, in which case all final causal series are unified in a single ultimate end.

Clearly my account here presupposes that what appear to be different ends of otherwise identical causal series are in fact unified as descriptions of the good of the primary cause of the series. But perhaps there are plausible causal series with quite distinct ends whose means are identical. Such series would undermine the account offered here, since it would entail that the ends are really distinct and not just descriptively so, in which case the problem of identical series with distinct ends reemerges.

As an example consider a teacher marking end of term papers. One end of that series could be that the teacher finishes his marking so as to be finished for the holidays; another distinct end could be that the teacher provides illuminating feedback to the student. In the former case, the good involved is that of the teacher, in the latter it is that of the student. Here we seem to have two distinct goods of perfectly overlapping series which cannot be suitably unified as they were before.

There are two ways to resolve this situation. On the one hand it could be the case that the teacher cannot mark papers in a timely fashion *and* provide illuminating feedback. On the other hand the teacher is talented enough to finish his marking quickly and provide illuminating feedback. In the first case, I want to argue that we do not have perfectly overlapping series with distinct goods as ends, i.e. the good of the student and that of the teacher; rather we have two distinct causal series. In the second case, I wish to say that we still have a single good which explains the finality of the series, yet that good is multiply analysable at the descriptive level, in which case the problem is resolved as before.

First then take the case where the teacher cannot both mark in a timely fashion and provide illuminating feedback. Where the teacher aims at the student's good by providing illuminating feedback, the teacher aims at the good of teaching. One of the ends involved in this good is that of illuminating one's students, and one way to do this is by taking one's time to provide illuminating feedback. Thus, providing illuminating feedback is an intermediate end willed by the teacher for the further end, which is the good of teaching. Where the teacher aims at his own good by finishing his marking in a timely fashion and *not* providing illuminating feedback, the teacher is clearly not acting for the good of his students, but not only that, he is not even aiming at the good of teaching; rather he is aiming at some other good such as getting away early for summer holidays, family time, etc. Providing illuminating feedback is not an end necessary for the latter goods, and so it is not willed by the teacher. In this case, we have two different series with not only different ends (the good of teaching or some other good) but also different means (providing illuminating feedback, marking in a timely fashion without illuminating feedback); hence the series do not perfectly overlap.

Second, take the case where we have a talented teacher who can mark in a timely fashion and provide illuminating feedback; arguably here we have perfectly overlapping series with distinct goods as ends. But what is the finality at work here? Is the teacher working for the good of his students or for his own good? I answer that the good involved here is the good of teaching, which is necessarily a good of the student but also of the teacher. The good of teaching not only involves the illumination of one's students (hence good for the student) but is also a good for the teacher; for when a talented teacher pursues the good of teaching as a vocation (and not just a way of earning money), he himself is perfected and fulfilled. Such perfection of the teacher through pursuing the good of teaching is not simply the exercise of certain dispositions the individual has to be a teacher, thereby fulfilling him in some way (though this is certainly true); rather many talented teachers will say that the illumination of their students is their own greatest good with respect to teaching. Hence, marking in a timely fashion, i.e. with efficiency, and providing illumination are for a single good, that of teaching. So in the case of a teacher who does both, he pursues the good of teaching, and this good is itself multiply analysable into various goods which are for both students and teacher. In this case then we can say that we have a single causal series with a single end which is multiply analysable.

Now consider whether or not per se final causal series as I have considered them terminate in some ultimate end.

1.3 Finite Final Causal Series

I argued in Chapter 4 that in per se causal series unless there is some primary cause there would be no causality in the series. The same reasoning applies here in the order of finality, i.e. there must be some primary final cause which is the ultimate end for the series without which there would be no (final) causality in the series. In order to consider the reasoning for this, I will return to the case of Dr Smith.

In the Dr Smith example I stopped at some arbitrary end—impressing the dean. But as is clear from the discussion, especially in conscious situations, I could have added further ends to which impressing the dean is simply proximate. Thus, just as improving one's swing is proximate to impressing the dean, so too impressing the dean is proximate to getting a promotion, which may itself be proximate to buying a bigger house, and this may be proximate to some greater goal. Hence Dr Smith hits balls *in order to* improve his swing *in order to* impress the dean *in order to* get a promotion *in order to* buy a bigger house *in order to* . . . So many (proximate) ends, and the question is whether they are finite or infinite, that is to say, in the order of final causal series, do such series terminate at some ultimate final cause itself uncaused in respect of the final causality of the series?

This question is a manifestation of a similar one which is considered when focussing on efficient causal series; just as we can project further and consider further efficient causes, can't we project (infinitely) further and consider further final causes?

I respond that just as my model of the per se efficient series permitted me to hold that in such series there must be some primary cause; so too the same model, suitably construed, will show that there is some ultimate final cause.

Take the per se series that I have been considering, that is, Dr Smith impressing the dean:

$$[[w \rightarrow (x \rightarrow (y \rightarrow z))] \leftarrow B] \leftarrow A.$$

It is not difficult to extend its scope and adjust the symbolism accordingly. Hence we write:

$$[\ldots[[w \rightarrow (x \rightarrow (y \rightarrow z))] \leftarrow B] \leftarrow A] \ldots \leftarrow n.$$

As is clear, in this case A now comes within the scope of some indefinite number of final causes (n), each of which is proximate to another. The question then is whether n is finite or infinite.

Draw to mind the argumentation that closed off the infinity of per se causal series when considering efficient causality in Chapter 4. In per se series the posterior causal relata are such that they do not essentially possess the causality of the series in question, in which case their causality is caused. Given the latter, if such a series were without a primary cause, that is, if it were infinite, there would be no cause of the causality of the series, in which case every member of the series would be causally inefficacious. Consequently, an infinite per se series would be lacking in causality and thus would not be a causal series. Granting some per se series, we must grant its necessary finitude.

The same reasoning applies to per se series in which final causality is operative. If such a series goes to infinity, i.e. if there is no ultimate final cause of the series, then there is nothing that causes the causality of the primary efficient cause; for as outlined above, secondary or intermediate final causes have their causality through participating in the causality of some final cause that is ultimate in respect of the given series in question. If there is no ultimate final cause, but just an infinite set of intermediate final causes, then there is no cause for the causality of the intermediate final causes, in which case there is no final causality. But if there is no final causality, then there is no cause for the causality of the primary efficient cause. So granting per se causal series with a primary efficient cause whose causality is derived from some final cause, there must be an ultimate or primary final cause from which the causality of all intermediate final causes is derived and consequently the causality of the efficient cause. Per se final causal series are necessarily finite.[12]

Now when we consider the final cause of any final causal series, that cause, as the terminus of the causality of the efficient cause, is the perfection of the series. This is because insofar as the activity of the efficient cause is brought into operation by the end, that end itself is the completion of the activity of the efficient cause. The work of the efficient cause as it were comes to perfection in the end—it achieves its goal. So in final causal series, the causality of the series is imperfect or incomplete until it comes to rest in the end, the final cause.[13]

Now, final causal series necessarily come to an end in some ultimate final cause, and hence the ultimate final cause of every causal series is the perfection of the series. Given that the ultimate cause of any final causal series is the perfection of the series, every ultimate cause is for the good of that series insofar as it brings it to completion. All final causes then are final causes precisely because they are good in some way, in which case goodness is at the heart of all finality—the final cause has the nature of the good.[14] The cause of goodness then will be a final cause that is not for the sake of any further end but is the end for the sake of which are all other proximate ends. The cause of goodness will be the very essence of end, which is not to be for any other but to be for itself;[15] it will be the end of all ends, and this is the good itself. The good then is *the* ultimate final cause, the end of all ends, without which

---

12. See *In II Met.*, lect. 4, n. 318.
13. *In III Phy.*, lect. 11, n. 385: 'Nullum carens fine est perfectum; quia finis est perfectio uniuscuiusque.'
14. Aquinas, *In I Met.*, lect. 4, n. 70: 'Quarta causa est finalis, quae opponitur causae efficienti secundum oppositionem principiae et finis. Nam motus incipit a causa efficiente, et terminatur ad causam finale. Et hoc est etiam cuius causa fit aliquid, et quae est bonum uniuscuiusque naturae'; *In II Met.*, lect. 4, n. 317: 'Eadem enim ratio boni et finis est'; *Summa Theologiae*, Ia, qu. 5, art. 2, ad. 1: 'Bonum autem, cum habeat rationem appetibilis, importat habitudinem causae finalis, cuius causalitas prima est, quia agens non agit nisi propter finem, et ab agente materia movetur ad formam, unde dicitur quod finis est causa causarum.'
15. *In II Met.*, lect. 4, n. 316: 'finis est id quod non est propter alia, sed alia sunt propter ipsum.'

there would be no final causal series; hence the good ultimately is that which all desire.

Just as in efficient causality *esse* is the absolute causal property without which there would be no causality in any efficient causal series, so too in final causality goodness is the causal property without which there would be no finality in any final causal series. Hence, just as the primary cause of *esse* (God) will be absolutely primary and hence absolutely uncaused in respect of efficient causality, so too will the cause of goodness (the good) be absolutely uncaused in respect of final causality. So whereas all proximate final causes are always 'in order to . . .' something else, that to which they are 'in order to' is something good. Hence the good is never 'in order to . . .' anything further; it is the single ultimate cause in all final causal series.

In the case of God, there is nothing independent of Him that could be His cause, since anything that is independent of God derives its *esse* from God and so cannot be the cause of God. Nevertheless, given the metaphysics of causality (and what was observed about God in Chapter 2), God's causality must be exercised in respect of the good, for the good is the ultimate final cause. Hence, if there is nothing other than God which can be the cause of God, yet God's causality must be exercised in respect of the good, God must Himself be the good that He wills as end.[16] Hence just as God is *esse* itself from which all beings flow, so too is God the good itself towards which all beings tend. God is thus both primary cause and ultimate end.

---

16. *Summa Theologiae*, Ia, qu. 19, art. 2, ad. 2: 'Et sic, sicut alia a se intelligit intelligendo essentiam suam, ita alia a se vult, volendo bonitatem suam'; *Summa Contra Gentiles*, Lib. 1, Cap. 86: 'Finis enim est ratio volendi ea quae sunt ad finem. Deus autem vult bonitatem suam tanquam finem, omnia autem alia vult tanquam ea quae sunt ad finem. Sua igitur bonitas est ratio quare vult alia quae sunt diversa ab ipso'; Cap. 87: 'Quamvis autem aliqua ratio divinae voluntati assignari possit, non tamen sequitur quod voluntatis eius sit aliquid causa. Voluntati enim causa volendi est finis. Finis autem divinae voluntatis est sua bonitas. Ipsa igitur est Deo causa volendi, quae est etiam ipsum velle. Aliorum autem a Deo volitorum nullum est Deo causa volendi.'

When it comes then to the unity of the origin and preservation of causality (*esse*) in creatures, God originates such causality in creating, but His creation is for the sake of the good which He Himself is, so creatures are preserved in such causality, that is, they are preserved in *esse* until they achieve their end. Now consider that end.

2 THE END OF CREATION

God is the primary cause and final end of all creation; He is that from which all beings flow and that to which they all return. The being of all things is directed towards God as their end. Hence all creatures exist as part of the per se causal series, with God as both primary and final cause. Given that God's creation is an expression of His goodness, the very act of creating orders creatures to the divine goodness as their end; this is clear from the metaphysics of per se series since the primary cause in such series causes the causality of the series so that it may reach its end. Hence creatures are not only originated in their being by God but directed to Him as their end and preserved therein by God Himself. All creatures then are governed by God in their existing to achieve their end, which is to be assimilated to the source of goodness, i.e. God.[17]

As creator then God governs all created things in preserving them in their end.[18] Nothing that exists escapes such divine ordering.[19] Nevertheless, this is not to undermine the role of secondary causes in God's governance of things. Recall that in per se causal series all intermediate causes participate in the causality imparted to them in the series (whether that is efficient or final causality), and as so participating they specify the causality of the series in their own particular domain. Hence God can order all

17. *Summa Theologiae*, Ia, qu. 103, art. 2, ad. 2, and art. 4.
18. Ibid., art. 1.
19. Ibid., art. 5.

creation and direct things to their ends by means of secondary causes which not only are directed to their end in God but also direct others to their end.[20] St Thomas puts this as follows:

> Order in ends follows the order of agents; for just as the supreme agent moves all secondary agents, so too the ends of secondary agents must be ordered to the end of the supreme agent, since the action of the supreme agent is for the sake of His own end. Now the supreme agent brings about [agit] the actions of all inferior agents by moving them all to their own actions, and consequently to their ends. Hence it follows that the ends of secondary agents are ordered by the primary agent for His own proper end. God is the primary agent of all things . . . [and] there is no other end for His will than His own goodness. . . . All things then, whether made by Him immediately or by mediating secondary causes, are ordered to God as to their end. This pertains to all beings, since nothing can be unless it has being from God. Everything then is ordered to God as its end.[21]

God is the end of all things, and as such He is the end to which all creatures are ordered. But given that God is the source of being of all creatures, He is not the kind of end which is sought but not yet existing; rather he is an end sought and already existing. God then is an end attained not through achievement, as a doctor brings about health in a patient, but through assimilation.[22] This assimilation to God by creatures can only occur through their becoming like God. How creatures can become like God I will explore hereafter, but the point to bear in mind is that for any creature to achieve its end it must strive to become like God.[23] This stands to reason because God is the source of all actuality,

20. Ibid., art. 6.
21. *Summa Contra Gentiles*, Lib. 3, Cap. 17.
22. Ibid., Cap. 18.
23. Ibid., Cap. 19.

the end of all things, and the being of things is directed to Him; all beings strive to become like God in order to achieve their own individual ends.

Now given that God is the final cause of things yet there are secondary nonultimate final causes to which creatures are ordered, there is a hierarchy of creatures. This hierarchy is determined by the degrees of goodness or perfection attainable by creatures of various kinds. Some kinds of creatures can only attain certain goods, whereas other creatures can attain the same goods and more. The hierarchy of goods attainable by creatures will therefore provide the measure by which creatures are ordered to the final cause—the greater the goods that can be attained by a creature of a kind, the greater assimilation that creature may have to God, Who fulfils the capacity for those goods.[24]

It should be made clear that I am not here discussing perfectabilty, that is to say, I am not discussing the 'journey' of the rational creature towards God or the coming to completion of one individual of a kind as opposed to another of the same kind. Rather, what I am discussing is the very constitution of creatures themselves as capable of various goods (or not) and so as being on a scale of being, the great chain of being. Hence no matter how close the rational creature comes to God or no matter how mature the nonrational creature grows, one will not draw closer to God than one's nature permits. Hence a St Dominic or a St Thomas can be very close to God, but they are close to God *qua* human; neither the *vir evangelicus* nor the Angelic Doctor can experience the closeness to God that an angel can enjoy, precisely because they are

24. Ibid., Cap. 20: 'Non omnes creaturae in uno gradu bonitatis constituuntur. Nam quorundam substantia forma et actus est: scilicet cui secundum id quod est, competit esse actu et bonum esse. Quorundam vero substantia ex materia et forma composita est: cui competit actu esse et bonum esse, sed secundum aliquid sui, scilicet secundum formam. Divina igitur substantia sua bonitas est; substantia vero simplex bonitatem participat secundum id quod est; substantia autem composita secundum aliquid sui.'

not angels. So the question of how one creature, particularly a rational creature, grows close to God within the confines of its nature is not my concern at the moment.[25]

There are two kinds of hierarchy in creatures. The first is what I will call a metaphysical hierarchy and pertains to the analogy of being. The second I will call a natural hierarchy and pertains to the essences of things.

The metaphysical hierarchy signifies the many ways in which being is said: (i) as substance, (ii) as accident, (iii) as relation, (iv) as privation and negation. Each of these expresses a way of being, and the ordering of them is hierarchical, moving from the stronger to the weaker.[26] This metaphysical hierarchy focuses on the constitution of things that exist; it does not give an indication of the hierarchical ordering of the kinds of things that exist, since it equally applies to cabbages and to angels. What we want is a consideration of the ordering of the things that exist, hence an ordering of them in terms of their goods; this will only be exhibited through the natural hierarchy.

A division necessarily implies multiplicity, and multiplicity occurs through composition; this is because the degree to which act is received by potency will signify the limitation placed on act by that potency. The greater the potency, the greater the limitation, and the greater the limitation, the greater the multiplicity. Thus,

---

25. For what I take to be an excellent study of man's attainment of perfection in his journey to God in the thought of Aquinas see Jean-Pierre Torrell OP, *St Thomas Aquinas: Vol. 2–Spiritual Master* (Washington, DC: Catholic University of America Press, 2003). For historical details of the hierarchy of being in the thought of Aquinas et al. and the tracing of its roots to the Neoplatonic tradition, see Edward Mahoney, 'Metaphysical Foundations of the Hierarchy of Being According to Some Late-Medieval and Renaissance Philosophers.' Mahoney's treatment is useful insofar as it distinguishes the medieval treatment of the hierarchy of being in thinkers like Albert, Aquinas, and even Siger of Brabant from Lovejoy's somewhat problematic treatment in *The Great Chain of Being*.

26. For discussion see Gyula Klima, 'The Semantic Principles Underlying Saint Thomas Aquinas's Metaphysics of Being', *Medieval Philosophy and Theology*, 5 (1996), pp. 87–141, Section 3. For a representative text from Aquinas, see *In IV Met.*, lect. 1, n. 539.

that which has a greater degree of potency will be more limited and thus more subject to multiplication. Practically speaking, the more layers of composition there are in a creature, the greater is its degree of potency and hence distance from God.[27] Hence, creatures are more or less distinct from God on the basis of the limitations brought about by the degrees of potency they have.

God is pure *esse*, and in creating He grants *esse* to others. God's *esse* is limited by nothing since there is no potency in Him. On the other hand the *esse* of creatures is limited in some way since it actuates some essence standing in potency to it. So all creatures are fundamentally composites of essence and *esse*, in which case every creature is inferior to God in some way, depending on Him for being and goodness; so much is clear.

Now it is the case that in some creatures the essence with which their act of existence is united is not a composite essence, that is to say, it is not composed of matter and form but is pure form. These creatures are immaterial, and whilst what they are is distinct from their existing, they do not participate in some species of which they are individuals. Hence, every such immaterial creature is a species in itself. Such creatures are closest to God in their actuality insofar as the only potency limiting their actuality is that of an essence subject to existence; the essence itself is not limited in its various individuals the way the essence of several material things is limited. These immaterial beings are the angels. Such beings are manifestations of God's creative activity in a most sublime way, since their only difference from God is

---

27. *Summa Contra Gentiles*, Lib. 1, Cap. 43: 'Omnis actus alteri inhaerens terminationem recipit ex eo in quo est: quia quod est in altero, est in eo per modum recipientis. Actus igitur in nullo existens, nullo terminatur'; Lib. 2, Cap. 52: 'Esse autem, in quantum est esse, non potest esse diversum: potest autem diversificari per aliquid quod est praeter esse; sicut esse lapidis est aliud ab esse hominis'; *De Potentia Dei*, qu. 2, art. 2, p. 6: 'Esse enim hominis terminatum est ad hominis speciem, quia est receptum in natura speciei humanae; et simile est de esse equi, vel cuiuslibet creaturae.' For a discussion of the principle that act is received and limited by potency see Wippel, 'Thomas Aquinas and the Axiom That Unreceived Act Is Unlimited'.

in respect of being composed of essence and *esse* with the various gradations of essence (the angelic hierarchy) that obtains therein; such things are not further removed from God by means of materiality.

Next we have creatures that are not only limited through being composites of essence and existence; the essence of such creatures too is limited through being composed of matter and form. Such creatures are not only existing things with essences; they are also individuals having some essence in common. So whereas with immaterial creatures each such individual is a species in itself, material creatures are individuals of a species. Material creatures thus have an added layer of potency over immaterial creatures and so are a further step removed from God. Material creatures are thus a less intense realization of God's creative activity than immaterial creatures are.

Within the domain of material creatures we have more or less diversity in two ways: (i) on the basis of the degree of actuality that the form gives to matter, and (ii) on the basis of the complexity of the form actuating the matter.

Concerning (i), there are some material things whose form completely actualizes the potentiality of their matter so that there is no potency left to be actualized, and, according to medieval physics, these are the heavenly bodies. Whilst it may seem that such heavenly bodies are magnificent instances of God's creative power, they are in fact very slight manifestations thereof. This is because whilst they are fundamental constituents of the material universe, they do nothing but simply be as the kind of material things that they are. They are not alive and they are not like elements whereby they can be components of mixed bodies. Thus, they are quite static in their being and so are quite significantly removed from God.

Next, there are some material things whose form does not fully actualize the potency of their matter, leaving some potency to be actuated, and these are nonheavenly or mundane bodies, the most fundamental of which are the elements, and then things composed of the elements.[28] The elements present a slightly greater manifestation of God's creative power than the heavenly bodies, and this because they are capable of entering into composition with other things to produce more complex things, and so they are not static in their being like the heavenly bodies, but actually contribute to the being of others.

Amongst mundane things there is an exhaustive division between the inanimate and the animate. Inanimate mundane things have a kind of form simply making them to be the kind of things that they are, whereas animate things have a form making them to be living things, a form by which they enjoy life, i.e. anima or soul. It follows then that animate things are a richer expression of God's creativity than inanimate things.

Amongst living things there is more or less complexity given the form of life of the living thing in question. So there are some living things that are merely alive and do nothing more than gain nutrition (vegetative life); then there are living things that not only live but live out their lives in interaction with an environment (sensitive life); then there are living things that not only live and live within an environment, but transcend the limits of the environment in which they live by coming to know the truth about themselves, the world, and God (rational life).[29]

28. *Summa Contra Gentiles*, Lib. 3, Cap. 20: 'In hoc autem tertio gradu substantiarum iterum diversitas invenitur quantum ad ipsum esse. Nam quorundam ex materia et forma compositorum totam materiae potentiam forma adimplet, ita quod non remanet in materia potentia ad aliam formam: et per consequens nec in aliqua alia materia potentia ad hanc formam. Et huiusmodi sunt corpora caelestia, quae ex tota materia sua constant. Quorundam vero forma non replet totam materiae potentiam: unde adhuc in materia remanet potentia ad aliam formam; et in alia materiae parte remanet potentia ad hanc formam; sicut patet in elementis et elementatis.'

29. *Summa Contra Gentiles*, Lib. 3, Cap. 22: 'In actibus autem formarum gradus quidam inveniuntur. Nam materia prima est in potentia primo ad formam elementi. Sub forma vero elementi existens est in potentia ad formam mixti: propter quod elementa sunt materia mixti. Sub forma autem mixti considerata, est in potentia ad animam vegetabilem: nam talis corporis anima actus est. Itemque anima vegetabilis est potentia ad sensitivam; sensitiva vero ad intellectivam. Quod processus generationis

Rational living material things then are the highest of all material things since they encompass all lower forms of life and materiality in themselves and add something to it by their rationality. Amongst material things then rational creatures are the greatest expression of God's creative power. Yet we can go further than that. All other creatures, including angels, express God's creative activity in one way or another, whether as pure spirits, or material existents, or living things; but man embodies in himself all aspects of God's creative activity, since he has both material and immaterial (intellectual) aspects and so touches on every degree of divine creativity; God pours forth into man as it were all aspects of creation. Accordingly, man is the highest of material beings and the lowest of immaterial beings. He is a frontier or horizon between the material and the spiritual and so unites the two in himself. Without man, creation would be radically incomplete; there would be a chasm separating the material from the immaterial with nothing to join it. In him is expressed by a certain similitude the entire order of created reality. Man is thus appropriately referred to as a microcosm, harmonizing all aspects of created reality.[30]

Now, as noted above, this hierarchy of created things is an ordered hierarchy. Inferior creatures are for the sake of superior

ostendit: primo enim in generatione est fetus vivens vita plantae, postmodum vero vita animalis, demum vero vita hominis. Post hanc autem formam non invenitur in generabilibus et corruptibilibus posterior forma et dignior.'
30. *Summa Contrra Gentiles*, Lib. 2, Cap. 68: 'Semper enim invenitur infimum supremi generis contingere supremum inferioris generis. . . . Est igitur accipere aliquid supremum in genere corporum, scilicet corpus humanum aequaliter complexionatum, quod attingit ad infimum superioris generis, scilicet ad animam humanam, quae tenet ultimum gradum in genere intellectualium substantiarum, ut ex modo intelligendi percipi potest. Et inde est quod anima intellectualis dicitur esse quasi quidam horizon et confinium corporeorum et incorporeorum, inquantum est substantia incorporea, corporis tamen forma.' *In III Sent.*, Proem: 'homo enim est quasi orizon et confinium spiritualis et corporalis naturae, ut quasi medium inter utrasque, bonitates participet et corporales et spirituales.' For a discussion of the notion of man as a horizon see Gerard Verbeke, 'Man as Frontier According to Aquinas', in *Aquinas and Problems of His Time*, ed. by G. Verbeke and D. Verhelst (Leuven: Leuven University Press, 1976), pp. 195–223.

creatures. For instance, the laws of the universe are for the sake of the things in the universe, the most fundamental of which are the elements, which are for the sake of mixed bodies, and mixed bodies for the sake of living bodies, and living bodies for the sake of rational living things.[31] Creatures thus form an ordered community with man, the microcosm, as the highest member of that community. The perfection of man then will be the perfection of creation, since creation is completed in him. Man's perfection, and hence that of creation, comes through his perfection as the rational animal that he is, and, like all other creatures, he will be perfected through being assimilated to God. Only when man, the summit of God's creative causality, returns to God as his end will creation itself be perfected and return to God.[32] To this issue I now turn.

3 MAN'S END

Whereas before I considered the natural hierarchy amongst things whereby things are ordered on the basis of the kinds of things they are, I am now considering the perfection of things as things of a kind, and the kind of things I am considering are human beings, rational animals. Hence, in this section I shall consider what man's end is and how it is to be attained.

The assimilation of a creature to God is for the perfection of the creature. The perfection of a creature cannot override the creature's

---

31. *Summa Contra Gentiles*, Lib. 3, Cap. 22: 'Ultimus igitur finis generationis totius est anima humana, et in hanc tendit materia sicut in ultimam formam. Sunt ergo elementa propter corpora mixta; haec vero propter viventia; in quibus plantae sunt propter animalia; animalia vero propter hominem. Homo igitur est finis totius generationis. . . . Si igitur motio ipsius caeli ordinatur ad generationem; generatio autem tota ordinatur ad hominem sicut in ultimum finem huius generis: manifestum est quod finis motionis caeli ordinatur ad hominem sicut in ultimum finem in genere generabilium et mobilium.'

32. *Summa Theologiae*, Ia, qu. 73, art. 1: 'Ultima autem perfectio, quae est finis totius universi, est perfecta beatitudo sanctorum; quae erit in ultima consummatione saeculi.'

nature but must be in accord with it. Any attempt to override the creature and act against its nature to perfect it would in fact undermine its nature, and so be detrimental to the creature. Thus, man's perfection as an assimilation to God must be in accord with man's nature and not an eradication thereof.

Man is a rational animal; his rationality is the specifying difference of his nature, so that whereas other animals enjoy a particular mode of animality, man's particular mode is rationality. Man's perfection must consist in the assimilation of his rational animality to God. The end of man then is an end or a good proper to the rational nature, i.e. proper to an animal which has the use of intellect and will; and this end is called happiness. Happiness then is man's final end.[33]

Now man's happiness cannot consist in any created good; for no such good is the good for which man was created, since all things are created as an expression of the divine goodness. Hence man's happiness, his good, must be in God alone. Since man is distinguished from all other animals on the basis of his intellect, his assimilation to God must be through the intellect. It follows then that man's happiness consists in knowing God, and through knowing Him and the good that He essentially is, loving Him. The greater a man can come to know and love God, the greater will be his happiness. It is thus by means of knowing and loving God that man is perfected and made happy, and this is his final end.

The knowledge of God in which man's intellect takes rest is ultimate; for it must be capable of arresting man's desire to know. Man

---

33. *Sentencia Libri Ethicorum*, Lib. 1, lect. 9, n. 106: 'necesse est enim unum esse ultimum finem hominis inquantum est homo, propter unitatem humanae naturae, sicut est finis unus medici inquantum est medicus propter unitatem medicinalis artis; et iste unus ultimus finis hominis dicitur humanum bonum, quod est felicitas.' *Summa Contra Gentiles*, Lib. 3, Cap. 25: 'Ultimus autem finis hominis, et cuiuslibet intellectualis substantiae, felicitas sive beatitudo nominatur: hoc enim est quod omnis substantia intellectualis desiderat tanquam ultimum finem, et propter se tantum. Est igitur beatitudo et felicitas ultima cuiuslibet substantiae intellectualis cognoscere Deum.'

can have knowledge of God in this life, whether through pushing against the upper limits of philosophy, or through faith by which he believes truths about God because He has revealed them to him. In neither case can man be said to have attained that knowledge, that understanding of God, that arrests his desire; for in both cases his intellect can know more, as is clear from the following.

Man's natural knowledge of God, whilst reaching the truth, is often gained by only a few people over a long period of time and accompanied by many errors; such cannot be the knowledge by which all of a person's intellectual yearning is brought to completion.[34] Not only that, the knowledge of God attained in philosophy does not provide a direct knowledge of His essence, but only an indirect knowledge. Thus, if the knowledge of God stopped only with the knowledge philosophy can provide, one would still stop short of knowing God in Himself and thus stop short of the final end.

The revealed knowledge that God gives to man and to which he assents through faith, whilst of a more fundamental nature than what is found in philosophy and indeed providing a knowledge of God's essence, is nevertheless incomplete. This is because revealed knowledge only lets man see in a glass darkly, to use St Paul's evocative phrase. Furthermore, the knowledge provided by faith does not disclose God in Himself but provides certain promissory notes as to what God is like, notes rendered certain given the veracity of the One providing them, yet promissory nonetheless. The knowledge of faith awaits the full knowledge of God that is to be revealed to man when he comes to see God face to face as it were. Thus, not even the knowledge of faith is enough to fulfil man's intellect; rather it anticipates the ultimate fulfilment in man's direct and immediate apprehension of God in Himself.

It follows from all this that man cannot reach his ultimate end in this life, because in this life he must satisfy himself with knowing God by means of philosophy and faith. Neither provides

34. *Summa Theologiae*, Ia, qu. 1, art. 1; *Summa Contra Gentiles*, Lib. 3, Cap. 38–39.

that assimilation to God that is necessary for man's happiness. Nevertheless, man can take steps towards assimilating himself to God whilst still in this life, and this he does through cultivating his intellect and will so as to draw closer to God.[35] As a wilful agent, a cause of his own actions, man already bears some likeness to God. By conforming his actions to the good, man will in turn draw closer to God in that likeness, anticipating thereby the full assimilation to God that will come about in the next life.[36] Thus, not only must man seek out the truth by means of his intellect, he must so form himself and be formed by the virtues, both cardinal and theological, so that he will live a life consonant with his nature and pleasing to God. In cultivating both the intellect and will, man can take steps along the way towards assimilation to God and thereby achieve a degree of happiness possible here in this life, which in turn anticipates the full happiness which is man's end in the next life.

Humanity's ultimate happiness consists in God alone, and given that humans are intellectual creatures it consists in the intellectual vision (and the attendant enjoyment) of the divine essence. Nothing but the divine essence will ultimately make man happy. Immediately this raises two issues; the first is whether or not the divine essence can be envisaged by the human intellect, and the second is how that in fact takes place.

To begin with the first, it is no doubt the case that no intellect other than God's could fully comprehend the divine essence. This is because no created intellect is identical with the being that the creature is, so a created intellect is dependent in some way and therefore lesser than the divine intellect. Only the divine intellect can comprehend fully being itself because only the divine intellect is being itself. All other intellects come to know something of

---

35. *Summa Contra Gentiles*, Lib. 3, Cap. 63: 'Huius autem ultimae et perfectae felicitatis in hac vita nihil est adeo simile sicut vita contemplantium veritatem, secundum quod est possibile in hac vita.'
36. *Summa Theologiae*, IaIIae, Proem.

being itself, but they do not comprehend it; they only apprehend it. Hence, so long as we bear in mind that an intellectual vision of the divine essence could never possibly exhaust the divine essence (that essence being limitless), we can grant that there can be an apprehension of God by created intellects, for humans no less than for angels, in which case it is possible for a created intellect to see God's essence yet not fully comprehend it.

Now insofar as man's beatitude is in God alone, it must be the divine essence that the human intellect apprehends and not some representational intermediary or reflected impression thereof. Ordinarily in the affairs of knowledge we distinguish between what we know (*id quod*, e.g. a tree within our perceptual field), and the means by which we know it (*id quo*, some conceptual content, the intellectual species, by means of which we grasp the thing in reality). But the *id quo* is not the *id quod*; what is known is a thing in reality, and it is known by means of the species, the conceptual content, but such content is not the object that is known. Nevertheless, the species does conform thought to reality, so that one's thinking is true when the form of the species is in accord with the form of the thing. When it comes to the vision of God, however, there is a problem, and this is because no created species, no conceptual content, could ever disclose to humans the divine essence, since the divine essence is incomprehensible to finite intellects.

Nothing but a direct intellectual apprehension of God Himself unmediated by any created species will make humans ultimately happy. Only God has such an unmediated knowledge of Himself. So in order to attain beatitude, the human intellect must come to know God as He knows Himself. If humans are to attain beatitude then, the divine essence must be not only the object of humanity's intellectual vision (the *id quod*) but also the means by which one may have such vision (the *id quo*). It follows then that in creating humans not only does God will their happiness, their good, but in creating them as specifically rational and capable of being happy through enjoying Himself, God wills humans, to use Torrell's expression, 'to be happy with the happiness with which He Himself is happy'.[37] This is to share in His divine life.

We are led nicely into the second issue of how beatitude can come about. Humans suffer the tragedy of sin. We were originally created in a state of grace, but with sin we have lost that grace, and whilst we retain our nature, that nature is wounded, and suffers, amongst other things, ignorance, weakening of the will, and lack of integrity between body and soul, which results in death. Sin distances humans from God and turns us away from Him; it is a weakness in humans that does not eradicate the goodness of their nature but certainly distorts within them what is good, turning them from God and disposing them to shun the true good that they ought to choose.[38] In the Catholic theological vision, God provides the remedy for sin through the work of Christ, whereby sanctifying grace, the attendant infusion of the virtues of faith, hope, and charity, and the gifts of the Holy Spirit restore fallen human nature. On this account, the second person of the Trinity, the Word, becomes man so as to show man that God loves him to such a degree that He would willingly suffer the consequence of sin (death) and thereby effect a return of man to God.[39]

The work of this atonement has the twofold effect of exhibiting to man the reality of God's love for him in spite of sin and of presenting to God a perfect instance of man.[40] As such the

---

37. Torrell, *Saint Thomas Aquinas: Vol. 2–Spiritual Master*, p. 339.
38. For a discussion of the effects of original sin on human nature in the Thomistic outlook see Thomas Joseph White, *The Incarnate Lord: A Thomistic Study in Christology* (Washington, DC: Catholic University of America Press, 2017), pp. 131–144.
39. I highly recommend Stump's presentation of Aquinas's position on the atonement, 'Atonement According to Aquinas', in *Oxford Readings in Philosophical Theology, I, Trinity, Incarnation, and Atonment* (New York: Oxford University Press, 2009), pp. 267–293. In this article Stump does an excellent job in disassociating Aquinas's account of the atonement from a more legalistic one whereby God is conceived as a collector of debts and the debt of sin is simply transferred onto Christ; the thrust of Aquinas's teaching, and Stump's presentation, is that the focus is taken away from God's being wronged and the emphasis is placed more on man's having gone astray and in need of a return to God. See also White, *The Incarnate Lord*, Part 2.
40. *Summa Theologiae*, IIIa, qu. 48, art. 2; qu. 49, art. 4.

effect is the removal of sin from the human race and the grace by which humans may remain free from sin.[41] Such grace is achieved through Christ, so that other humans may access that grace only through him; and herein Aquinas sees the need for the sacraments of the Catholic Church, principally baptism but fundamentally the Eucharist, by which the members are united with Christ.[42] Through participation in the sacramental life, Aquinas holds that the theological virtues of faith, hope, and charity, which perfect the cardinal virtues (and in turn all virtues subordinated to them), are infused in us and that such infusion of theological virtues directs us to our supernatural end in God.[43] Only through incorporation into Christ by means of the sacramental life can any human being hope to achieve salvation from sin and thereby enjoy the beatitude that is the perfection of man and hence the end of creation.

Given the incarnation of Christ, Aquinas sees union with Christ as the Word of God the special end of man, and this is owing to (i) man's dignity, and (ii) a certain necessity pertaining to the condition of man. With regard to (i), human nature is in itself apt to be assimilated to the Word of God by means of its proper operation of knowing and loving God. But (ii) human nature is subject to sin and so depends on the Word of God for the reparation of sin.[44] Man's total end as assimilation to God then is found in Christ since it is in Christ that man is assimilated to God by knowing and loving Him and through whom remission for sin is made. Christ is the destiny and true end of all men.

Christ then represents the point of creation where human nature is restored to God and the beatific vision can be attained. But if this is so, then Christ's incarnation brings creation to completion, since with him man, the apex and richest expression of

41. Ibid., IIIa, qu. 8, art. 6; qu. 48, art. 1.
42. Ibid., IIIa, qu. 61, art. 1, qu. 63, art. 6, qu. 73, art. 3.
43. Ibid., IaIIae, qu. 62, art. 1, qu. 63, art. 3.
44. *Summa Theologiae*, IIIa, qu. 4, art. 1.

divine creativity, is brought to a point where he can achieve his final end in the vision of God. The whole process of creation, whose successive temporal regions have moved through one moment until the next since the beginning, has been brought to its completion with the incarnation of Christ and the restoration of man to God.

So God as creator brings into existence all things, presupposing nothing. But as the good itself, God's action in bringing things into existence is motivated by the goodness that He sees in Himself. Just as there is a sense in which all creation is a participation in and thereby an expression of God's being, so too all creation is a participation in and an expression of God's goodness; indeed more so since creation is brought about with a view to that goodness. Creation then ought not to be thought of only as an act of sheer power but as an act of goodness making use of omnipotent power in its expression.

To will the good for another is to love the other for which that good is willed; to will the good of another which other has done nothing to merit that good is to love the other unconditionally. In creating God wills the good for things that did not even exist prior to His creating them, in which case God's willing of the good for creatures, i.e. His bringing them into being, is an act of unconditional love.

In Aquinas's metaphysical thought we can thus think of creation as an act of love, an unconditional act of love from the creator to the creature. This idea should cause us to stop and think, since whilst it does not deny the sheer power implicit in the act of creation, if one were to think of it solely in terms of power, one would belittle creation as nothing more than an awesome magic trick. But to think about creation as an act of sheer unconditional love is to render the act of creation meaningful on an entirely new level; for once creation takes on the significance of a loving act, rational creatures, who are themselves capable of love, must realize that in their love they are elevated to the nobility of the special mark of the creator as loving, and so the only appropriate response they can offer the creator is to love Him in return.[45] The existence, the solidity, the durability, the sheer thereness of all that is would be nothing if not for the love of God. We rational creatures exist precisely because we are loved, and our final end is the enjoyment appropriate to us as such creatures. We can achieve this through assimilation to God through Christ. Hence Christ is the end of man and of creation.

45. The same sentiment is expressed in a number of places in scripture and religious authors: 1 Jn 4:7–12, Wis. 11:24, Pope Francis, *Laudato Si*, n. 77. Dante forcefully captures the notion of God as the love from which all things come and to which all they return in *The Divine Comedy: Paradiso*, Canto 33, 142–145: 'At this point high imagination failed; but already my desire and my will were being turned like a wheel, all at one speed, by the love which moves the sun and the other stars.'

BIBLIOGRAPHY

Acar, R. 2010: 'Creation: Avicenna's Metaphysical Account', in David Burrell, Carlo Cogliati, Janet M. Soskice, and William R. Stoeger eds., *Creation and the God of Abraham* (Cambridge: Cambridge University Press), pp. 77–91.

Adams, R. 1974: 'Theories of Actuality', *Noûs*, 8:3, pp. 211–231.

Adler, M. J. 1980: *How to Think about God: A Guide for the 20th Century Pagan* (New York: Collier/Macmillan).

Alberston, J. 1954: 'Instrumental Causality in St Thomas', *New Scholasticism*, 28, pp. 409–443.

Anderson, J. 1952: *The Cause of Being: The Philosophy of Creation in St. Thomas* (London: Herder).

Aquinas 1926: *Summa Theologiae* (Turin: Marietti).

Aquinas 1927: *Quaestio Disputata De Anima* (Turin: Marietti).

Aquinas 1927: *Quaestio Disputata De Spiritualibus Creaturis* (Turin: Marietti).

Aquinas 1927: *Quaestiones Disputatae De Malo* (Turin: Marietti).

Aquinas 1927: *Quaestiones Disputatae De Potentia Dei* (Turin: Marietti).

Aquinas 1927: *Quaestiones Quodlibetales* (Turin: Marietti).

Aquinas 1929: *Scriptum Super Libros Sententiarum* (Paris: Lethielleux).

Aquinas 1935: *In Metaphysicam Aristotelis Commentaria* (Turin: Marietti).

Aquinas 1950: *In Librum Beati Dionysii De Divinis Nominibus Expositio* (Turin: Marietti).

Aquinas 1952: *In Aristotelis Libros De Caelo et Mundo* (Turin: Marietti).

Aquinas 1954: *Compendium Theologiae* (Turin: Marietti).

Aquinas 1954: *De Articulis Fidei* (Turin: Marietti).

Aquinas 1954: *In Octo Libros Physicorum Aristotelis Expositio* (Turin: Marietti).

Aquinas 1955: *In Librum De Causis Expositio* (Turin: Marietti).

Aquinas 1961: *Summa Contra Gentiles* (Turin: Marietti).

Aquinas 1962: *Tractatus De Substantis Separatis* (West Hartford, CT: St Joseph College).

Aquinas 1968: *Expositio Super Primam Decretalem* (Rome: Leonine).

Aquinas 1976: *De Ente et Essentia* (Rome: Editori di San Tommaso).

Aquinas 1976: *De Mixtione Elementorum* (Rome: Editori di San Tommasso).

Aquinas 1976: *De Principiis Naturae* (Rome: Editori di San Tommasso).

Aquinas 1984: *Sentencia libri De Anima* (Rome: Commissio Leonina).

Aquinas 1992: *Super Boethium De Trinitate et Expositio Libri Boethii de Ebdomadibus* (Rome: Commissio Leonina).

Aquinas 2006: *Lectura Romana in primum Sententiarum Petri Lombardi*, ed. by Leonard Boyle and John Boyle (Toronto: Pontifical Institute of Mediaeval Studies).

Aristotle 1984: *The Complete Works of Aristotle*, ed. by Jonathan Barnes (Princeton: Princeton University Press).

Baldner, S. E., and Carroll, W. E., trans. 1997: *Aquinas on Creation: Writings on the 'Sentences' of Peter Lombard Book 2, Distinction 1, Question 1* (Toronto: Pontifical Institute of Mediaeval Studies).

Beadouin, J. 2007: 'The World's Continuance: Divine Conservation or Existential Inertia?', *International Journal for Philosophy of Religion*, 61, pp. 83–98.

Bobik, J. 1954: 'Dimensions in the Individuation of Bodily Substances', *Maynooth Philosophical Studies*, 4, pp. 60–79.

Bobik, J. 1998: *Aquinas on Matter and Form and the Elements: A Translation and Interpretation of the 'De Principiis Naturae' and the 'De Mixtione Elementorum' of St Thomas Aquinas* (Notre Dame, IN: University of Notre Dame Press).

Bonansea, B. 1974: 'The Impossibility of Creation from Eternity According to St Bonaventure', *Proceedings of the American Catholic Philosophical Association*, 48, pp. 121–135.

Brown, B. 1985: *Accidental Being: A Study in the Metaphysics of St Thomas Aquinas* (Lanham: University Press of America).

Burrell, D., et al., eds. 2010: *Creation and the God of Abraham* (Cambridge: Cambridge University Press).

Da Cruz Pontes, J. M. 1964: 'Le problème de l'origine de l'âme de la patristique à la solution Thomiste', *Recherches de Théologie ancienne et médiévale*, 31, pp. 175–229.

Davidson, H. 1982: *Proofs for Eternity, Creation and the Existence of God in Medieval Islamic and Jewish Philosophy* (New York: Caravan Books).

Davies, B. 1992: *The Thought of Thomas Aquinas* (Oxford: Clarendon Press).

Davies, B. 2012: 'The Limits of Language and the Notion of Analogy', in Eleonore Stump and Brian Davies eds., *The Oxford Handbook of Aquinas* (Oxford: Oxford University Press), pp. 390–397.

de Finance, J. 1960: *Être et agir dans la philosophie de Saint Thomas* (Rome: Librairie Éditrice de l'Université Grégorienne).

Fabro, F. 1950: *La nozione metafisica di partecipazione scondo s. Tommaso d'Aquino* (Turin: Società Editrice Internazionale).

Fabro, F. 1961: *Participation et Causalité* (Louvain: Publications Universitaires de Louvain & Paris: Éditions Béatrice-Nauwelaerts).

Feser, E. 2011: 'Existential Inertia and the Five Ways', *American Catholic Philosophical Quarterly*, 85, pp. 237–267.

Feser, E. 2017: *Five Proofs of the Existence of God* (San Francisco: Ignatius Press).

Freddoso, A. J. 1988: 'Medieval Aristotelianism and the Case against Secondary Causation in Nature', in Thomas Morris ed., *Divine and Human Action: Essays in the Metaphysics of Theism* (Ithaca, NY: Cornell University Press, 1988), pp. 74–118.

Freddoso, A. J. 1991: 'God's Concurrence with Secondary Causes: Why Conservation Is Not Enough', *Philosophical Perspectives*, 5, pp. 553–585.

Garrigou-Lagrange, R. 1943: *De Deo Trino et Creatore* (Turin: Marietti).

Geiger, L.-B. 1942: *La participation dans la philosophie de s. Thomas d'Aquin* (Paris: Libraire Philosophique J. Vrin).

Gilson, É. 1940: *The Spirit of Medieval Philosophy* (New York: Scribner).

Gilson, É. 1952: *Being and Some Philosophers* (Toronto: Pontifical Institute of Medieval Studies).

Gilson, É. 1956: *The Christian Philosophy of St Thomas Aquinas* (Notre Dame, IN: University of Notre Dame Press).

Gilson, É. 1971: *D'Aristote à Darwin et retour: Essai sur quelques constantes de la bio-philosophie* (Paris: Librairie Philosophique Vrin).

Gilson, É. 1974: 'Quasi Definitio Substantiae', in *St Thomas Aquinas 1274–1974: Commemorative Studies* (Toronto: Pontifical Institute of Medieval Studies), pp. 111–131.

Gracia, J. J. E., ed. 1994: *Individuation in Scholasticism: The Later Middle Ages and the Counter Reformation* (New York: State University of New York Press).

Haldane, J., and Lee, P. 2003: 'Aquinas on Human Ensoulment, Abortion, and the Value of Life', *Philosophy*, 78:304, pp. 255–278.

Haldane, J., and Lee, P. 2003: 'Rational Souls and the Beginning of Life (A Reply to Robert Pasnau)', *Philosophy*, 78:306, pp. 532–540.

Hankey, W. 2012: 'Aquinas, Plato, and Neoplatonism', in Eleonore Stump and Brian Davies eds., *The Oxford Handbook of Aquinas* (Oxford: Oxford University Press), pp. 55–65.

Hawking, S. 1998: *A Brief History of Time* (London: Bantam Press).

Henninger, M. G. 1987: 'Aquinas on the Ontological Status of Relations', *Journal of the History of Philosophy*, 25:4, pp. 491–515.

Irwin, T. 1988: *Aristotle's First Principles* (Oxford: Clarendon Press).

Jaeger, W. 1947: *The Theology of the Early Greek Philosophers* (Oxford: Clarendon Press).

Johnson, M. 1989: 'Did St Thomas Attribute a Doctrine of Creation to Aristotle', *New Scholasticism*, 63:2, pp. 129–155.

Johnson, M. 1992: 'Aquinas's Changing Evaluation of Plato on Creation', *American Catholic Philosophical Quarterly*, 66:1, pp. 39–46.

Kahn, C. 1982: 'Why Existence Does Not Emerge as a Distinct Concept in Greek Philosophy', in Parviz Morewedge ed., *Philosophies of Existence* (New York: Fordham University Press), pp. 7–18.

Kenny, A. 1969: *The Five Ways* (London: Routledge & Kegan Paul).

Kerr, G. 2008: 'The Meaning of *Ens Commune* in the Thought of Thomas Aquinas', *Yearbook of the Irish Philosophical Society*, pp. 32–60.

Kerr, G. 2012: 'Aquinas's Argument for the Existence of God in *De Ente et Essentia* Cap. IV: An Interpretation and Defense', *Journal of Philosophical Research*, 37, pp. 119–121.

Kerr, G. 2012: 'Essentially Ordered Series Reconsidered', *American Catholic Philosophical Quarterly*, 86:4, pp. 155–174.

Kerr, G. 2012: 'A Thomistic Metaphysics of Creation', *Religious Studies*, 48, pp. 337–356.

Kerr, G. 2015: *Aquinas's Way to God: The Proof in 'De Ente et Essentia'* (New York: Oxford University Press).

Kerr, G. 2015: 'Thomist *Esse* and Analytical Philosophy', *International Philosophical Quarterly*, 55:1, pp. 25–47.

Kerr, G. 2016: 'Aquinas, Stump, and the Nature of a Simple God', *American Catholic Philosophical Quarterly*, 90:3, pp. 441–454.

Kerr, G. 2017: 'Essentially Ordered Series Reconsidered Once Again', *American Catholic Philosophical Quarterly*, 91:2, pp. 541–555.

Klima, G. 1996: 'The Semantic Principles Underlying Saint Thomas Aquinas's Metaphysics of Being', *Medieval Philosophy and Theology*, 5:1, pp. 87–141.

Klima, G. 2002: 'Aquinas's Theory of the Copula and the Analogy of Being', *Logical Analysis and History of Philosophy*, 5, pp. 159–176.

Klima, G. 2007: *Medieval Philosophy: Essential Readings with Commentary* (New York: Wiley-Blackwell).

Klima, G. 2012: 'Theory of Language', in *The Oxford Handbook of Aquinas*, ed. by Eleonore Stump and Brian Davies (Oxford: Oxford University Press), pp. 371–390.

Kretzmann, N. 1997: *The Metaphysics of Theism: Aquinas's Natural Theology in Summa Contra Gentiles I* (Oxford: Clarendon Press).

Kretzmann, N. 2001: *The Metaphysics of Creation: Aquinas's Natural Theology in Summa Contra Gentiles II* (Oxford: Oxford University Press).

Kripke, S. 1981: *Naming and Necessity* (Oxford: Blackwell).

Lonergan, B. 1997: *Verbum: Word and Idea in Aquinas* (Toronto: University of Toronto Press).

Lovejoy, A. O. 1960: *The Great Chain of Being: A Study of the History of an Idea* (New York: Harper and Row).

Mahoney, E. 1982: 'Metaphysical Foundations of the Hierarchy of Being According to Some Late-Medieval and Renaissance Philosophers', in Parvis Morewedge ed., *Philosophies of Existence* (New York: Fordham University Press), pp. 165–257.

Maimonides, M. 1956: *Guide for the Perplexed*, trans. M. Friedländer (New York: Dover).

Maurer, A. 1951: 'Form and Essence in the Philosophy of St Thomas', *Mediaeval Studies* 13, pp. 165–176.

Maurer, A. 1986: *Thomas Aquinas: The Divisions and Methods of the Sciences* (Toronto: Pontifical Institute of Medieval Studies).

Maurer, A. 2004: 'Darwin, Thomists, and Secondary Causality', *Review of Metaphysics*, 57:3, pp. 491–514.

McMullin, E., ed. 1986: *Evolution and Creation* (Notre Dame, IN: Notre Dame University Press).

McMullin, E., ed. 2011: 'Darwin and the Other Christian Tradition', *Zygon*, 46:2, pp. 291–316.

Michon, C., et al. 2004: *Thomas d'Aquin et la controverse sur 'L'Éternité du monde'* (Paris: Flammarion).

Montagnes, B. 2004: *The Doctrine of the Analogy of Being according to Thomas Aquinas)*, trans. E. M. Macierowski (Milwaukee: Marquette University Press).

Morewedge, P., ed. 1982: *Philosophies of Existence* (New York: Fordham University Press).

Morris, T., ed., 1988: *Divine and Human Action: Essays in the Metaphysics of Theism* (Ithaca, NY: Cornell University Press).

Morris, T., and Menzel, C. 1986: 'Absolute Creation', *American Philosophical Quarterly* 23:4, pp. 353–362.

Norris Clarke, W. 2001: *The One and the Many* (Notre Dame, IN: University of Notre Dame Press).

Oderberg, D. 2008: *Real Essentialism* (New York: Routledge).

O'Rourke, F. 2004: 'Aristotle and the Metaphysics of Evolution', *Review of Metaphysics* 58:1, pp. 3–59.

Owens, J. 1988: 'Thomas Aquinas: Dimensive Quantity as Individuating Principle', *Mediaeval Studies*, 50, pp. 279–310.

Owens, J. 1994: 'Thomas Aquinas (b. ca. 1225; d. 1274)', in J. J. E. Gracia ed., *Individuation in Scholasticism: The Later Middle Ages and the Counter Reformation* (New York: State University of New York Press), pp. 173–194.

Peghaire, J. 1932: 'L'Axiome "Bonum est diffusivum sui" dans le néoplatonisme et le thomisme', *Revue de l'Université d'Ottawa*, 1, pp. 5–30.

Pegis, A. 1939: *St. Thomas and the Greeks* (Milwaukee: Marquette University Press).

Pegis, A. 1946: 'A Note on St. Thomas, *Summa Theologica*, I, 44, 1–2', *Mediaeval Studies*, 8, pp. 159–168.

Pennock, R. T., ed. 2001: *Intelligent Design Creationism and Its Critics: Philosophical, Theological, and Scientific* (Cambridge, MA: MIT Press).

Phelan, G. 1957: 'The Being of Creatures', *Proceedings of the American Catholic Philosophical Association*, 31, pp. 118–125.

Plantinga, A. 1973: 'Which Worlds Could God Have Created?', *Journal of Philosophy*, 70:17, pp. 539–552.

Plantinga, A. 1974: *The Nature of Necessity* (Oxford: Clarendon Press).

Plantinga, A. 2001: 'When Faith and Reason Clash: Evolution and the Bible', in Robert T. Pennock ed., *Intelligent Design Creationism and Its Critics: Philosophical, Theological, and Scientific* (Cambridge, MA: MIT Press), pp. 113–147.

Quine, W. V. O. 1964 : 'On What There Is', in *From a Logical Point of View* (New York: Harper and Row), pp. 1–20.

Quine, W. V. O. 1964: *From a Logical Point of View* (New York: Harper and Row).

Rea, M. 2009: *Oxford Readings in Philosophical Theology: Vol. 1– Trinity, Incarnation, and Atonement* (New York: Oxford University Press).

Robbins, F. E. 1912: *The Hexaemeral Literature: A Study of the Greek and Latin Commentaries on Genesis* (Chicago: University of Chicago Press).

Roland-Gosselin, M-D. 1948: *Le 'De Ente et Essentia' de s. Aquinas d'Aquin* (Paris: Librairie Philosophique J. Vrin).

Sartre, J.P. 2007: *Existentialism is a Humanism* (York, England: Methuen).

Seligman, P. 1982: 'Being and Forms in Plato', in Parvis Morewedge ed., *Philosophies of Existence* (New York: Fordham University Press), pp. 18–33.

Selner-Wright, S. C., trans. 2011: *On Creation: Quaestiones De Potentia Dei Qu. 3* (Washington, DC: Catholic University of America Press).

Sorabji, R. 1982: *Time, Creation, and the Continuum* (London: Duckworth).

Sosa, E., ed. 1975: *Causation and Conditionals* (Oxford: Oxford University Press).

Stump, E. 1995: Stump, 'Non-Cartesian Substance Dualism and Materialism without Reductionism', *Faith and Philosophy*, 12:4, pp. 505–531.

Stump, E. 2003: *Aquinas* (London: Routledge).

Stump, E. 2009: 'Atonement According to Aquinas', in Michael Rea ed., *Oxford Readings in Philosophical Theology: Vol. 1–Trinity, Incarnation, and Atonement* (New York: Oxford University Press), pp. 267–294.

Stump, E., and Davies, B., eds. 2012: *The Oxford Handbook of Aquinas* (Oxford: Oxford University Press).

Stump, E., and Kretzmann, N. 1981: 'Eternity', *Journal of Philosophy*, 78, pp. 429–458.

Taylor, R. 1975: 'The Metaphysics of Causation', in Ernest Sosa ed., *Causation and Conditionals* (Oxford: Oxford University Press, 1975), pp. 39–44.

Te Velde, R. 2006: *Aquinas on God: The 'Divine Science' of the 'Summa Theologiae'* (Aldershot: Ashgate).

Te Velde, R. 1995: *Participation and Substantiality in Thomas Aquinas* (Leiden: Brill).

Torrell, J-P. 2003–2005: *St Thomas Aquinas: Vol. I–The Person and His Work; Vol. II–Spiritual Master*, trans. Robert Royal (Washington, DC: Catholic University of America Press).

Van Steenberghen, F. 1974: 'La controverse sur l'éternité du monde au XIIIe siècle', in *Introduction à l'étude de la philosophie médiévale* (Louvain: Publications Universitaires & Paris: Béatrice-Nauwelaerts).

Van Steenberghen, F. 1980: *Le problème de l'existence de Dieu dans les Écrits de s. Thomas d'Aquin* (Louvain: Éditions de l'institut supérieur de philosophie).

Verbeke, G. 1976: 'Man as Frontier According to Aquinas', in G. Verbeke and D. Verhelst eds., *Aquinas and Problems of His Time* (Leuven: Leuven University Press), pp. 195–225.

Vollert, C., et al., eds. and trans. 1964: *St Thomas Aquinas, Siger of Brabant, St Bonaventure, On the Eternity of the World* (Milwaukee: Marquette University Press).

White, T. J. 2017: *The Incarnate Lord: A Thomistic Study in Christology* (Washington, DC: Catholic University of America Press).

Williams, C. J. F. 1960: '"Hic autem non est procedure in infinitum..."', *Mind* 69, pp. 403–405.

Wippel, J. 1981: *The Metaphysical Thought of Godfrey of Fontaines* (Washington, DC: Catholic University of America Press).

Wippel, J. 1982: 'The Relationship between Essence and Existence in Late Thirteenth Century Thought: Giles of Rome, Henry of Ghent,

Godfrey of Fontaines, and James of Viterbo', in Parviz Morewedge ed., *Philosophies of Existence* (New York: Fordham University Press), pp. 131–165.

Wippel, J. 1984: *Metaphysical Themes in Thomas Aquinas* (Washington, DC: Catholic University of America Press).

Wippel, J. 1984: 'Thomas Aquinas and the Problem of Christian Philosophy', in *Metaphysical Themes in Thomas Aquinas* (Washington, DC: Catholic University of America Press),

Wippel, J. 1984: 'Thomas Aquinas on the Possibility of Eternal Creation', in *Metaphysical Themes in Thomas Aquinas* (Washington, DC: Catholic University of America Press), pp. 191–215.

Wippel, J. 2000: *The Metaphysical Thought of Thomas Aquinas* (Washington, DC: Catholic University of America Press).

Wippel, J. 2003: 'Norman Kretzmann on Aquinas's Attribution of Will and Freedom to Create to God', *Religious Studies*, 39:3, pp. 287–298.

Wippel, J. 2007: *Metaphysical Themes in Thomas Aquinas II* (Washington, DC: Catholic University of America Press).

Wippel, J. 2007: 'Thomas Aquinas and the Axiom That Unreceived Act Is Unlimited', in *Metaphysical Themes in Thomas Aquinas II* (Washington, DC: Catholic University of America Press), pp. 123–152.

Wippel, J. 2007: 'Thomas Aquinas on Creatures as Causes of *Esse*', in *Metaphysical Themes in Thomas Aquinas II* (Washington, DC: Catholic University of America Press).

Wippel, J. 2011: 'Thomas Aquinas on the Ultimate Why Question: Why Is There Anything At All Rather Than Nothing Whatsoever', in John Wippel ed., *The Ultimate Why Question: Why Is There Anything At All Rather Than Nothing Whatsoever?* (Washington, DC: Catholic University of America Press), pp. 84–106.

Wippel, J. 2011: *The Ultimate Why Question: Why Is There Anything at All Rather Than Nothing Whatsoever?* (Washington, DC: Catholic University of America Press).

Wippel, J. 2014: 'Aquinas on Creation and Preambles of Faith', *The Thomist* (2014), 78:1, pp. 1–36.

Wolterstorff, N. 1970: *On Universals: An Essay in Ontology* (Chicago: University of Chicago Press).

INDEX